FROM
CONCEPTION
TO   BIRTH

Roberts Rugh, Ph.D.

Landrum B. Shettles, Ph.D., M.D.

with Richard Einhorn

drawings by Rhoda Van Dyke

FROM
CONCEPTION
TO BIRTH

the drama of life's beginnings

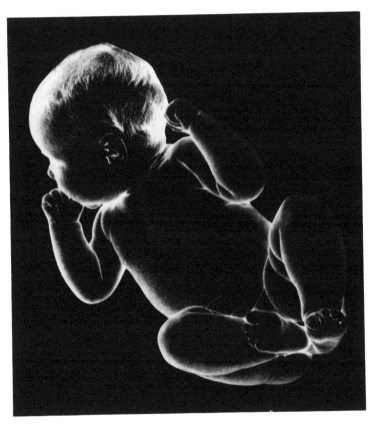

HARPER & ROW, Publishers

1817

New York, Hagerstown, San Francisco, London

DESIGNED BY CHARLOTTE THORP

LIBRARY OF CONGRESS CATALOG CARD NUMBER: 77–96803

78 79 80 10 9 8 7 6

contents

Color photographs follow page 54.

preface

There are at least two aspects of the population problem. No one will deny its importance when, for instance, we learn that each month the population in India is increased by more than one million babies to be fed and cared for. The first aspect is therefore purely quantitative, simply the need to avoid having the world's inhabitants outstrip both space and food for survival. The second consideration is equally important, namely, the need to improve the quality of human life through education of the prospective mother concerning her pregnancy. Infant and maternal mortality must be reduced. Also, those babies that do survive must be secure, able to cope with a changing world, and above all, must be wanted.

The impetus for writing this book was not primarily to help in controlling or reducing the world's population, but rather to give those who are to be born the best possible beginning in life. It is our hope that the prospective mother will wish to know all that she can about how this microscopic speck of protoplasm grows and develops rapidly for nine months.

If we could point to a single major thesis in this book it

would be simply that life on this planet, which arose millions of years ago, has survived in its various forms until today. Most people have inherited the ability to pass that life along to another individual. But every such individual is a chance composite of two distinct lines of inheritance and is thus in every way unique, different from all other individuals. Since each child possesses a heritage from the past and is a link with the future, this privilege of life is to be cherished, guarded, and nourished with all the modern resources and knowledge available. In such manner life on this earth can be improved.

With the realization that a purely scientific treatise on the subject of human development would presuppose a vast scientific vocabulary foreign to the majority of possible readers, we found it necessary to revise the original draft into more popularly acceptable language, yet always to be scientifically accurate.

The facts of this book have been gleaned from many sources, as well as from research of the authors—one an experimental embryologist, researcher, and teacher, and the other an obstetrician and gynecologist of wide experience. It has therefore been a collaborative effort which ensures a broad base from several related disciplines.

To the authors there is no more exciting or dramatic event than that of birth, when the child of nine months' development emerges into the atmosphere to take its first breath, utter its first cry, and reach for its first object, and thus be launched on its uniquely individual path through life. But the processes by which a child develops from a single fertilized ovum until it is a sizable and relatively independent infant are no less miraculous. Samuel T. Coleridge, more than 130 years ago, wrote: "The history of man for nine months preceding his birth would, probably, be far more interesting, and contain events of greater moment, than all the threescore and ten years that follow it." It is these events which we describe, and which constitute the substance of this book.

Roberts Rugh, M.A., Ph.D.
Landrum B. Shettles, M.D., D.Sc., Ph.D.

PART 1

chapter 1

prelude to pregnancy

The perpetual flame of life was kindled on earth about 4 billion years ago, when just the right combinations of chemical elements were slowly formed under ideal conditions in that vast laboratory known as the seas. What developed first from the primordial brew were not full-blown animals or plants but unusually large and complex molecules containing tens of thousands of atoms. In the course of time these enormous molecules developed lifelike properties, such as the ability to duplicate their own chemical constituents down to the last atom and to produce other chemicals.

At some point the gap between an organic compound and an organism was bridged, and the first tiny, single-celled living creatures appeared. To this day unicellular plants and animals have survived. The amoeba is one. The bacteria that cause tuberculosis or pneumonia or boils are others. Even the most complex organisms—men, whales, and elephants—consist of aggregates of these units known as cells.

Vital functions in the human body are carried out by trillions of somatic (body) cells. These cells are organized into a

Diagram of a typical living human body cell

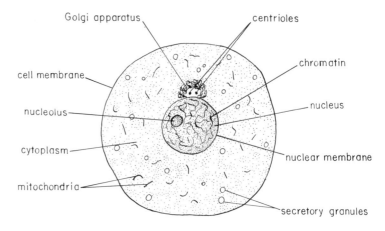

complexity that almost defies comprehension. Your brain alone contains more than 10 billion neurons (nerve cells) interconnected by pathways that dwarf the Bell Telephone System or IBM's biggest computers. Other cell clusters cover the internal and external surfaces of your body, provide a rigid frame so that you don't ooze like a jellyfish, see to it that every part of your body is nourished, bring you oxygen, or permit you to move.

All of your somatic cells, whether they be blood, bone, muscle, or nerve, are basically alike. They consist of units of protoplasm walled off by a porous membrane. Each cell is subdivided into a semifluid portion called the cytoplasm and a denser kernel called the nucleus. There are two categories of giant organic molecules in every cell: one is named protein, derived from the Greek word for primary, and the other is named nucleic acid because it is particularly abundant and active in the nucleus. Proteins control the growth and metabolism of the cells, but the nucleic acids control the formation of proteins, and thus they occupy an even more exalted position in the hierarchy of life. The nucleic acids in the nucleus of every human body cell at certain definite times align themselves into 46 elongated and worm-shaped bodies known as chromosomes. Chromosomes are the bearers of hereditary traits, and in any species their number and configuration are constant.

Your body continually replaces worn-out somatic cells; if it were unable to do so you would die as soon as your vital component parts were depleted. Your cells sustain life by growing to about twice their normal size and then splitting in half. This division, known as mitosis, results in two "daughter" cells which are identical to the parent cell in chromosomal make-up, and in every other way.

In the bridge between generations all of these marvelous somatic cells are discarded with no more ceremony than a scab on your kneecap—they die with you. But in your germ cells—sperm or ova—resides the stuff of physical immortality. A single-celled fertilized egg that can barely be seen without a magnifying lens carries all the genetic information needed to create a whole new organism with trillions of somatic cells of its own.

How, you may ask, was it possible for you to have developed so many specialized cells from one dividing ancestral cell? After all, doesn't a primitive nerve cell produce only nerve cells, and primitive muscle cells only muscle cells? Why aren't all our cells like the original one?

The answer lies in the chromosomes. The entire blueprint for the construction of a person is contained in the chromosomes of the fertilized egg cell. When you were an embryo the cytoplasm of your dividing cells began to differentiate under the influence of the nucleic acids (particularly one called DNA, by a process which is discussed further in Chapter 13) until you became what you are today. The process was completely regulated—everything appeared in definite stages and stopped when it was supposed to. Scientists now believe that every body cell of an individual contains a complete set of identical biological blueprints, no matter what its destination.

This book is concerned with how the gift of life is passed on from one generation to the next. Today you are the torchbearer. You yourself are a composite of the genetic material of your two parents, and they in turn of your four grandparents. Eight great-grandparents contributed to your make-up. If you traced your ancestry for only 32 generations you would arrive at a figure of 4.3 billion, which is greater than the total number of all the people who ever were alive at one time. Yet 32 generations span only half the Christian era, a fraction of man's tenure as a species.

How do we account for this? Obviously everyone must have ancestors in common with a large number of other human beings. Somewhere, somehow, you must be related to much of mankind through intermarriage and common ancestry. With each future generation more and more human beings will be able to claim you as an ancestor. But your direct hereditary contribution to any one of your descendants will be diluted from generation to generation, just as the chromosomal legacy

Diagrams of the stages of mitosis in a typical body cell having five chromosomes   (Human cells have 46 chromosomes.)

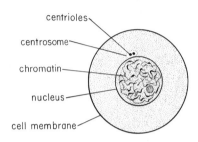

centrioles
centrosome
chromatin
nucleus
cell membrane

Late interphase

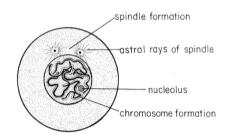

spindle formation
astral rays of spindle
nucleolus
chromosome formation

Early prophase

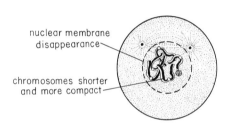

nuclear membrane disappearance

chromosomes shorter and more compact

Late prophase

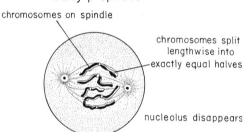

chromosomes on spindle

chromosomes split lengthwise into exactly equal halves

nucleolus disappears

Early metaphase

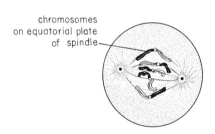

chromosomes on equatorial plate of spindle

Metaphase

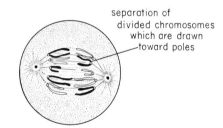

separation of divided chromosomes which are drawn toward poles

Anaphase

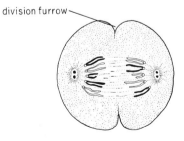

division furrow

Early telophase

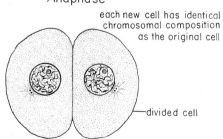

each new cell has identical chromosomal composition as the original cell

divided cell

Late telophase

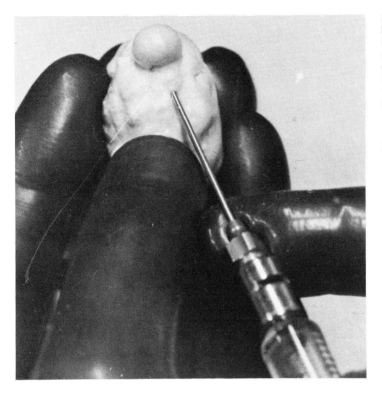

Mature egg (Graafian follicle) in human ovary (Aspiration by hypodermic syringe removes egg.) Occasionally a woman may be operated upon at the moment an egg is being released from her ovary. In such a case the egg appears in a bubblelike projection from the surface of the ovary which would shortly rupture freeing it in a rush of follicular fluid into the tube. In order to obtain this mature egg, which is very much smaller than this follicle (actually about the size of the period at the end of this sentence), the surgeon can pass a hypodermic needle through the ovary and into the follicle and then draw fluid and egg into the syringe. In this case the surgeon did just that, placed the fluid containing the egg on a slide and under a microscope and added some human spermatozoa whereupon the egg was fertilized. Such a fertilized egg cannot survive or develop very far because it requires certain chemicals in its normal environment, the reproductive channels of the woman. Each month one such egg will rupture from one of the woman's ovaries, and generally the next month from the other. The egg itself would be too small to be seen with the naked eye. The moment of ovulation has been reported electrically, may be associated with the change in the basal body temperature, and some women are so sensitive that they can feel the event. Vaginal smears may give a clue to the time of ovulation.

from your own forebears has been spread out among others. So, whether you look backward or forward you see that any life is part of a vast biological reservoir.

Nevertheless, since you are alive you are part of an unbroken chain. Had a single one of your ancestors been sterile or had he died before reaching sexual maturity you wouldn't be here today. For the continuance of humankind fertility is as important as life itself.

Man has been around for a long time, perhaps a million years. In the course of evolution various features have been built into the human reproductive process to safeguard the perpetuation and future of the species.

One such safeguard is the great length of the fertile period: more than thirty years for the female, virtually lifelong for the male. Once every 28 days or so, after the onset of puberty, a single ovum matures in the average woman's ovaries. This is but one of about 400 ova that will become available for fertilization before she reaches her menopause. If no opportunity for pregnancy were missed, and if the woman somehow retained her health and sanity, she could become a mother more than 30 times.

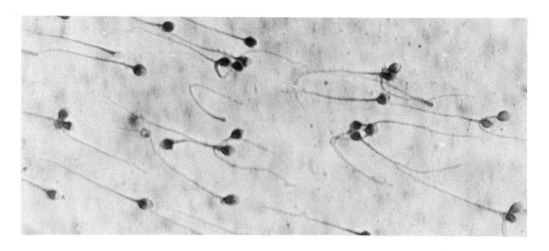

Living human sperm each 1/800 inch in length, which swim toward the ovum at the rate of an inch in 16 minutes. A single normal semen specimen may contain 300 million sperm per cubic millimeter.

Prolific as this may seem, there is no comparison with the ability of a human male to sire children. A mature, healthy man produces more than 300 million active spermatozoa in each cubic centimeter of semen (a mixture of sperm and other fluids) that he ejaculates at the climax of the sexual act. Therefore, he might release millions of spermatozoa simultaneously, all in quest of one fertilizable ovum. Allowing time for his body to replenish the supply at the rate of about several hundred million a day, a man could go on producing sperm throughout his lifetime, even if he lived to be one hundred years old.

This may seem like superabundance, extravagance, or even wastage on the part of nature, but it has been estimated that if a man ejaculated fewer than about 20 million sperm cells at a time he would for all practical purposes be sterile. Even though only one sperm is necessary to fertilize an ovum, most of the available sperm fail to survive the trip. A certain minimum number is considered necessary to ensure that one reaches the ripe ovum.

The human race has survived primarily because the first thing an embryo does, even before it begins to form heart, lungs, brain or digestive tract, is to set aside a savings account of cells for the exclusive purpose of producing another generation about 20 years later, *if* the embryo develops into a fetus, is born, and reaches sexual maturity. This is the epitome of preparedness or insurance.

Associated with each embryo is an undeveloped yolk sac. Probably it served our distant forebears as a prenatal source of food, but mutations must have occurred somewhere along the line, and in modern man the embryo (or fetus, as it is called in the later stages of development) receives nourishment directly from its mother. Nevertheless this yolk sac has been retained to play a role quite different from its former one: about 21 days after conception, when the embryo is less than one-eighth inch long and totally unrecognizable as a human being, the yolk sac gives rise to about 100 primordial (primitive) germ cells. These cells migrate a considerable distance (by crawling like an amoeba) toward the site at which the reproductive organs will later develop.

By the 38th day they reach their destination and begin to organize in the forming testes or ovaries. At this time the testes or ovaries aren't functional. They couldn't even be recognized as such; nor could the primordial germ cells be distinguished as sperm or ova. Yet you as an embryo were already preparing for your own pregnancy many years later. This was your first altruistic deed when you were an embryo.

By 50 days after conception human embryonic development has progressed far enough for certain external features to provide telltale evidence that the child is to be a girl or a boy. These features are known as secondary sexual characters, and they arise in response to certain chemicals released by the body. Although these characters distinguish a male from a female, they themselves are *not* the prime difference between the sexes. The primordial germ cells are what distinguish a boy from a girl, and this determination was made by the chromosomes at the moment of conception, as will be shown in a later chapter.

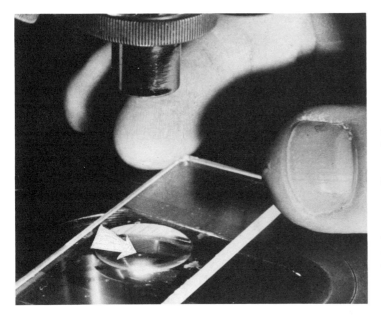

Human ovum just after ovulation On this microscopic slide has been placed a single human egg (ovum) with its cluster of small surrounding cells (corona radiata) as seen with the naked eye at the point of the arrow. Note the relative size of the human thumb and forefinger. The ovum measures 1/175 of an inch in diameter and weighs about one twenty-millionth of an ounce as it is released from the ovary.

In the case of a girl the baby develops paired ovaries, a vagina, a uterus, a cervix, and two oviducts (Fallopian tubes) which connect the uterus with the paired ovaries. The girl baby at birth has all the germ cells that will ever form in her ovaries.

Similarly, the boy baby develops his own reproductive organs. In addition to paired testes the boy develops sperm-carrying ducts, such as the epididymis and vas deferens, and the prostate and other glands—all of which are paired—and a single phallus (penis). During the migration of the primordial germ cells they multiply and reach the hundreds of thousands. Before he is born his testes house millions of potential spermatozoa.

In both sexes neither the secondary sexual characters nor the germ cells mature before puberty, even though the potential is there before birth. At 50 days the female embryo's developing ovaries teem with about 600,000 primitive germ cells (potential ova), all the descendants of the original colony of about 100 which migrated to the ovaries from the yolk sac about 3 weeks earlier. By the end of the fifth month these ova will have produced about 7 million descendants of their own (now called oögonia). From this point on, the savings account of egg cells dwindles, as though the woman were living off her principal. When a girl is born she has about 2 million oöcytes, all of which could become ova. At seven years of age she has 500,000, and at twenty only 300,000. Of these, only about 400 mature to the stage (ova) when they can be fertilized. This number is further reduced with every menstrual cycle. Moreover, the body of a girl just entering puberty is still not mature enough to nurture a baby through nine months of pregnancy, and she and her child would most certainly suffer as a consequence. The boy, though

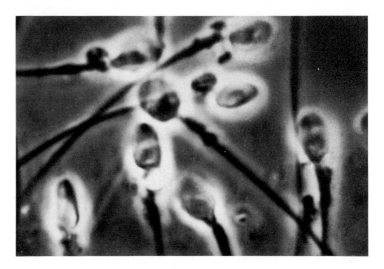

Living human spermatozoa
(Dark field illumination)

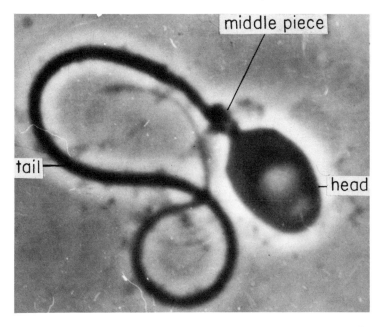

middle piece

tail

head

Human spermatozoa highly magnified This is a very much magnified mature human spermatozoon. It measures about 1/500 of an inch in length, and most of this length consists of a tail. The oval head which contains the nucleus is the important structure in fertilization of the egg and in its development. There is a collar or middle piece which contains elements that aid in the motion of the spermatozoon, and a long filamentous tail whose function is solely to propel the spermatozoon toward the egg. The head is flat from one view, but is actually concave on both sides. From the surface view it appears to be oval. This specimen is normal but in any sample one may find bizarre shapes or types which are probably useless in fertilization.

usually reaching puberty later than the girl, is then biologically ready to impregnate a female.

Sperm and ova are specially adapted for the task of reproduction. The mature ovum, unlike a hen's egg, is a tiny sphere only 1/175 inch in diameter and weighing about 1/20 of a millionth of an ounce. All the ova that produced the present world's population would fit in a shoebox.

But in this microcosm the ovum is relatively gigantic. Its mate, the sperm cell, consists of a tiny oval head, a whiplike tail, and a middle piece that connects them. It is only about 1/500 inch long, and most of that is tail. It would need about 90,000 of its fellows to balance a single ovum on the scales. And the 3 billion-plus sperm necessary to fertilize that shoeboxful of ova would fit into a thimble.

The ovum, like any other egg, contains some yolk that can sustain life. The spermatozoon, on the other hand, is stripped to the hereditary essentials and carries no food. It depends entirely on the hospitality it receives on its journey.

The fate of all these tiny protagonists in the battle for survival is influenced by a biological clock present in the body of every woman. This timepiece runs for an average of 28 days before repeating itself. It is known as the menstrual cycle (named after the menses, the 28-day lunar months). However, scientists prefer the term estrous cycle (named after estrogen, a hormone or chemical secreted by the ovary to regulate the process). In the chart of the menstrual cycle, the events in the ovary, associated with the rapid growth and maturation of

Mature human ovum (egg) ready for fertilization The human egg as it leaves the ovary takes with it many of the nurse cells that have been associated with it for many years, since before the woman was born. It is believed that any of the many nurse cells seen surrounding the egg could, at one time, have developed in a like manner into an egg cell. No one knows why one cell is selected for this special attention, to eventually enlarge and become fertilizable.

This egg which is highly magnified under special lighting conditions, is about 1/175 of an inch in diameter and is surrounded by a protective envelope called the zona pellucida, a transparent membrane. This envelope will be removed a few days after the egg is fertilized and has started dividing and developing into an eventual fetus and child. But to fertilize this egg the successful spermatozoon must penetrate through a thick phalanx of cells. However, the sperm is provided with a chemical which helps to clear a path between these cells which are not really enemies to the sperm—they just get in its way. However, they do protect the egg from certain kinds of injury.

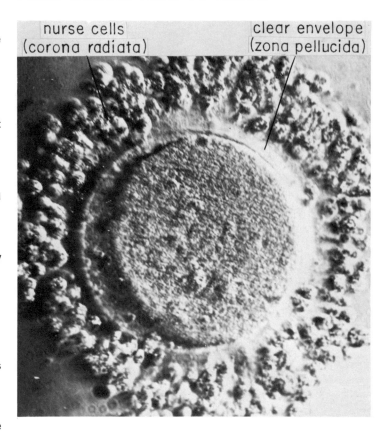

nurse cells (corona radiata)

clear envelope (zona pellucida)

the ovum, are grouped around the inner circle. Note that the ovum matures in the middle of the cycle (reckoned from the start of menstruation). Only when the ovum leaves the ovary can it be reached and fertilized by invading spermatozoa. The time of ovulation varies in individual women, but the general average is the 14th day after the onset of menstruation. It is associated with changes in the body temperature and electrical potentials between parts of the female reproductive system. Some women claim they can feel when they are ovulating. If an ovum is fertilized, events follow the course outlined in the outer circle of the chart, and described in this book. If not, the egg dies in about 12 hours and is eliminated.

Profound changes are constantly taking place throughout this menstrual cycle. Purely for the sake of convenience let us assume it starts with menstruation. The first step is the expulsion from the body of an overripe ovum and with it the mucous membrane that lines the uterus. This membrane, which is richly supplied with blood, may be likened to a bed of nutritious earth in which a fertilized ovum can be implanted. If the ovum is not fertilized the body starts all over again by grooming a new ovum for release and by slowly relining the uterus.

The mature ovum grows out of what is known as a secondary oöcyte. This round speck is surrounded by an entourage of about 6,000 nurse cells, each of which was also an oöcyte that might have become an ovum. What distinguishes the successful candidate from the also-rans that protect it and nourish it is an unsolved mystery.

Before egg cells leave the ovary they must undergo further maturation. The primary oöcyte divides asymmetrically into a discarded nucleus with a minimal amount of cytoplasm (the

Hormone relations in human reproduction This chart shows how the master gland, the pituitary, lying beneath the center of the brain, controls the various parts and functions of the reproductive system of the human female. The organs that are interrelated include the thyroid, adrenals, mammary glands, ovaries, uterus, and vagina. The pituitary also secretes chemicals which affect the uterus and vagina. Progesterone stimulates the follicles of the ovaries through the pituitary and inhibits LH and LTH production. Estrogen, on the other hand, stimulates production of LH and LTH in the pituitary gland and inhibits FSH (the follicle stimulating hormone) so that ovulation is suspended during pregnancy.

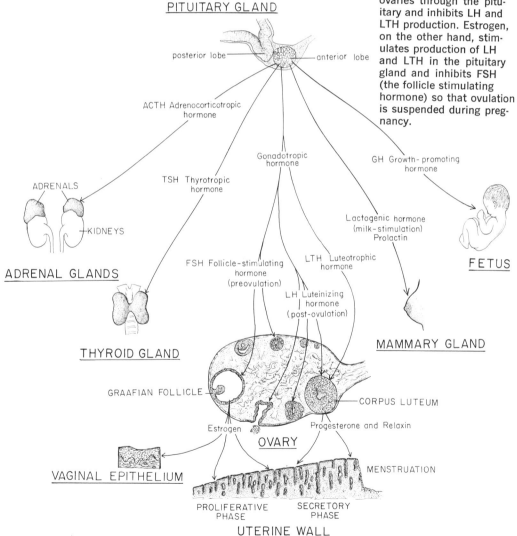

PITUITARY GLAND

posterior lobe — anterior lobe

ACTH Adrenocorticotropic hormone

Gonadotropic hormone

GH Growth-promoting hormone

ADRENALS

TSH Thyrotropic hormone

KIDNEYS

Lactogenic hormone (milk-stimulation) Prolactin

ADRENAL GLANDS

FSH Follicle-stimulating hormone (preovulation)

LTH Luteotrophic hormone

FETUS

LH Luteinizing hormone (post-ovulation)

THYROID GLAND

MAMMARY GLAND

GRAAFIAN FOLLICLE

CORPUS LUTEUM

Estrogen

Progesterone and Relaxin

OVARY

VAGINAL EPITHELIUM

MENSTRUATION

PROLIFERATIVE PHASE   SECRETORY PHASE

UTERINE WALL

Events of the human female cycle resulting in pregnancy   The events in the human female body relating to the reproductive process are called the menstrual cycle because they tend to occur in regular sequence beginning about every 28 days. This chart shows (on the outside) the events in the uterus, changes in preparation for the reception of a fertilized egg. On the inside of the circle are the events relating to the egg in the ovary and its liberation (ovulation). Note the timing of these events so that the egg is ready to be fertilized at a certain time, but at a time appropriate for the implantation of that egg in the receptive uterus. In the event no fertilized egg reaches the uterus at the correct time, the lining of the uterus is discarded in what we call menstruation. The uterus then begins again to prepare for the next ovulation, and possible fertilization.

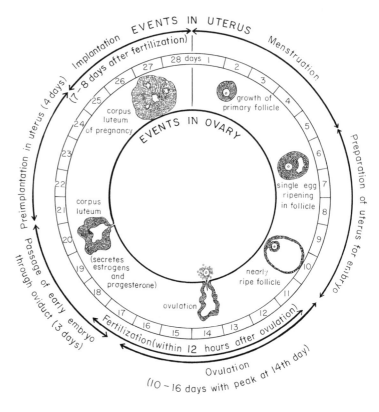

first polar body) and a secondary oöcyte containing an extra ration of cytoplasm and yolk. The secondary oöcyte then divides to give rise to the second polar body and a mature ovum, with still more cytoplasm and yolk.

The entire cluster of maturing ovum and surrounding nurse cells forms into what is known as a Graafian follicle, a bloated, fluid-filled structure that protrudes from whichever of the two ovaries is supposed to release an ovum that month (the ovaries do not necessarily alternate). Occasionally two ova are released and, if fertilized, result in fraternal twins.

Somewhere between the 10th and 16th days of the average woman's menstrual cycle ovulation takes place. Under pressure from the accumulated fluid the follicle ruptures, expelling the by now fully ripened ovum along with its accompanying nurse cells into the body cavity. The bevy of nurse cells and ovum do not have much chance to escape, however, for in all but rare cases they are quickly drawn into the oviduct (Fallopian tube) by microscopic, moving, hairlike projections called cilia which line the entrance to the tube (ostium tubae). This undulating structure partially surrounds the ovary. Its cilia all beat in the same direction, creating a current that whisks the ovum into the upper portion of the Fallopian tube. There the ovum rests for a few hours. Then it is propelled farther downward toward the uterus, not only by the ciliary currents but also by muscular contractions of the wall of the tube.

Meanwhile, the ruptured Graafian follicle has by no means surrendered. Now known as the corpus luteum because of its newly acquired yellow color, it rapidly fills with a mass of cells that secrete hormones (estrogens and progesterone). These hormones have three main effects in the event of pregnancy: they prepare the mucous lining along the inner wall of the uterus for implantation of the fertilized ovum, they prevent any other egg from ovulating, and they signal the breasts to prepare for lactation (the formation of milk). If pregnancy does not occur, the corpus luteum shrinks, and by the start of the next menstruation it has disappeared entirely.

In all of these changes that occur throughout the menstrual cycle the actions of the ovaries play a highly important part. However, even the ovaries are merely acting under the direction of the pituitary, a pea-sized gland located in the base of the brain. The pituitary is the master gland that controls many bodily functions, such as growth (a midget or a giant characteristically has a malfunctioning pituitary gland). The relationship of various glands that produce hormones is shown in the diagram on page 11.

In a basically similar manner spermatozoa are produced or matured at the rate of an average of 300 million a day. (The production of spermatozoa is under the influence of vitamin E, and a deficiency of this vitamin may cause male sterility.) One reason for the large population of spermatozoa is that no nuclei are discarded in the maturing process, as they are in the production of ova. Every dividing primitive sperm cell provides two equal surviving cells, then four, and so on, not a sleek prima donna and an undernourished polar body.

Within the testes of any normal, mature male there may be found thousands of primitive spermatogonia, some of which are constantly growing until they reach a stage at which they are known as primary spermatocytes. These cells have a full complement of 23 *pairs* of chromosomes, a total of 46. The primary spermatocyte undergoes a special cell division to form two equal secondary spermatocytes, which in turn form four spermatids. One of these divisions results in cells having only 23 chromosomes apiece (one member of each of the original pairs). But these spermatids are still nonfunctional and must undergo a further stage of metamorphosis into spermatozoa. In the process they lose most of their cytoplasm and develop a middle piece and a long, lashing tail that permits them to swim relatively great distances. Each spermatozoon has a meager amount of protoplasm from which to derive energy for its movements; therefore its life is limited.

If coitus (sexual intercourse with ejaculation of semen into the vagina) occurs at an inopportune time—that is, too far in advance of ovulation or too long after it—the fate of the hundreds of millions of spermatozoa is sealed. They will perish, victims of innumerable pitfalls that make the vicissitudes of spawning salmon seem like a pastime.

The first barrier is sheer distance. The farthest reaches of the upper oviduct are less than a foot away. This may not seem very great, but for the microscopic sperm it is the equivalent of miles. The violence of the ejaculation is necessary to propel the spermatozoa through the vagina. From that point on, they migrate upward by whiplike motions through the genital tract toward the ovary, aided in their ascent by the orgasm and also by activity of the cervix.

Normally the vagina is slightly acidic, and acid is lethal to

Meiosis (unequal cell division) The production of sperm or ova; black from one parent, clear from other parent. Meiosis refers to cell division which results not only in unequal daughter cells, but cells which possess half the original number of chromosomes. This reduction in number is achieved by each pair splitting and separating, so that the resulting cells possess but a single member of each pair usually found in the cells of the human. This type of division occurs only in the production of germ cells (ova or sperm) and when they later come together in fertilization the full number of chromosomes (and pairs) is restored.

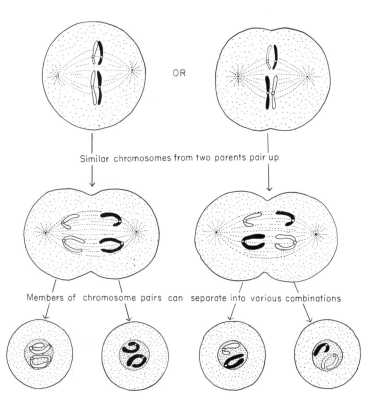

OR

Similar chromosomes from two parents pair up

Members of chromosome pairs can separate into various combinations

sperm. At ovulation, however, the vagina becomes slightly alkaline. Similarly, the cervix, the uterus, and the Fallopian tubes become progressively more alkaline. Even so, the period during which the sperm could survive the passage would be extremely short if it weren't for the fact that the semen, the viscous medium in which the sperm are immersed, is markedly alkaline itself.

As though the acid bath weren't bad enough, in sailing through the cervix the sperm would become entangled in a Sargasso Sea of thick mucus that is constantly in motion, powered by the kinetic energy provided by body temperature (98.6 degrees Fahrenheit). At ovulation the mucous plug thins and becomes far less resistant to the passage of sperm. Their migration through the mucus is like that of fish struggling upstream at their greatest possible speed.

Should the spermatozoa be hardy enough to surmount these obstacles they would enter the uterus, where they must do some powerful long-distance swimming with the aid of their whiplike tails. For those which possess the stamina to hold out, there is an unappetizing dilemma: if they enter the wrong oviduct (the one associated with the ovary that wasn't ovulating that month), they forfeit their chance for survival, and even if they enter the right one they are faced with perhaps their greatest tribulations.

The ciliary currents and muscular contractions that propel the ovum downward present a countercurrent to the spermatozoa. Like the spawning salmon, they must swim upstream after all. But unlike a river, the 5- to 7-inch-long oviduct is not a straight, broad channel. The wall of the oviduct has many folds and crannies in which some of the spermatozoa may be entrapped, never to emerge. In addition, there is evidence that any foreign material in the uterus or oviduct will call forth thousands of scavenging white blood cells to devour the trapped or lingering sperm. Thus, it is no wonder that of the hundreds of millions deposited in the vagina only a few hundred arrive at the vicinity of the ripe ovum in the oviduct. The surviving spermatozoa then compete to penetrate the ovum.

A sperm cell has an average life of about 48 hours inside the female tract. If it has not found and fertilized an ovum by then, it will die. As has already been pointed out, the unfertilized ovum lives for about 12 to 24 hours. Thus, if coitus occurs more than 48 hours before the egg reaches the oviduct, the lifetime of the sperm will have expired. But if it occurs more than about 22 hours after the appearance of the egg (allowing 2 hours for the sperm to reach the ovum), the egg will have expired. Therefore, an ovum can be fertilized in a particular woman over a maximum range of 72 hours each cycle, contrary to popular opinion! Someday it may be possible to know exactly when these 72 hours occur for any particular woman, that is, when we could say she is fertile.

What is the likelihood of pregnancy? you may ask.

In a recent study of couples who desired children and who did not use contraceptives, it was found that only 33 per cent achieved pregnancy in the first month, 60 per cent by three months, and 75 per cent within six months. It is also estimated that 30 per cent of fertilized ova do not survive. Thus the barriers to pregnancy are far greater than you may think.

Now that you have been introduced to the changes that prepare one for pregnancy, we will go on to the fertilization of the ovum and the dramatic development of the child.

the first month
of life

During the first month after conception only the exceptional woman would be aware of the minute creature she is harboring.[1] But in these 720 hours the embryo increases its size about 40-fold and its weight almost 3,000-fold. More remarkable than mere size or weight gain is the transformation of a single cell into an embryo with a head, a trunk, and the rudiments of organs, and the establishment of a close working association with the body of the mother. The embryo begins to form blood cells at seventeen days and a heart as early as eighteen days after the sperm invades the ovum. This embryonic heart, no more than a simple tube, starts a slow, irregular pulsation at 24 days which in one more week smooths into a rhythmic contraction and expansion. The heart eventually beats more than 100,000 times each day and will continue to do so, without interruption, for seventy, eighty, or maybe ninety years.

1. Margaret Shea Gilbert, in her excellent book *Biography of the Unborn* (Hafner, 1963), says: "Life begins for each of us at an unfelt, unknown, and unhonored instant when a minute wriggling sperm plunges headlong into a mature ovum or egg."

Fertilization First polar body divided into two. (Note excess spermatozoa.) A photograph of another human egg just recently fertilized, showing rejected spermatozoa still clinging to the outermost membrane. This also shows the discarded small cell with nucleus (called a polar body) which has divided into two, which always occurs shortly after sperm penetration. Actually the maturing egg discards three-quarters of its chromosome material, but retains half of every one of its original chromosomes.

Note here that a new space has developed around the egg, due, it is believed, to a slight shrinkage of the egg. This space is filled with a fluid. Such an egg has been properly stimulated and supplemented by a spermatozoon so that it is ready to begin the rapid process of development into a human being.

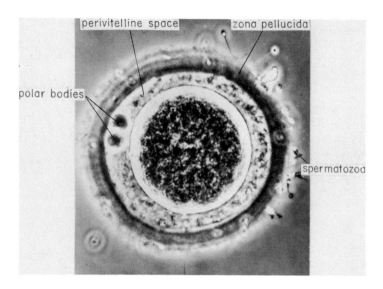

It is difficult to imagine these changes because they occur slowly and continuously and they cannot be seen by the naked eye.

In the United States another baby begins its development about every 3 seconds. Each second ticked off by a watch represents an average of 3¾ babies conceived around the world. The day of your child's birth will be shared by 16,000 other American babies. Three and a half million of them are born each year, out of four and a quarter million pregnancies (82 per cent success).

Not one of these babies will be identical to any other either in appearance or in potentialities.[2] And since each person is a composite of characteristics contributed by two parents, he or she cannot be a carbon copy of either of them.

Who, then, will that baby be?

It will be a combination of the genetic content of one of the mother's 400 ova with those of one of, say, 360 million spermatozoa released at the same time. The child you conceived might have been any one of about 144 billion distinct human beings, assuming that all of the spermatozoa really had an equal chance to fertilize that ovum. The slightest difference in the timing of the sex act would have tipped the odds in favor of a different spermatozoon—and resulted in a different child. No other couple could produce a child identical to yours.

2. The only exception is the rare instance when a fertilized ovum divides equally to form identical twins.

fertilization of the ovum

When the armada of spermatozoa, after battling through a murderous obstacle course at a speed of one inch in 20 minutes, finally arrives in the vicinity of the ovum, only about 2,000 of the original hundreds of millions remain in the running. The nose-cone-like cap (the acrosome) of each sperm produces an enzyme called hyaluronidase, which digests the protective cumulus cells in its path around the ovum. Now the finalists in the race confront the zona pellucida, the clear, gelatinous, but firm cover of the ovum. A mature spermatozoon bores with

Drawing of a mature human spermatozoon Note the distinct head, the intricate middle piece, and the long and filamentous tail which propels it toward the mature egg or ovum. Its nucleus contains all of its hereditary contributions as well as the determiners of sex of the resulting child. Sex is determined entirely by which of two kinds of sperm fertilizes the egg, but these influences are invisible.

The entering spermatozoon has brought into the egg half of the hereditary genes so that there is now an equal influence from the father and the mother.

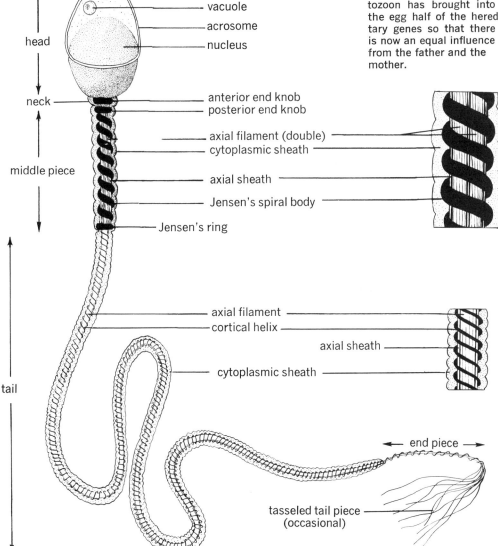

head

neck

middle piece

tail

vacuole

acrosome

nucleus

anterior end knob
posterior end knob

axial filament (double)
cytoplasmic sheath

axial sheath

Jensen's spiral body

Jensen's ring

axial filament
cortical helix

axial sheath

cytoplasmic sheath

end piece

tasseled tail piece
(occasional)

Fertilized human egg with two polar bodies This is a special view through a phase contrast microscope of a human egg 12 hours after it was fertilized by a single spermatozoon. By this time most of the surrounding cells and extra spermatozoa have disappeared, and the two polar bodies (the discarded and divided nuclei) are seen floating freely in the (perivitelline) space. There is no external evidence of the very dynamic changes that are occurring inside of the egg in preparation for its first division into two cells.

some effort through the zona pellucida, apparently with the cooperation of the ovum, and finally it pierces the cell membrane itself at any point on the surface. *As soon as this occurs the ovum rejects all other spermatozoa,* although many may try to attach themselves to the zona pellucida.

In the process of penetrating the ovum the successful spermatozoon loses its acrosomal cap. Once inside, it loses its tail as well, leaving just the sperm head, which is basically a nucleus containing 23 chromosomes. Only a mature spermatozoon can stimulate the otherwise dormant ovum. Now there begins a complicated process known as development, which never really ceases until the death of the individual many years later.

The protoplasmic content of the ovum begins to vibrate. If you could examine such an ovum alive under very high magnification, you might describe the activity of its cytoplasm as relatively violent, only everything would be taking place on a drawn-out time scale, like an exaggerated slow-motion picture. The ovum, which in the course of its maturation had discarded some nuclear material (the first polar body), now prepares to discard a second polar body. The remaining nuclear material, the pronucleus, containing 23 chromosomes (half the normal complement, because a previous division had taken place within the ovary), then moves slowly toward the center of the ovum. There it meets the pronucleus of the sperm, which also contains 23 chromosomes. The two pronuclei become enlarged and lose their enclosing nuclear membranes. Within 12 hours they merge, so that the fertilized ovum, now called a zygote, has its requisite 23 *pairs* of chromosomes (one member of each pair from each parent) restored and is ready to develop into a baby. Soon the protoplasm of the fertilized ovum becomes much less agitated, and an observer would get the impression that an orderly sequence of events will follow.

division of the fertilized ovum (cleavage)

Little in biology is more thrilling to watch or more significant in its implications than the first division of the zygote into two equal parts by the process known as cleavage. It is through this process that a single fertilized ovum will give rise to the more than trillions of cells of the newborn baby. Cleavage is not at all comparable to a simple knife stroke that cuts an egg in two; it involves a sequence of preparatory events, called mitosis. Prior to the division of the egg each chromosome doubles its hereditary materials (DNA molecules) by a process of synthesis that is characteristic of all living things (this will be discussed in Chapter 13). Then each chromosome splits lengthwise to provide two qualitatively equal half-chromosomes that regroup into two distinct nuclei, one of which goes with each half of the divided egg. *Every daughter cell is therefore identical in chromosomal make-up, and hence in hereditary potential, to the original zygote.* Thus each cell of the developing baby, right from the beginning, contains an equal number of chromosomes from each of the parents, and it is these chromosomes that carry the all-important hereditary units known as genes (see Chapter 13).

The first cleavage of the zygote takes about 36 hours, but each succeeding division takes slightly less time. Finally the proliferation levels off to a fairly constant rate.

The process of cleavage has been observed in the fertilized eggs of many lower animals, from sea urchins to mice, and it never fails to amaze the observer. At one moment there is a spherical mass of protoplasm. Then, almost imperceptibly, it begins to flatten on one side where lines of tension appear on the surface. This indicates some potent but regulated inner force. Finally the cell seems to be pinched in the middle, as though by an invisible drawstring that is being pulled to separate the mass into two halves, each enclosed in its own outer membrane and each containing its own nucleus.

Although the cells are structurally separate they seem to be held together by some cohesive force. The strength of this

Human egg at two-cell stage A two-cell human embryo is rarely seen because it is so very small and lies within the folds of the oviduct. This is a slice (section) through the two cells which has been stained with a dye to bring out the inner structures, namely the two nuclei. Each nucleus is found near the center of the cell and the two are actually identical in size although in this section they are not both cut exactly through the center so that one appears to be slightly larger than the other. Surrounding the embryo is a transparent membrane which helps to keep the cells together during very early development. Within each nucleus are 23 pairs of hereditary structures known as chromosomes, but they cannot be seen here because they are not specifically stained. In every nucleus of every cell of the human body there are 46 such chromosomes.

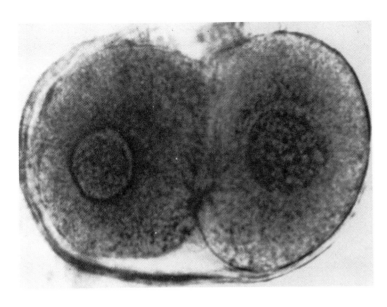

Mitosis (Cleavage—equal cell division) Each cell of a child's growing body has 46 chromosomes (23 pairs) of which only 4 (2 pairs) are shown here; black from one parent, clear from other parent.

Mitosis is the process by which a single living cell divides into two equal daughter cells. This occurs following fertilization of the ovum until this single cell gives rise to the 800 billion or more cells of the body of the human being. Note that in this hypothetical case where there are only two pairs of chromosomes shown in the nucleus, each division is preceded by a splitting of the chromosomes so that the daughter cells each have the same set of chromosomes with which the original cell started.

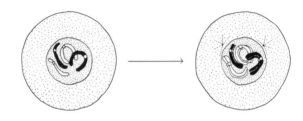

Chromosome growth occurs here   Each chromosome and its genes split lengthwise

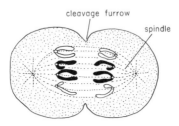
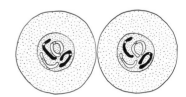

cleavage furrow

spindle

Cell dividing into exactly equal parts including all 46 chromosomes

Division complete (two cells from one)

In this way the fertilized egg produces the trillions of cells of the newborn, all having identical sets of chromosomes

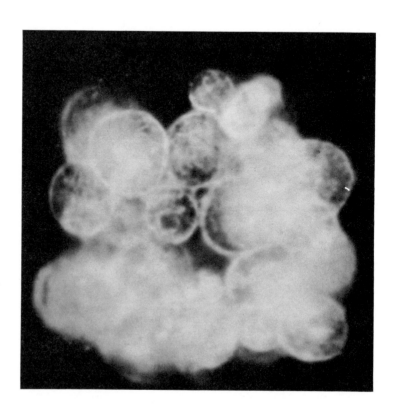

Human embryo in morula stage at 3½ days

attraction becomes more obvious later on, when there are many cells in the cluster.

Occasionally the first two daughter cells arising out of the zygote separate completely and each divides independently, giving rise to two separate individuals known as identical twins. They are identical in hereditary potential, physical make-up, susceptibility to disease, and life expectancy because both are formed from exactly the same hereditary blueprint contained in their genes. We don't know why this separation occurs after the first division of the fertilized egg, but the tendency to twinning itself may be hereditary. From experimental studies on animals and from what we have observed of multiple human births, we believe that at least for the first few divisions the human ovum provides daughter cells that are "totipotent," meaning that any one of them could independently give rise to a complete person if it were separated from the zygote. This may account for identical multiple births—by the separation of, say, the four cells resulting from the first two cleavages into four separate embryos. It is much more common, however, for twins to arise through double ovulation, or the simultaneous liberation of two mature ova (possibly one from each ovary). Since they would have to be fertilized independently by two different spermatozoa, these ova develop into fraternal twins that are no more alike than any other siblings; they merely happen to share the uterus at the same time.

The second cleavage is completed by 2 days after conception. By the end of 3 days there are 16 to 32 cells, and by 4 days there may be 60 to 70 cells. The earliest divisions tend to be synchronous (this is, all of the cells divide simultaneously), but soon the divisions of the constituent cells become asynchronous, and the rate of these repeated mitotic divisions is accelerated. In a few days there are enough cells to form a sphere called a morula, which looks like a mulberry encased in a transparent envelope called the zona pellucida.

The cells of the morula are functionally integrated. They have already lost some of their independence, and if one cell were separated from the cluster it could no longer give rise to a separate individual. As the number of cells increases, the morula moves away from the site at which the original ovum was fertilized, down through the ciliated oviduct, and, on about the third day, through a narrow opening into the uterine cavity, where there is more room. (At this age, if the embryo were examined under a special microscope, the prospective sex could already be ascertained.) This is where the embryo (and later the fetus) will grow and develop for the next nine months. We have provided a drawing to illustrate these events, but it must be borne in mind that the drawing is only schematic and represents events that occur over quite a few days.

The proliferation of cells by successive division leads one to wonder whether there is any limit to this process. There must be, since the population of cells comprising the whole lies within a certain range of size and weight. When unbridled proliferation occurs later in life in certain regions of the body, it is superficially similar to early proliferation, but it is uncontrolled (and therefore malignant) cancer.

The mature ovum is one of the largest cells in the body. It is unique among all human cells in that it stores yolk, which is used for nutrition during division. In the first few days after conception, the total mass of protoplasm does not increase and its over-all size does not change. Instead, it is subdivided into smaller and smaller daughter cells and there is less and less yolk left for survival. A hen's egg is so richly provided with yolk that the developing chick embryo can sustain itself for the 21 days prior to hatching; after that the chick must peck for itself. But all mammalian embryos soon outgrow the yolk supply and begin to derive nourishment from the mother's tissues. Once this happens, the trend toward miniaturization is reversed. The cells now give rise to other cells of fairly uniform size, although small in comparison with the original ovum. Fluid begins to accumulate among the morula cells, and a central cavity begins to form.

blastulation

By the time the morula enters the uterus the dense cluster of cells has been altered to form a single-layered, hollow sphere known as a blastula or blastocyst around a fluid-filled cavity known as a blastocoel. This hollow spherical formation gives the illusion of a greatly enlarged embryo. Such a stage is characteristic of the development of most animals, and in man it lasts until the sphere is implanted in the wall of the uterus. It is during blastulation that the cells begin to differentiate.

The blastocoel expands and some of the cells around the hollow ball congregate on one side. This thickened mass of cells forms the embryonic disc or blastoderm. It is these cells that will develop progressively into the embryo, the fetus,[3] and the

3. The term "fetus" is used to designate the unborn human 5 or more weeks postconception, to distinguish it from the embryo up to this time. It does not imply ability to survive independently of the mother, but rather the first resemblance to a human.

child. The rest of the cells around the sphere (called the trophoderm) will provide the covering (chorion) and protective membranes associated with the developing baby. The chorion, the placenta, the amnion ("bag of waters"), and the yolk sac all play an important role in embryonic development but are not physically a part of the baby.

The blastoderm comprises two distinct layers of cells. The original outer and thicker layer (called the ectoderm) will develop into the brain, the spinal cord, all the nerves and sensory organs, and the skin. The newer and innermost layer (called the endoderm) will become the lining of the entire digestive tract from pharynx down through the esophagus, stomach, liver, and intestines to the anus. Later an intermediate layer (called the mesoderm) will appear which gives rise to the skeleton, muscles, and many internal organs. These three layers of cells appear in the development of all higher animals. As the blastula is forming it is being propelled by ciliary currents and muscular contractions downstream in the oviduct and into the uterus, where it will grow and develop for the remaining 260 days of the pregnancy. All of this occurs before a woman could possibly be certain that she is pregnant.

Human blastocyst at 5 days
By 4 days the human embryo is like a large cyst, with more cells clustered at one side than at the other. This cluster of cells will become the embryo while the other thin layer of cells will help the embryo to invade the lining of the uterus there to develop and grow. The cluster of cells is called the embryonic disc, now seen as only two cells thick.

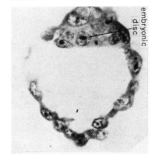

implantation in the uterus

About 7 to 9 days after conception, when there are several hundred cells, the thicker or embryonic end of the sphere makes contact with the uterus, usually with the back wall. This contact is not casual, since the blastocyst appears to be "glued" to the wall. Soon it vigorously erodes through the uterine lining as

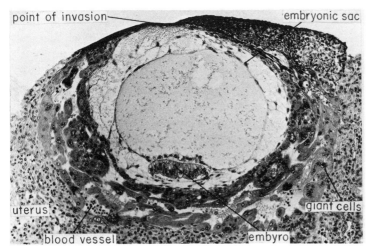

Human embryo at 12 days
Human embryo at 12 days sectioned to show its relation to the mother's uterine tissues. Note that surrounding the invading embryos numerous cells are being destroyed and there are many loose blood cells. The embryo will continue to penetrate deeper and deeper.

Schematic drawing of one side of human female reproductive system showing egg development and early embryonic growth This drawing follows one human egg as it matures in the ovary, ruptures from the ovary (at ovulation) into the surrounding space, is picked up by the fingerlike folds in the opening of the oviduct, and is carried into the oviduct by ciliary currents. Shortly after moving into the oviduct it meets spermatozoa, one of which fertilizes it there. Polar bodies are extruded from the egg and then it begins the process of dividing into two cells, at about 36 hours after it is fertilized. Such an early embryo continues down the oviduct as it divides further into smaller and smaller cells so that by the time it reaches the uterus it is a ball of cells (morula). This morula then acquires an inner cavity, with a cluster of cells to one side. This is a blastula which is next seen invading the lining of the uterus just as a parasite might force its way into the body. Actually the human embryo does develop a parasitic relationship to the mother, the wall of the uterus providing the nesting place for development.

The changes that occur in relation to one human egg pictured here take place about two weeks in the ovary and another week in the oviduct and uterus. Fertilization occurs in the oviduct at the end of the first two weeks of this process. It is of interest to remember that this particular egg was present in the woman's ovary long before she was born, and has been protected, nursed and allowed to develop until this particular time when it matured and became ready for fertilization. In this way it is freed from the ovary and moves to the oviduct to meet the oncoming spermatozoa to accomplish fertilization.

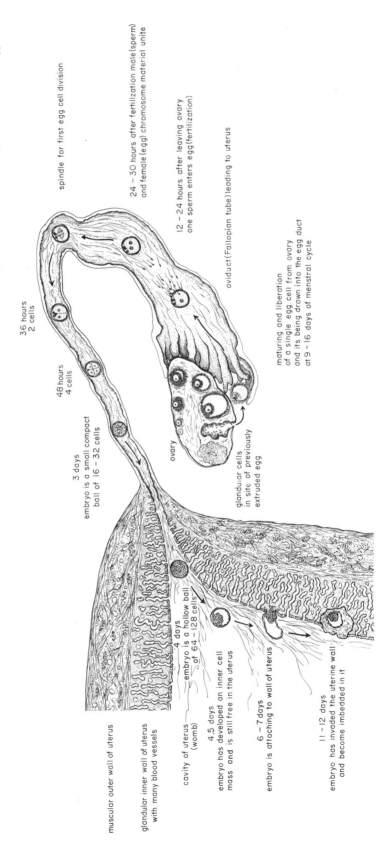

spindle for first egg cell division

24 – 30 hours after fertilization male (sperm) and female (egg) chromosome material unite

12 – 24 hours after leaving ovary one sperm enters egg (fertilization)

oviduct (Fallopian tube) leading to uterus

maturing and liberation of a single egg cell from ovary and its being drawn into the egg duct at 9 – 16 days of menstrual cycle

36 hours 2 cells

48 hours 4 cells

ovary

glandular cells in site of previously extruded egg

3 days embryo is a small compact ball of 16 – 32 cells

muscular outer wall of uterus

glandular inner wall of uterus with many blood vessels

cavity of uterus (womb)

4 days embryo is a hollow ball of 64 – 128 cells

4.5 days embryo has developed an inner cell mass and is still free in the uterus

6 – 7 days embryo is attaching to wall of uterus

11 – 12 days embryo has invaded the uterine wall and become imbedded in it

Surface lining of the uterus about 12 days after conception This very unusual photograph shows where the embryo is implanting, being surrounded by the tissues of the uterus as it penetrates deeper and deeper.

though it were an invading parasite intent on nesting down for the next nine months. The uterus at first reacts to this invasion of the blastocyst as it would to the presence of an enemy. The lining tissues actively swell outward to engulf the embryo, and at the same time marshal thousands of white blood cells to clean up any debris. Then resistance turns to welcome. The blood vessels of the uterus become greatly engorged with blood, the lining glands secrete their fluids more actively, and the uterine tissues seem to make a place for the embryo—some tissues even form a protective cordon around the embryo.

In the relationship between the embryo and the uterus the embryo seems to dominate, although with the acquiescence of the mother's body. The embryo ruptures many of the small maternal blood vessels in its path and is literally bathed in the blood. The hemorrhaging tissues of the uterus liberate a starch called glycogen, which, when broken down into glucose, serves as food for the embryo. This is the first outside source of nutrition for the early embryo, and it immediately gluts itself. The embryonic mass is still only a scarcely visible dot, but it begins to grow at an astounding rate—it doubles its size every day for a few days because of the sudden availability of rich nourishment—and causes a major and continuing adjustment in the tissues of the uterus. (This will be described more fully in conjunction with the placenta.) At this stage the mass of active cells couldn't be distinguished from a mouse embryo or an elephant embryo at a corresponding stage of development. At one week after conception the little human parasite is only about 1/100 inch long.

In summary, up to this point the embryo makes contact with the lining of the uterus and begins by erosion to embed itself into that lining. This is a gradual process lasting several

weeks. By the eighth day after conception the embryo begins to
form an enclosing membrane, the amnion, and secretes into this
sac the amniotic fluid, which cushions the embryo against any
jolt the mother might suffer. The fluid distributes any impact
widely over the body. This is the origin of the term "bag of
waters." The embryo's outermost membrane, the chorion,
makes direct contact with the mother's uterine blood vessels, or
else may be immersed in blood that has hemorrhaged out of the
mother's vessels. A seemingly insignificant structure, known as
the yolk sac, is formed on the opposite side of the disc from the
amnion. It contains no yolk but is so called because it is comparable to the yolk-containing sac of many lower forms, and
possibly of the ancestors of present-day humans. It has a new
significance, however (suggested in Chapter 1), of giving rise to
the primitive germ cells at a very early stage of human development. It also produces blood cells for the embryo until the liver,
spleen, and bone marrow take over. The yolk sac usually disappears during the second month.

Up to this point we have been describing events which
occur at the microscopic level and go unsuspected by the
mother. Increasingly intricate mechanisms gradually transform
this cluster of apparently similar cells into a child. The most
important new aid to this growth and transformation is the
placenta, which serves as an intermediary between mother and
embryo. The placenta may be regarded as a multiservice organ
substitute for the immature digestive system, kidneys, liver,
lungs, and endocrine glands of the embryo. It exchanges stale
blood for fresh, waste products for digested food, embryonic
hormones for maternal hormones. It acts as a barrier against
infection and it aids in maintaining pregnancy against the
tendency to rejection. We will describe the placenta and its
functions now, even though it develops almost throughout the
course of pregrancy, because it begins to form shortly after
implantation and is vital to survival and growth. Then we will
pick up the embryo proper and trace its development for the
first month.

the placenta: exchange device par excellence

The placenta is a disc-shaped mass of tissues. In it capillaries
(tiny blood vessels) from both mother and fetus intertwine
without joining. Materials are exchanged between mother and
embryo through membranes which keep out relatively large

particles but through which dissolved nutrients and waste products can diffuse readily. The placenta presents many square yards of contact surface for this exchange.

By three weeks the placenta covers 20 per cent of the uterus; and by five months, 50 per cent. The placenta grows until about seven months after conception, then remains static until the eighth month, when it begins to regress a bit. At 24 weeks the placenta weighs about 250 grams (roughly 8 ounces) and at birth about 640 grams (almost 1½ pounds). When the baby is delivered, the placenta follows as the afterbirth. The uterus then regenerates its lining in preparation for any future pregnancy.

The placenta begins to form as soon as implantation takes place. The thinner side of the embryo (called the trophoblast) eats its way into the uterine lining and forms an ever expanding surface contact with the capillaries of the uterus. By 12 days after conception the chorion, the outermost membrane of the embryo, begins to form folds which develop into the many-fingered projections known as villi. These villi rupture uterine capillaries to form pools of blood. In each villus are blood vessels which pick up digested food and infuse it into the embryo's blood vessels. The ruptured uterine capillaries are still connected with the intact blood vessels of the mother, and therefore pooled blood can be returned to the mother's circulatory system. There the waste products and gaseous carbon dioxide are removed and the blood recharged with oxygen and nutrients for the embryo (and later for the fetus).

While the uterus is most cooperative, the trophoblast apparently initiates it all by enzyme action, since the embryo could become embedded in the linings of other organs if transplanted there; all it needs is a high-density capillary network to bring it nourishment. In rare cases the fertilized ovum escapes the ciliary currents of the oviduct and spontaneously develops outside the uterus—in the oviduct (Fallopian tube) or even in the body cavity. These, of course, are abnormal sites, and although development and even the formation of a pseudo-placenta can begin, development cannot proceed for long, and therefore the embryo must be removed surgically to protect the mother. Such pregnancies are called ectopic.

From the beginning the placenta is connected to the embryo by the umbilical cord, which is a conduit carrying two fetal arteries and one fetal vein. The umbilical cord may measure from 5 inches to more than 4 feet in length. Its three blood vessels are cushioned in a substance known as Wharton's jelly; just before birth these vessels carry about 300 quarts of blood a day back and forth from placenta to fetus at a rate of about 4 miles per hour. The round trip of a single corpuscle from the cord to the baby's body and back takes about 30 seconds. The two arteries carry blood loaded with waste products from the fetus to the placenta while the single large vein carries oxygen and nutrients to the fetus. The force and volume of blood flow in the umbilical cord keeps it taut, like a filled hose, so that knots seldom form even though the baby may move in all directions in its fluid chamber. By analogy, the conduit that enables the space-walking astronaut to remain connected with his capsule has been called his umbilical cord.

Even immunities to certain diseases built up by the mother during her pregnancy can be passed through the placenta to the fetus. These immunities will persist for some six months after birth, granting the child temporary resistance against many of those infectious diseases so harmful to children.

The placenta also helps combat internal infection. It is selective about what materials will pass through it for the benefit of the fetus. Thus it is the main defensive barrier for the fetus. Moreover, just before birth, the placenta takes on the added function of altering the hormone balance, which is believed to be vital in initiating labor and birth.

Human fetal placenta
This is the treelike structure representing the fetal part of the placenta, namely two arteries and a vein, all injected so as to distend them as they might be seen in the living placenta. The maternal part of the placenta is quite similar, and would be intermeshed with this so that substances could diffuse from one to the other.

Substances are transferred through the placenta by physical diffusion (a process by which the molecules of two fluids flow back and forth between them without combining chemically). Particles with a molecular weight less than 1,000 (the equivalent of about 50 molecules of water) can pass through the walls of the blood vessels. The tiny particles diffuse from a region of high concentration to a region of low concentration until a balance is struck. The mother's blood, whether it flows in her capillaries or oozes in the spaces between them into which it has escaped by hemorrhaging, is usually higher in digested nutrients than the fetal blood on the other side of the membrane. Therefore these dissolved nutrients diffuse readily from mother to fetus. Such foods are predigested by the mother's enzymes, so that all the fetus need do is recombine them into its own type of protoplasm. Likewise, the waste products from food metabolism or from respiration (such as gaseous carbon dioxide), or from kidney waste products like uric acid, pass constantly from the fetal circulation to the mother's circulation and are excreted through her kidneys, lungs, and so forth.

This is purely a physical transfer and requires no special mechanism other than that the walls of the blood vessels be semipermeable, that is, they allow some but not all substances to pass. The rate of transfer and the quantity transferred is automatically regulated by the difference in concentration between the blood of the mother and that of her fetus. When the fetal blood is low in nutrients, and the mother's blood is high in those same nutrients, they will automatically pass from mother to fetus by diffusion. Digested food substances in the mother's blood can reach the fetus within an hour's time (see Chapter 9). The fetus becomes an increasingly efficient parasite in the uterus of its mother; if the nutritional needs of the fetus exceed what is normally supplied for both, *then the mother will suffer the consequences.* To avoid this the obstetrician may prescribe certain supplemental chemicals and vitamins for the pregnant woman.

There is one known exception to this explanation, namely, that vitamin C passes from mother to fetus via the placenta but cannot return to the mother, no matter what the concentrations. This suggests that there are probably devices other than the obvious one of simple physical diffusion for the transfer of materials between mother and fetus, and it also emphasizes the mother's own needs.

Respiration is also accomplished by diffusion. There is a one-way passage of oxygen from mother to fetus, where the concentration is always lower. On the other hand, since the fetal tissues have a higher carbon dioxide concentration than the mother's blood, this gas is passed to the mother by the fetus for her to exhale. The placenta is thus a miniature version of the mother's lungs. Should the mother live in a rarefied atmosphere high in the mountains, or go on an extended high-altitude flight with inadequate oxygen pressure conditions, the placenta would try to compensate for this by growing larger and thus provide more surface for the blood vessels to make the exchanges.

There is also a constant exchange of water between mother and fetus. The early fetus is about 90 per cent water by weight, and this is decreased to about 70 per cent by the time of birth. Some of this water is diffused from the mother's blood, but a portion is also swallowed by the fetus from the surrounding amniotic fluid. Water may be excreted by the fetus into the amniotic sac, and some of it will pass out by way of the mother's circulation and her kidneys.

development after the first week

Now we return to the events after conception. To review them briefly, the fertilized ovum has turned successively into zygote, morula, and blastocyst and has implanted itself in the uterine lining. One end of the hollow, spherical blastula has thickened and formed the disc-shaped blastoderm, while the thinner mass of cells on the other side constitutes the trophoblast. The embryo develops from the blastoderm, and the various membranes and protective sacs from the trophoblast.

At seven days the single-layered ball of cells folds over to form two—and then three—layers of cells. The resultant pouch-like structure is called the gastrula (literally, "little stomach"). The outermost layer, called the ectoderm, develops a bulge at 11 to 13 days that is called the primitive streak. This primitive streak is thought to be a marker for the main axis of the baby's body, along which it will later develop its spinal column. It is the first indication that the embryo will be a vertebrate and will have a left and a right side.

The period from days 18 to 28 is known as the neurula stage, when the emphasis is on development of the nervous system, even though other vital organs (such as the heart) develop at the same time. The neural groove—sort of a channel in which the spinal cord and spinal nerves will form—is laid down along the length of the primitive streak. By the third week

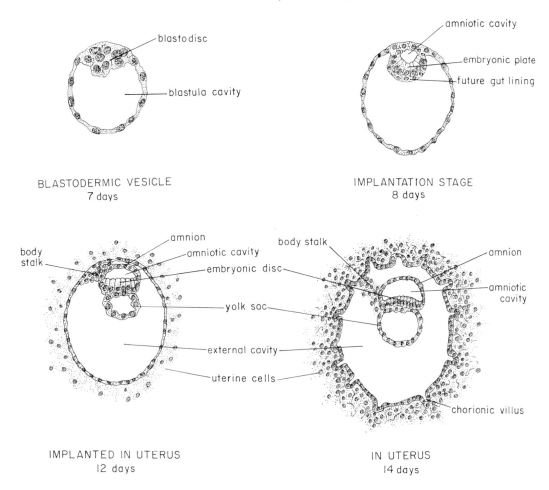

BLASTODERMIC VESICLE
7 days

IMPLANTATION STAGE
8 days

IMPLANTED IN UTERUS
12 days

IN UTERUS
14 days

the groove starts to close into a tube.

The nervous system begins to form very early (18 days), and it continues to develop until at least several weeks after birth. This is necessary because the nervous system integrates the actions of most other systems. At one month after conception the baby's head is the largest part of its body, presumably because its brain develops so early. By 20 days the foundation for the child's brain, spinal cord, and entire nervous system will have been established, as well as the rudiments of its eyes. The primordial nervous system at first will be made up of neuroblasts, or primitive neurons. These neurons, aggregated to form nerves, will permeate every minute region of the growing child's body to control it much like a telephone system reaching out from a central office to the most remote regions. But it is always a two-way system, for messages can be brought to as well as

The second week of human development

Human embryo (dorsal aspect) Estimated fertilization age: 21 days. C.R.L.: 2.1 mm. Streeter's horizon: 10.

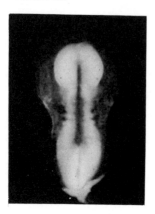

Human embryo (dorsal aspect) Estimated fertilization age: 24 days C.R.L.: 3.6 mm. Streeter's horizon: 11.

away from the brain. By 6 weeks after conception this system will have developed so well that it is controlling movements of the baby's muscles, even though the pregnant woman is still unable to feel such movements. The nervous system eventually comprises the most efficient cable system in the world for the transmission of messages. Ultimately each nerve fiber will be covered by a sheath of protective cells (sometimes 5,000 per fiber), and each will be able to carry messages at a speed of 150 yards per second, or 300 miles per hour. From these primitive cells, first distinguishable at 18 days after conception, the embryo will form more than 10,000 taste buds in its mouth. The fetus has many times the number of taste buds that it will have as a newborn infant, and there is ample reason to believe that it has a keen sense of taste. Some 12 million nerve endings will form in the baby's nose to help it to detect fragrances or odors in the air. More than 100,000 nerve cells will be devoted to reacting to Beethoven's Fifth Symphony or to the rasping of a riveter, the screeching of an auto, or the ticking of a Swiss watch. The piano has only 240 strings, but the baby's ears will have more than 240,000 hearing units to detect the smallest variations in sound. The baby's eyes, which begin to form at 19 days, will have more than 100,000 sensitive areas made up in turn of more than 12 million screen points per square centimeter; the retina, or light-sensitive portion, of its eye will have more than 50 billion such points. The composite picture the eyes record is homogeneous because these light-sensitive points blend into a whole. Take a hand lens and examine any picture in any daily newspaper. You will find it made up of hundreds of points, each light or dark, which together make up the picture as you look at it from a greater distance. This is exactly what the eye does, only in much finer detail. Where do these billions of cells in the nervous system come from? From the original fertilized ovum, which is still dividing after one month to form the tissues and organs that the child requires. *It has been estimated that all 2 billion of the specific nerve cells which make any individual educable are located in the outer covering of his brain, its cortex, and that these 2 billion cells could be stored in a thimble.* The nervous system comes from the original outer layer of embryonic cells known as the ectoderm, which arises first at about 8 or 9 days after conception. Development continues even after birth in certain parts of the brain. By the end of the first month of embryonic development none of these parts of the brain, spinal cord, nerves, or sense organs is completely formed, but the foundation for all of them has been laid.

During this period of the initial development of the nervous system, the embryo is simultaneously forming some of its basic muscles. By 28 days it has the building blocks for 40 pairs of muscles, situated from the base of its skull to the lower end of its spinal column. The 33 pairs of vertebrae that form the spinal column start as segments known as somites, which grow laterally out from the neural tube in the third week. To serve these nerves and muscles the embryo simultaneously forms its heart (as we pointed out earlier in this chapter) and the many blood vessels that will ultimately nourish and remove wastes from every cell of the growing body. The muscles of the heart must begin to pump the baby's blood around the closed circulatory system, through the walls of which will diffuse the nourishment the embryo's blood gets from the mother via the placenta.

Thus, by the end of the first month after conception the human embryo has gone from the one-celled state to millions of cells, from an unformed microscopic unit of protoplasm to intricately organized groups of cells which have specific assignments or functions in the incipient nervous, muscular, vascular (circulatory), digestive, and skeletal systems. The embryo forms first a tubular and then a chambered heart through which blood can be channeled to deliver nutrition or to eliminate waste, and begins the formation of a tubular system in which food can be digested for assimilation and growth. The embryologist often refers to the digestive system by the earthy name of "gut" or "food canal." At about the 22nd day the human embryo quickly develops the pronephros, a kidney-like structure that resembles the kidneys of primitive eels. The pronephros never functions in the human embryo but is displaced in several weeks by the mesonephros, a more posterior and truly kidney-like structure. The mesonephros, which actually functions for a time, is reminiscent of the kidneys of fishes and frogs and is in turn displaced by a much more advanced and efficient excretory organ, the metanephric kidneys of the newborn (and adult) human.

This, then, is the great planning period, when out of apparently nothing comes evidence of a well-integrated individual who will form along certain well-tried patterns, but who will, in the end, be distinguishable from every other human being by virtue of ultramicroscopic chromosomal differences. During these early days of development this embryo possesses 4 pairs of temporary gill arches which form in the same manner as they do in fishes, tadpoles, and birds, but they never function in its breathing. It also has a rudimentary tail, an extension of its

Circulatory system of human embryo at 4 weeks

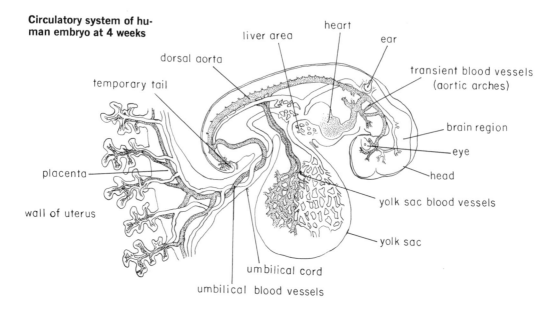

heart

liver area

ear

dorsal aorta

transient blood vessels (aortic arches)

temporary tail

brain region

eye

placenta

head

wall of uterus

yolk sac blood vessels

yolk sac

umbilical cord

umbilical blood vessels

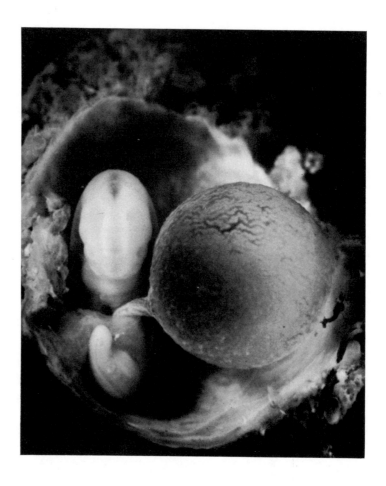

Human embryo and yolk sac 28 days; 5.2 mm. or 3/16 inch.

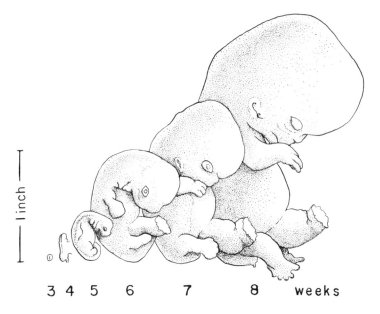

Human ova and embryos showing growth and body form from 3 to 8 weeks

1 inch

3 4 5   6   7   8   weeks

spinal column, which is absorbed and disappears in almost all (except 6 per cent) children. These, like many other temporary structures, are remnants of our ancestry, retained in embryonic life but useless in survival.

The second month of life is not quite as decisive as the first—indeed no period is—but it, too, is a period of great change and accompanying vulnerability.

the second month:
the embryo
becomes the fetus

In the second month of pregnancy a threshold is crossed: the embryo becomes a fetus, and the growing organism, small as it is, looks human even if quite unlike its parents. Before then it could easily be confused with the offspring of many other species—a pig, a mouse, an elephant, or a chick.

It has been said, "Ontogeny recapitulates phylogeny," or the development of an individual from conception to birth retraces the evolutionary history of the entire species. The evidence produced to support this theory is the fact that the embryo (and later the fetus) passes through various phases which resemble the embryonic forms of other species: It gives rise to a yolk sac, it develops gill-like visceral arches; its paired eyes appear first on the sides of the head; its kidneys undergo a metamorphosis in which initially structures similar to those found in primitive eels appear, to be superseded by a froglike set and finally by an unmistakably mammalian pair; it develops a tail that usually disappears, and so forth. Every human retains 27 vestiges of his ancestry—none presently useful to him. This theory of recapitulation has a very limited validity in that it demonstrates the similarity between the embryonic development of a human and that of any other vertebrate. But it would be a serious mistake to believe that the fetus passes through a proto-zoan phase (since the zygote superficially resembles a single-celled animal like the amoeba), a fish phase, an amphibian phase, a bird phase, a general mammalian phase and a monkey phase—from lowest to highest—before it becomes human. There are simply too many exceptions in the order in which features appear—and indeed in whether they appear at all—to support such a theory. And as for the question, "When does the embryo become human?" the answer is that it *always* had human potential, and *no other,* from the instant the sperm and the egg came together, because of its chromosomes.

Then why, you may ask, does the embryo develop extraneous structures? Well, the mature fish, the mature fowl, and the mature human are very different. Their evolutionary paths have diverged sharply, even though all three are vertebrates. But their *ontogeny,* or development, is not radically different, and many purposes are served by similar primitive structures in the embryo. In the fish, for example, the arches become gills, while in man they become the jaw, the larynx and pharynx, etc.

What marks the transition from embryo to fetus? It is not an abrupt one. Some features become obvious early, others late. Rather, it is the cumulative effect of many changes that bring the gleam of recognition to the observer.

The real significance of the transition is not the creature's appearance, although it is natural for the parent to identify more easily with the manlike fetus than the chick-like embryo. Rather, it marks a degree of completeness in that all the major organ systems have been started if not actually built, and coming out of the second month the fetus is far less vulnerable to the effects of disease, drugs, radiation, and other external influences (see Chapter 10) than the embryo was when it entered that month. The fetus is by no means out of danger, but now for the first time it is better able to survive certain conditions that would surely have been lethal or disabling earlier. Most of this increased resistance comes from the fact that the fetus has safely started to form all of its vital parts, but another consideration is its larger size: it would take larger doses or concentrations of toxic materials, more serious diseases, or more radiation to wreak havoc with the fetal constitution.

Let's take a closer look at that progress.

At the end of the first month after conception the human embryo is about a quarter of an inch in length from the top of its flat, bulbous head to the end of its temporary tail. Internally,

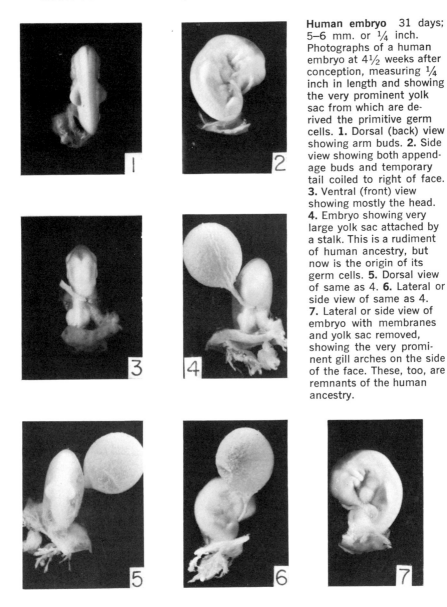

Human embryo 31 days; 5–6 mm. or ¼ inch. Photographs of a human embryo at 4½ weeks after conception, measuring ¼ inch in length and showing the very prominent yolk sac from which are derived the primitive germ cells. **1.** Dorsal (back) view showing arm buds. **2.** Side view showing both appendage buds and temporary tail coiled to right of face. **3.** Ventral (front) view showing mostly the head. **4.** Embryo showing very large yolk sac attached by a stalk. This is a rudiment of human ancestry, but now is the origin of its germ cells. **5.** Dorsal view of same as 4. **6.** Lateral or side view of same as 4. **7.** Lateral or side view of embryo with membranes and yolk sac removed, showing the very prominent gill arches on the side of the face. These, too, are remnants of the human ancestry.

most of the organs are just starting to form. Since the brain and the heart are needed much sooner than the digestive organs, the upper end of the body develops faster than the lower, and one-third of the embryo's length is taken up by the head. There is no distinguishable face—only the outlines of eyes appear on the sides of the head, just above the large but primitive mouth cavity. At 30 days the three primary parts of the brain are present, and the eyes, ears, and nasal organs have started to form. While the elements of the backbone have been laid down, the embryo is so bent that the head almost touches the tail—as in the development of the chick, mouse, pig, etc. There are no discernible arms or legs yet.

At this time the heart is an S-shaped bulge in the midriff that almost meets the forward-bent head, and its pulsation may be observable through the thin, transparent skin. Although the heart is still incomplete, it is now beating rhythmically, pumping blood cells through a closed but expanding vascular system, which includes not only the embryo's own blood vessels but also the umbilical cord and placenta. The blood itself is forming in the yolk sac.

The basic alimentary canal (digestive tract) forms downward from the mouth (which opens for the first time on the 28th day). The liver is the first of the gastric glands or organs to appear; liver cells begin to aggregate on the 21st day and can be recognized as the liver by days 27 to 30, when the gall bladder appears. The thyroid gland, which will play a vital role in metabolism, enters its initial phase of development, arising from

Human embryo (four aspects) Estimated fertilization age: 33 days. C.R.L.: 5.2 mm. Streeter's horizon: 13.

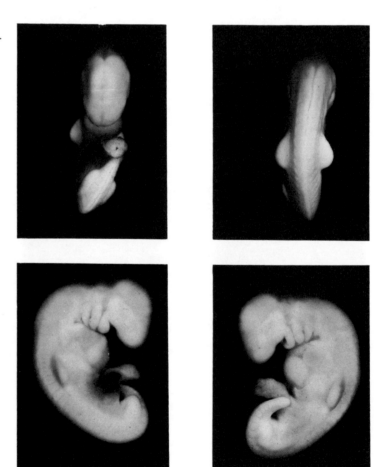

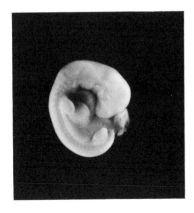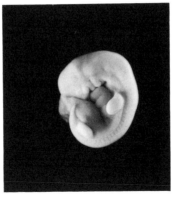

Human embryo 34 days;
8 mm. or 5/16 inch.

the food canal. The stomach, intestines, liver, and pancreas are defined, but there is no anal opening. The respiratory system (potential lungs) is still connected with the digestive tract. Lung buds may be seen on the 27th day, but the trachea (windpipe) does not form until a few days later.

During the second month the mother may gain or lose as much as 2 pounds, compared with the average of 1 pound she gains during the first month. At the same time the fetus increases its weight to 1 gram (about one-thirtieth of an ounce). While this is lighter than an aspirin tablet, it represents a 50-fold gain over what the four-week-old embryo weighed. The rest of the mother's weight gain is made up largely of fluids.

A diary of some of the events of the second month (starting with the 31st day) would usually read as follows:

day 31

Muscles appear in the pelvic region. Both arms and legs begin to form as protruding buds. The nerve root fibers of the spinal cord form, and the optic stalk (at the end of which the eyes will form) is prominent in the brain structure. The stomach and esophagus (food tube leading to the stomach) begin to form. The valve separating the upper and lower parts of the heart appears now or in the next few days, although the heart is still not divided into compartments. The germ cells are actively moving along the mesodermic tissue toward the genital ridges, where they will later form into ovaries or testes (see Chapter 1).

day 32

More caudal muscle blocks appear, and the fourth and last pair of vestigial gill arches forms.

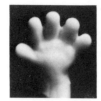

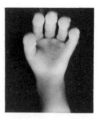

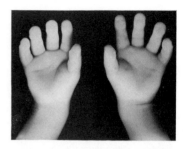

Hand plate
6 weeks

Finger ridges
7 weeks

Definite thumb and
fingers with pads
8 weeks

Regression of finger pads
13 weeks

Development of human hands

day 33

The brain is now a series of five cavities lined with embryonic nerve tissue that will grow and almost fill the cavities. The earliest differentiation of the cerebral cortex, the part of the brain that governs motor activity as well as intellect, may be seen. Tail muscles form, but since they are vestigial they never function to move the tail. The ear pits may be seen on the side of the head.

day 34

More tail muscles form, and the slender stalk separating the embryo from the yolk sac lengthens. The vestigial tail reaches its maximum length.

day 35

The primitive germ cells arrive in large numbers along the embryonic kidney ridge. The olfactory lobe (associated with the sense of smell) is present in the brain.

Development of human feet (Slightly later than hands)

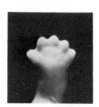

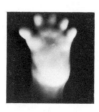

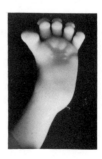

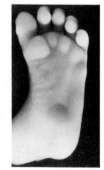

Foot plate
7 weeks

Toe ridges
Two days later

Heel development
8 weeks

Note walking pads
9 weeks

Regression of toe pads
13 weeks

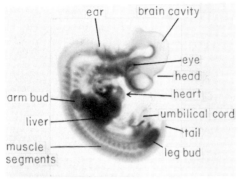

ear brain cavity

eye
head
arm bud
heart
liver
umbilical cord
tail
muscle segments
leg bud

Looking through a 5-week embryo This specimen was prepared by clearing in oil of wintergreen to make it transparent, thus revealing the inner structure.

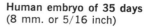

Human embryo of 35 days (8 mm. or 5/16 inch)

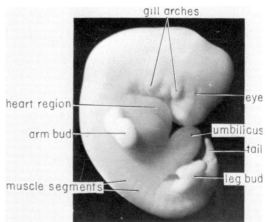

gill arches

heart region
arm bud
muscle segments
eye
umbilicus
tail
leg bud

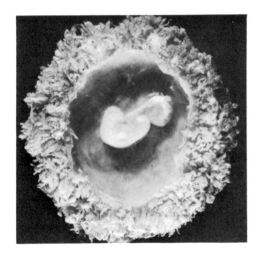

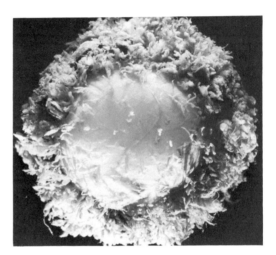

Human embryo at 5 weeks within its chorionic vesicle

Other remarks on the fifth week: The embryo is 8 milli-meters (one-third inch) in total length from crown to rump, and weighs only about 1/1,000 of an ounce.[1] The jaws are forming and the face begins to look human. The umbilical cord is prominent and is now the only part of the embryo that is con-nected to the placenta. The pituitary gland, so important in the control of bodily processes, is forming in the middle of the brain. The pharynx gives rise to two branches which will later form the bronchi (tubes that bring air to the lungs). The trachea

1. These measurements, like others reported in the book, represent averages of the specimens studied and may not apply to any specific case.

Human fetus at 38 days postconception This is about the time any woman would first suspect she is pregnant. At this stage it could easily be confused with fetuses of the mouse, rat, pig, etc. However, it is at the most critical stage so far as the production of congenital anomalies is concerned, because the organs have not yet completely differentiated. It is at this stage that the tranquilizer Thalidomide had its most devastating effects.

grows as the spleen and liver ducts are all forming, and the intestines elongate. Membranes begin to divide the trunk into separate cavities for the heart, lungs, and viscera (organs and glands of the digestive tract).

day 36

All of the muscle blocks have now appeared. The arm and leg buds are formed, and the tail begins to regress. The fetus may have started to move its body, but the movement cannot yet be detected by the mother or the obstetrician.

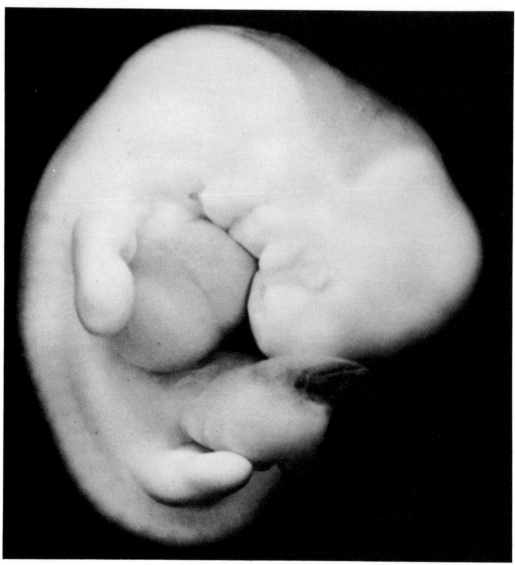

day 37

The intestines are growing and now begin to bend. The cavity that forms the outer ear chamber closes and recedes into the head. The brain stem is now recognizable.

day 38

The upper and lower jaw parts, each of which was formed in two symmetrical halves with a gap between them, now begin to fuse in the midline of the face. The delicate eye muscles begin to form. The larynx is temporarily obstructed, now or in the next few days. The hand plates (paddle-like rudiments of a hand) develop. The viscera have grown too rapidly for the body enclosure and are so enlarged that they project temporarily from the body in a sort of hernia. The germ cells reach the gonad region and end their migration.

Fetal membrane (chorionic villi) at 40 days (Uterus side)

day 39

Nerve fibers connect with the olfactory lobe of the brain, laying the groundwork for the sensation of smell.

day 40

The eyes become pigmented, as seen through the transparent skin. The jaws are now well formed, and the teeth and facial muscles begin to form. The vestigial gill arches disappear. The diaphragm forms, as do limb, back, and abdominal muscles. Partitioning of the heart into distinct chambers begins. The liver takes over the manufacture of blood cells from the yolk sac, which by now is separated from the digestive tract by its attenuated stalk.

day 42

The earliest reflexes begin. The rudiments of fingers and then toes become evident, and the first traces of undifferentiated gonads appear. In the male the penis begins to form.

Other remarks on the sixth week: the fetus is 13 millimeters (half an inch) long. Cartilage centers appear where bone will later develop. The head seems to be relatively larger even than it was at 5 weeks, and it is bent forward onto the chest. The fingers develop. Milk lines, which give rise to the mammary

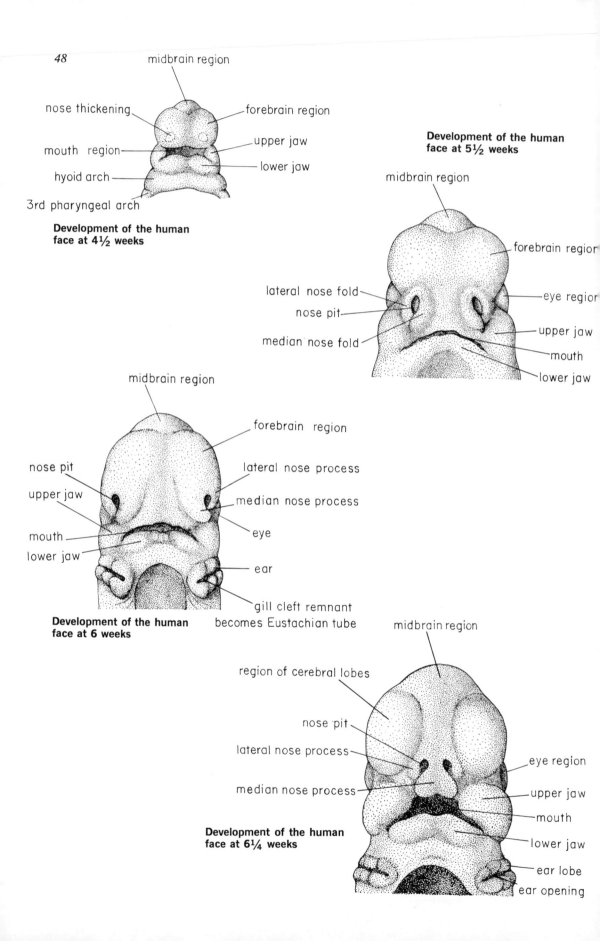

48

midbrain region

nose thickening

forebrain region

mouth region

upper jaw

lower jaw

hyoid arch

3rd pharyngeal arch

**Development of the human
face at 4½ weeks**

**Development of the human
face at 5½ weeks**

midbrain region

forebrain region

lateral nose fold

eye region

nose pit

upper jaw

median nose fold

mouth

lower jaw

midbrain region

forebrain region

nose pit

lateral nose process

upper jaw

median nose process

mouth

eye

lower jaw

ear

gill cleft remnant
becomes Eustachian tube

**Development of the human
face at 6 weeks**

midbrain region

region of cerebral lobes

nose pit

lateral nose process

eye region

median nose process

upper jaw

mouth

lower jaw

**Development of the human
face at 6¼ weeks**

ear lobe

ear opening

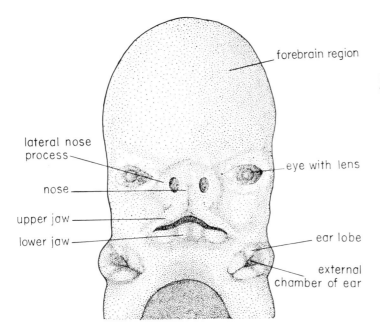

forebrain region

**Development of the human
face at 7 weeks**

lateral nose
process

eye with lens

nose

upper jaw

lower jaw

ear lobe

external
chamber of ear

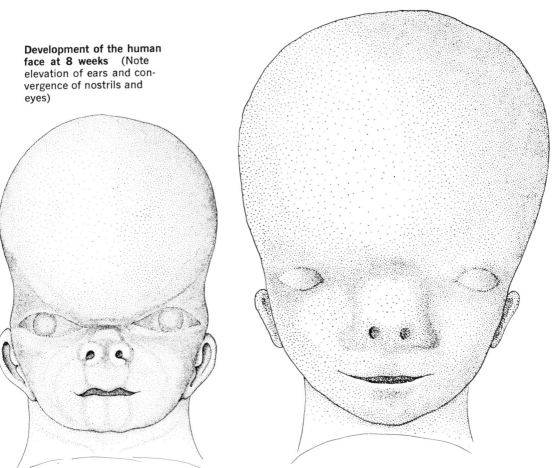

**Development of the human
face at 8 weeks** (Note
elevation of ears and con-
vergence of nostrils and
eyes)

**Development of the human
face at 10 weeks** (Eyes
still far apart, ears not
fully elevated, nostrils
coming together, mouth
open)

Human embryo (four aspects) Estimated fertilization age: 41 days. C.R.L.: 9.4 mm. Streeter's horizon: 15.

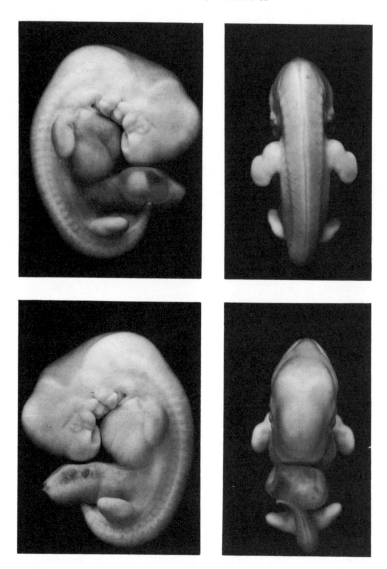

glands, appear in both sexes. The stomach and intestines begin to rotate as they must to fit into the abdomen and take up their final positions. Muscles throughout the body are lengthening, and both cartilage and bone may be seen in the forming skeleton. The pronephros (the first, and nonfunctioning, set of kidneys) has been replaced by the mesonephros (the second stage), and the metanephric kidneys (the final set) have started to form.

day 44

The nerve cells of the retina of the eye form, as do the palate of the mouth and the semicircular canals of the ear, which aid in maintaining balance. The jaw parts continue to grow and fuse, drawing largely on the remnants of the vestigial gill arches.

day 46

The gonads (ovaries or testes) have differentiated so that microscopic examination could reveal the sex of the fetus. The nasal passages open to the outside.

day 48

The face rounds out and begins to look human. All evidence of vestigial ancestral gills or gill arches disappears. The tongue forms from the floor of the mouth. The nerve connections from the retina to the brain are established.

Other remarks on seventh week: the fetus is 20 millimeters (four-fifths inch) long. The head continues to enlarge, and a distinct neck now connects the head with the body. The cerebral

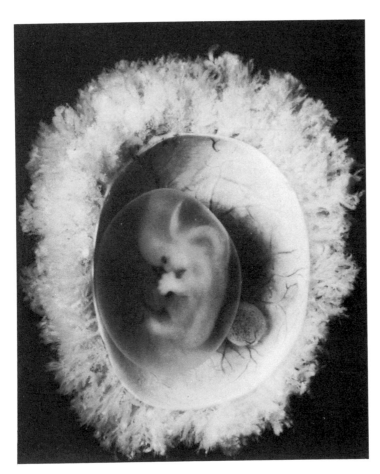

Forty-two-day human fetus —½ inch long—showing amnion, yolk sac, chorionic placenta This perfect specimen of a human fetus of about 42 days (½ inch body length) is seen within its amniotic sac, the attached yolk sac, the blood vessels lining the placenta, and the surrounding chorionic villi which make up the fetal part of the placenta.

hemispheres, the major part of the brain, begin to fill the forward part of the head. The back is now straighter, and the tail normally begins to regress. All the fingers are present, although they are not fully formed. The ears are developing rapidly, and the eyes even more so. The stomach is a miniature version of what it will be in the newborn infant; however, it is temporarily blocked at the point at which it joins the small intestine. All the body muscles are organizing well. The jaws, ribs, and vertebrae are all changing from cartilage to bone. The palate normally begins to close at this time. The temporary kidneys, soon to be replaced by the permanent ones, are helping to rid the fetus of metabolic wastes. By the seventh week the urogenital and rectal passages are completely separate, and an anal membrane appears. This ruptures during the eighth week to form the anus. Traumatic exposure to drugs or diseases at this time may lead to urological abnormalities which will have to be corrected later.

day 50

The hands are now far apart. The head is very large and is bent over the bulging heart. Bone begins to replace the cartilage in the jaws, shoulders, arms, legs, and, to some extent, the body skeleton. The neck muscles are actively forming. The clitoris appears in the female, and the ovaries begin to descend from the

Perfect two-month-old human fetus showing skeleton development

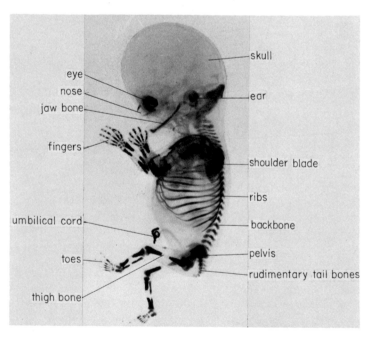

skull

eye
nose
jaw bone

ear

fingers

shoulder blade

ribs

umbilical cord

backbone

toes

pelvis

rudimentary tail bones

thigh bone

site of their origin. The testes begin to descend within the body of the male. The kidney tubules, which will function throughout life, appear in the permanent kidneys.

day 56

The eyes have moved from the sides of the head to the front, and the face appears to be quite human, except that the jaws are not yet fully developed. The heart continues to form its chambers. The umbilical abdominal hernia is still large (much of the viscera are exposed). The appendages are growing rapidly, and the fingers of both hands are usually found close to the nose. In areas where cartilage was previously found, many of the bones are forming (ossifying). A genital swelling in the male may be identified as the scrotum. All facial clefts (rudiments of the ancestral gill slits) close. The palate for the roof of the mouth is forming.[2] The stomach moves into its final position, and muscular layers of the esophagus, stomach, and intestines begin to proliferate. The major blood vessels of the body assume their final plan.

Other remarks on the eighth week: The fetus has grown to 30 millimeters (1¼ inches) in length from the top of its head to its buttocks (its sitting height) and it weighs about one-thirtieth of an ounce (1 gram). The hands and feet are well formed and distinctly human, and the mammary glands are identifiable. The taste buds in the mouth begin to form at this time. The upper and lower jaws are synchronized in development. Various endocrine (ductless) glands, such as the thyroid, thymus, and adrenals, are all developing. The lungs now not only have lobes but also extend into many-branched bronchioles (minute tubes). A diaphragm begins to separate the heart and lungs from the intestines. Direct electrical records (electrocardiograms) have been taken of a 23-millimeter human fetus showing that at 6 to 7 weeks the heartbeat ranged from 40 to 80 per minute; six minutes after the beginning of the recordings, all of the typical phases of the heart record were recognizable, traceable, and measurable. It now seems likely that even at 5½ weeks the fetal heartbeat is essentially similar to that of an adult in general configuration. The intrauterine heartbeat rate of the fetus is usually 117 to 157 per minute because of the warmer environment. The energy output is about 20 per cent that of the adult, but the fetal heart is functionally complete and normal by

2. When, in rare instances, this does not occur the result is a cleft palate and possibly a harelip.

7 weeks. The second set of kidneys (the mesonephros) now shows signs of degenerating, and the permanent kidneys (the metanephros, which will serve newborn and adult) are actively forming to take their place. Movements are possible now, since some of the major muscles are well developed, but such movements are too slight to be detected by the mother.

If one can imagine a one-inch miniature doll with a very large head but gracefully formed arms and legs, Oriental slitlike eyes and small ear lobes over slight depressions on the sides of the head, and a rather bulbous abdomen, he would have a fair mental picture of a two-month-old fetus. The face is unmistakably human but not like that of anyone you know. Since the head comprises almost half the fetus, one gets the impression that it is top-heavy and could not possibly maintain an upright position, which is true. The rapid growth of the head is conditioned in part by the early development of the brain. Growth of the fetus depends entirely upon nutrition from the mother, conveyed through the placenta, the umbilical cord, and its own blood vessels to its growing tissues. The prominent umbilical cord contains three large, visible blood vessels.

Neither the thoughts nor the experiences of the mother can affect the unborn child. The newborn child is the product of its genes. Since there is no nervous connection between the mother and her fetus, it would be impossible for any of her sensations to be transmitted directly to her child at any time. Up to the time of birth, the mother has scant influence on her child (aside from the condition of her own health). In human development the fetus is most sensitive to trauma or to physical injury during the first six weeks after conception, when the majority of women are not aware that they are pregnant. After the fetus forms its major organ systems there is little the mother can do to harm it before birth. Therefore, *there is no scientific basis for thinking that birthmarks, blemishes, or even congenital anomalies are the result of some harrowing nervous experience of the mother*. Development during the first two months is crucial. Once the fetus weathers this successfully, the odds are in its favor.

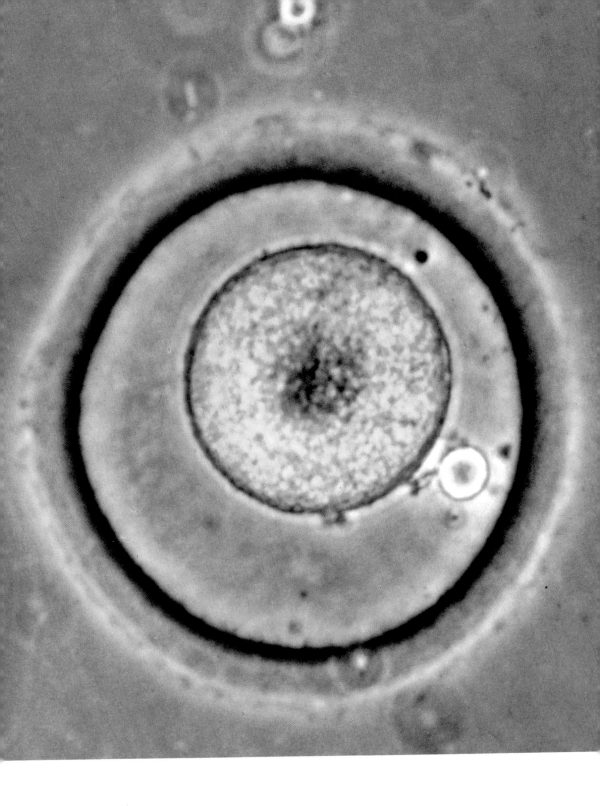

Human ovum Natural
color; 1/175 inch

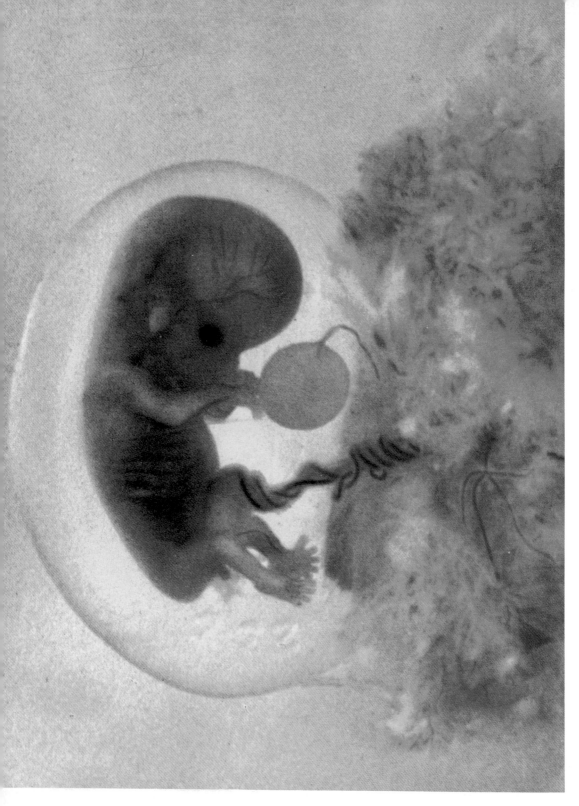

Human fetus at 8 weeks in sac Shows umbilical connection with placenta and persisting yolk sac

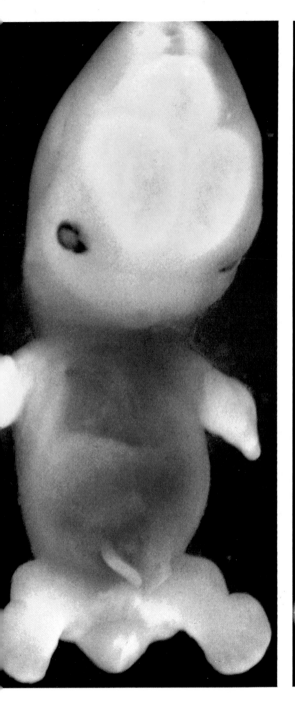
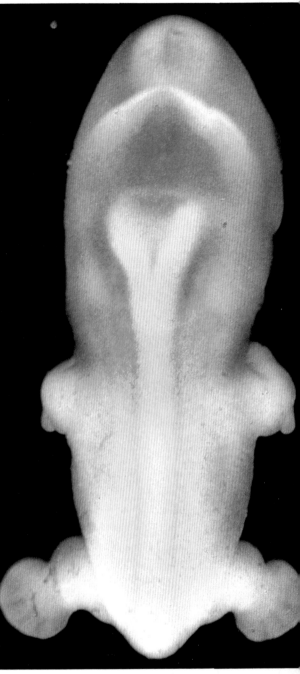

Human fetus at 40 days, front and back views Note spinal cord, brain, paddle-like feet.

OVER: Human fetus at 40 days, side view, natural color

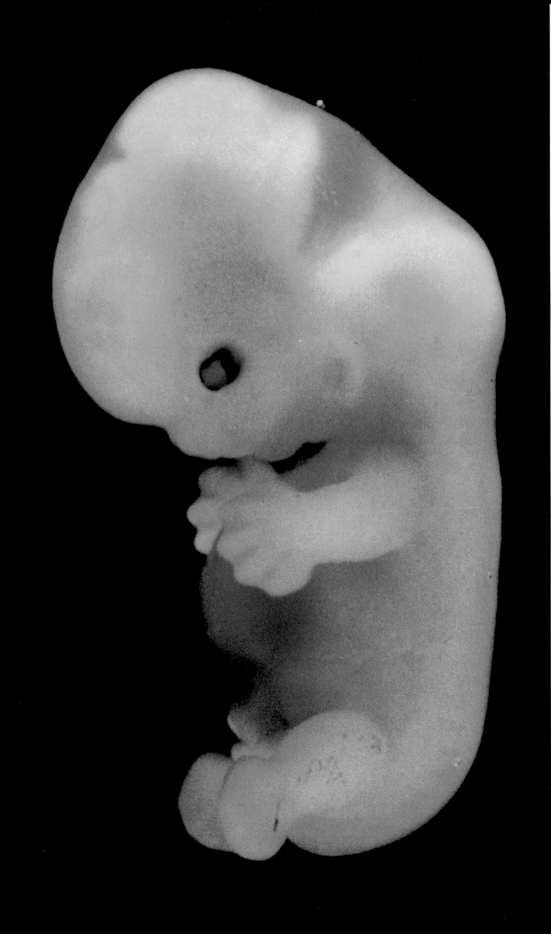

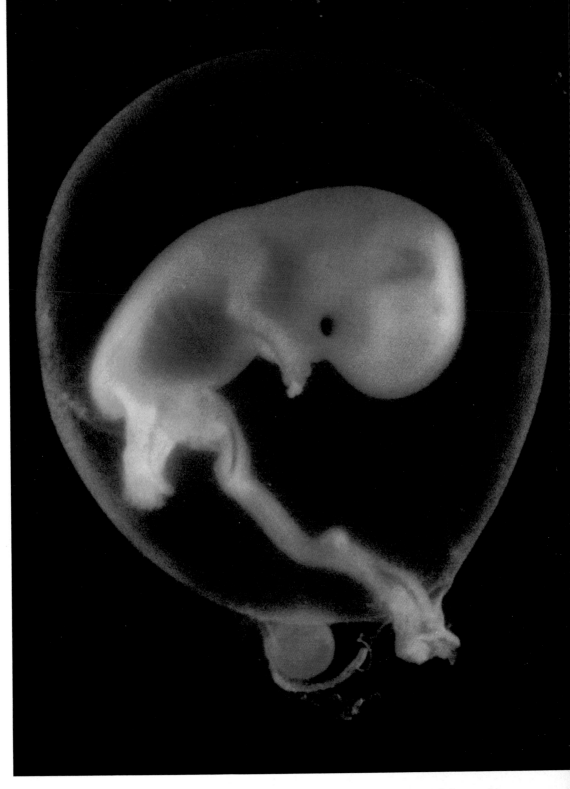

Seven-week human fetus
within amnion but removed
from placenta Note
umbilical cord and yolk sac

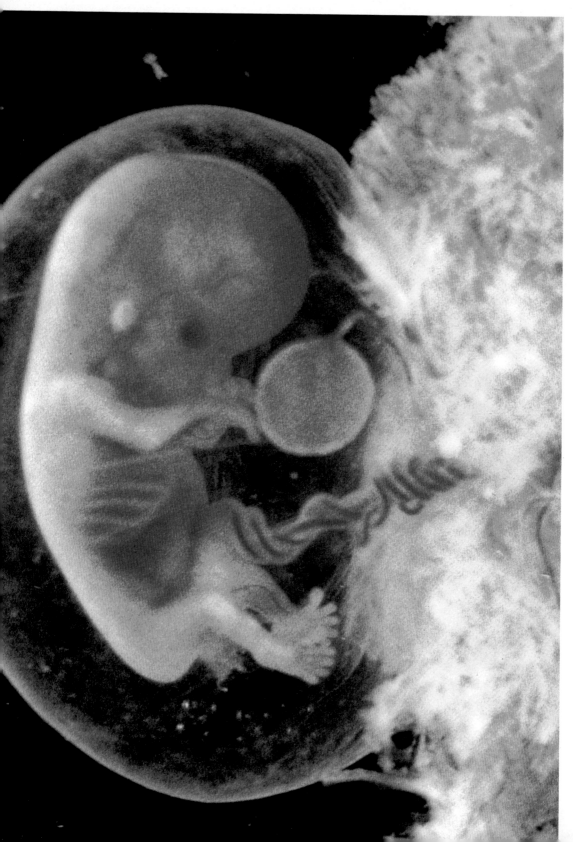

Two-month-old human fetus showing yolk sac, amnion, and placenta

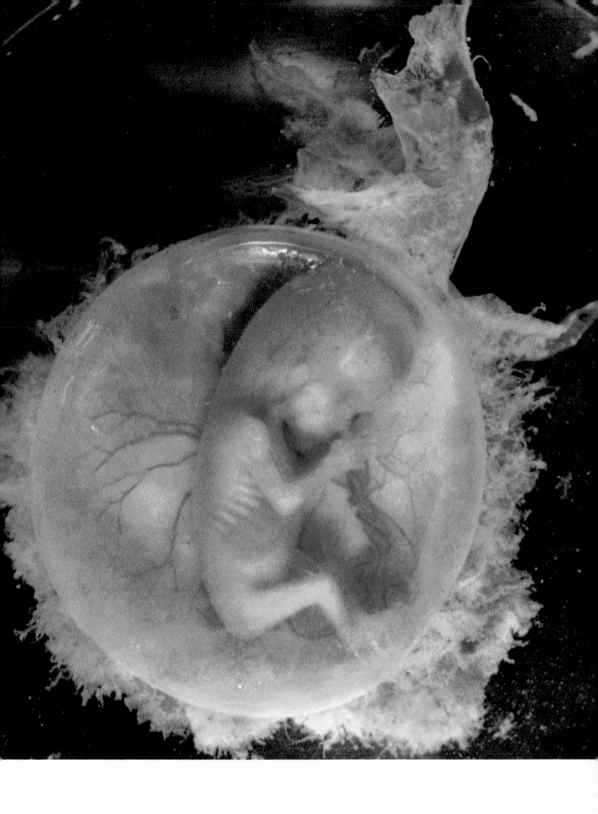

Two-month-old human
fetus in sac

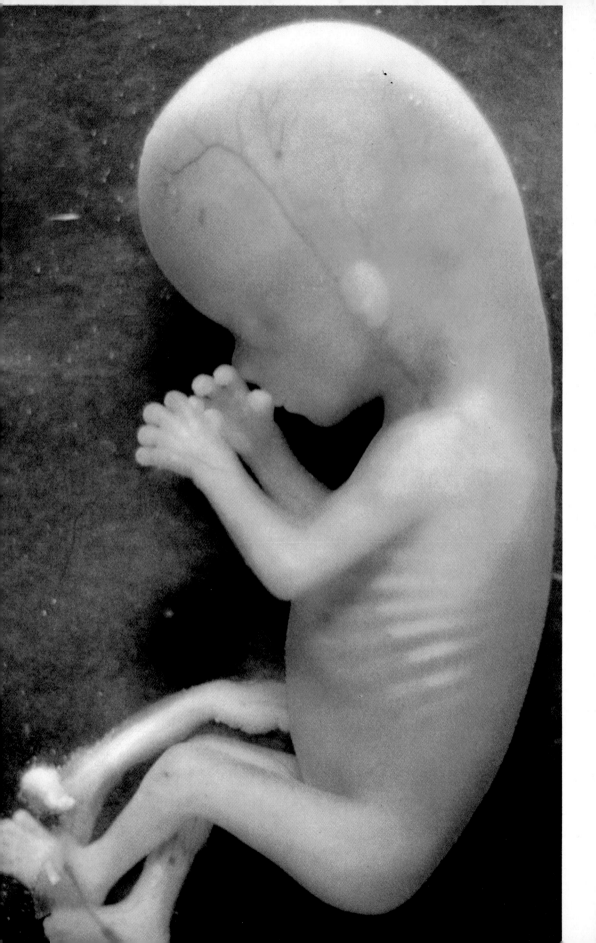

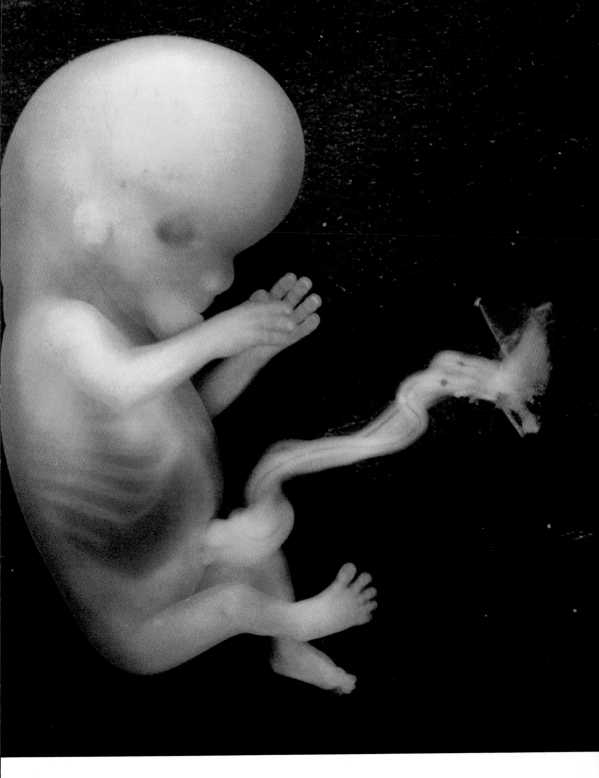

LEFT: Perfect two-month-old human fetus showing skeleton development

ABOVE: Ten-week human fetus, right side

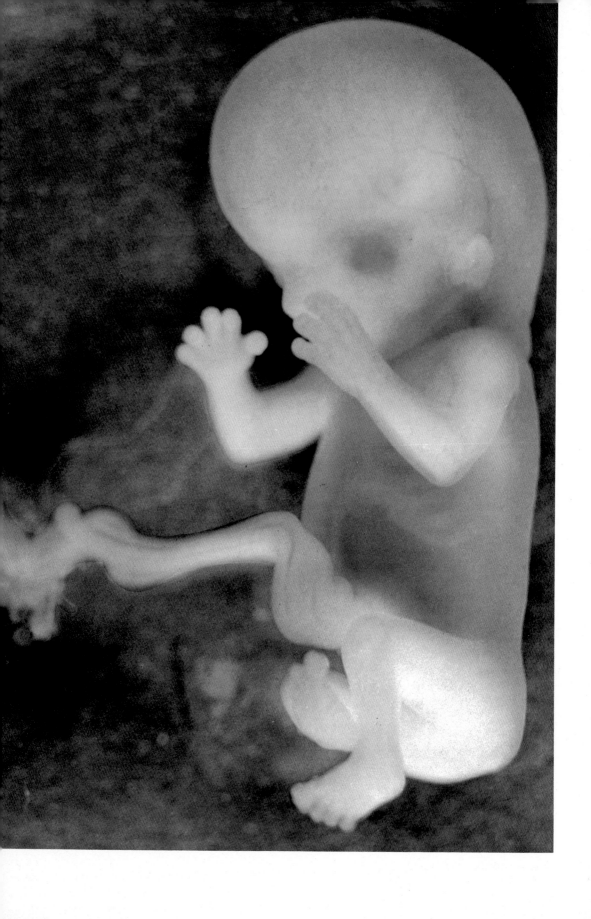

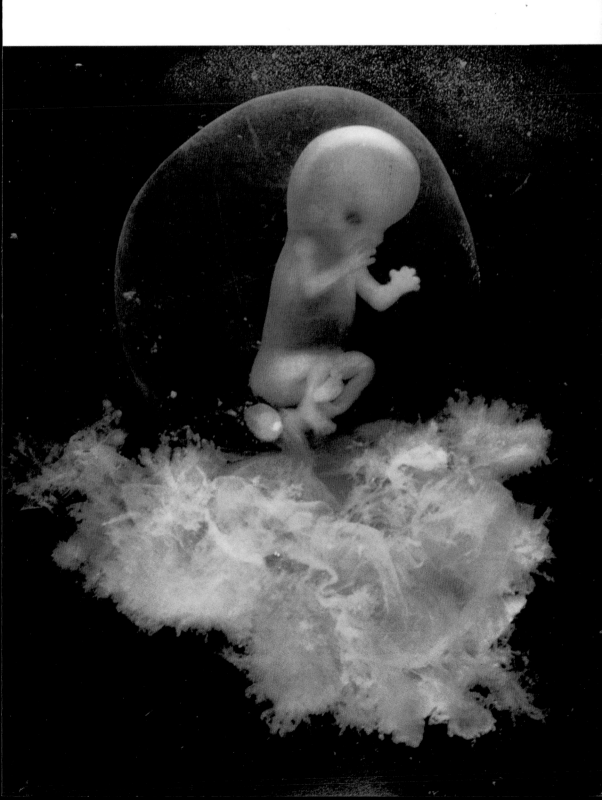

LEFT: Ten-week human fetus, left side

BELOW: Ten-week human fetus in sac

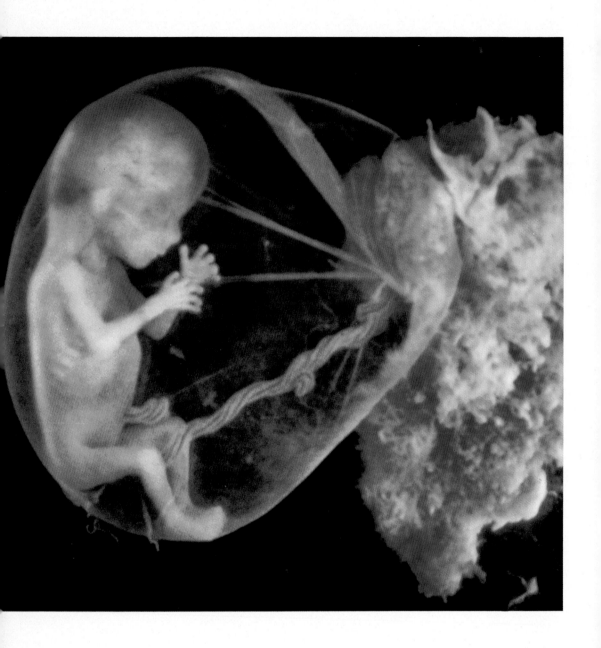

**Eleven-week human fetus
in sac (amnion) with
placenta**

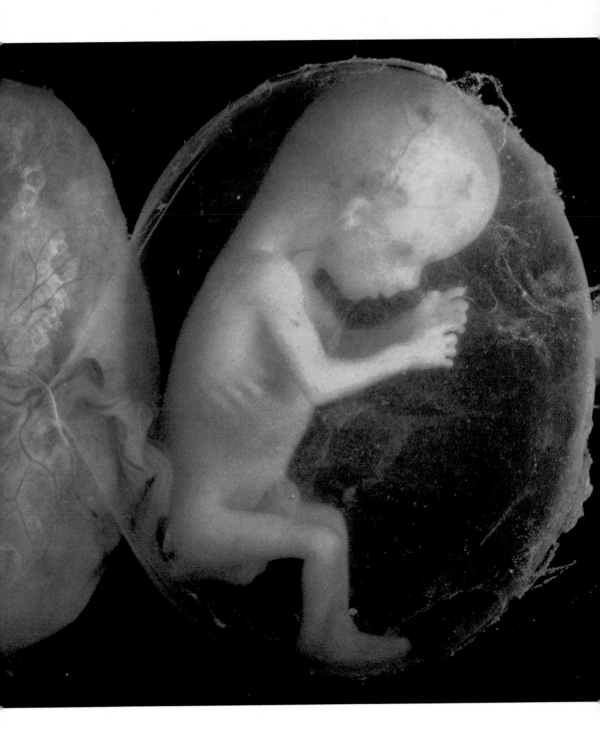

**Human fetus of 12 weeks
in amniotic sac** Note
umbilical cord connection
with placenta

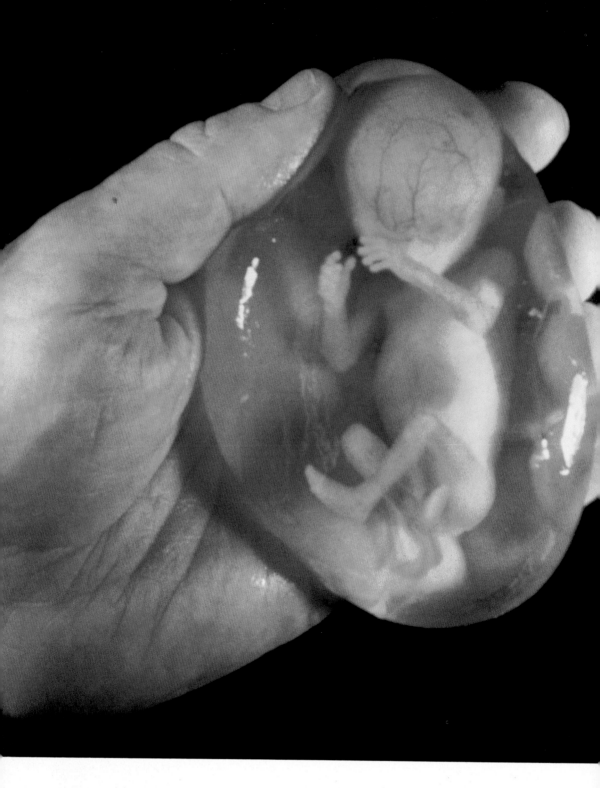

Twelve-week-old human
fetus in amniotic sac showing size relative to adult
human hand

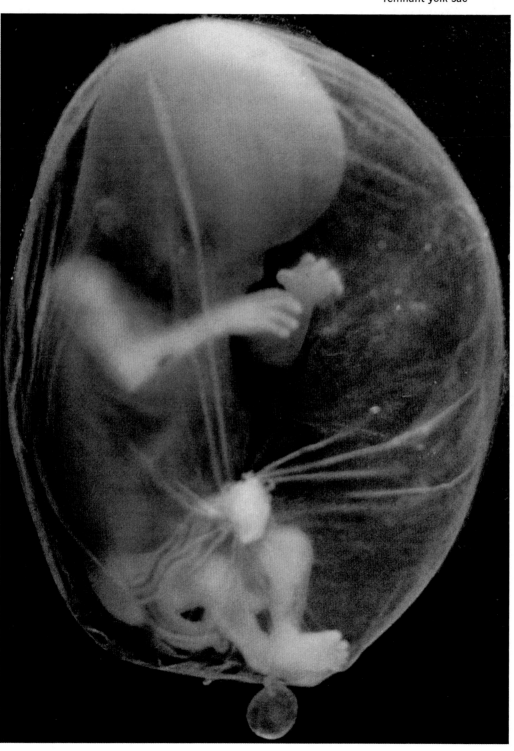

Twelve-week human fetus dissected away from the uterus, but still within its amniotic sac. Note small remnant yolk sac

Fourteen-week human
fetus in sac (amnion) still
attached by umbilical cord
to placenta

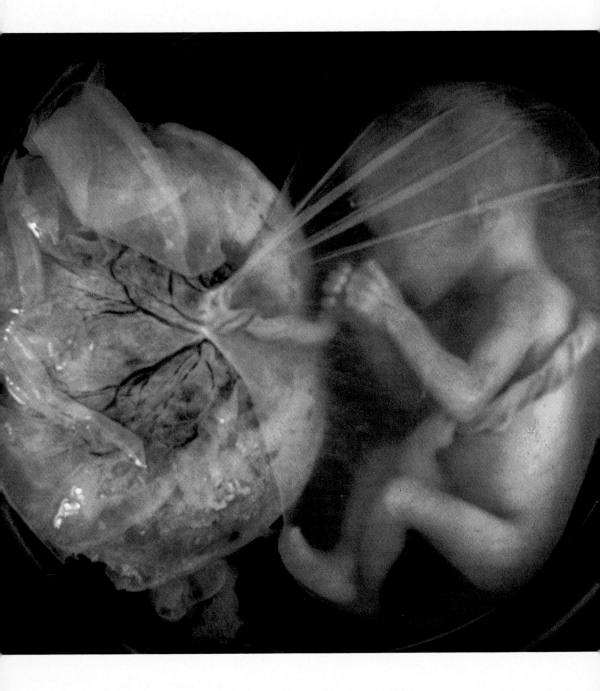

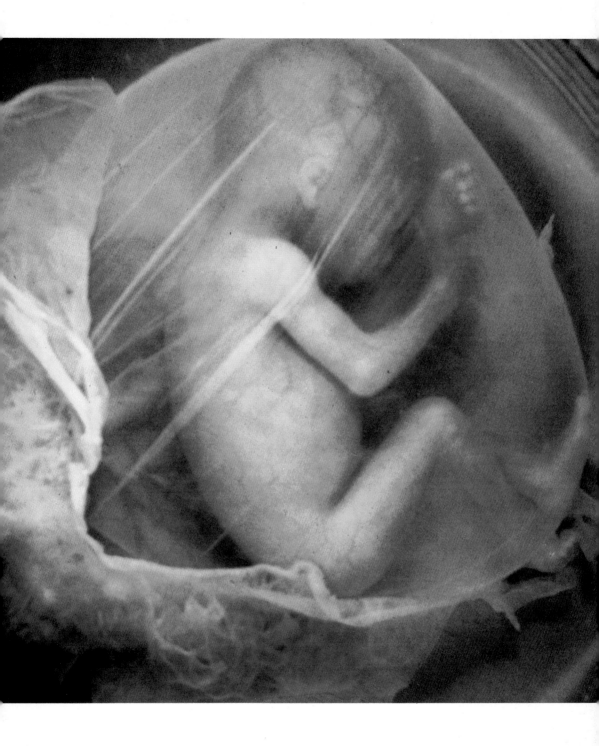

Sixteen-week human fetus

Human placenta at 20
weeks in natural color

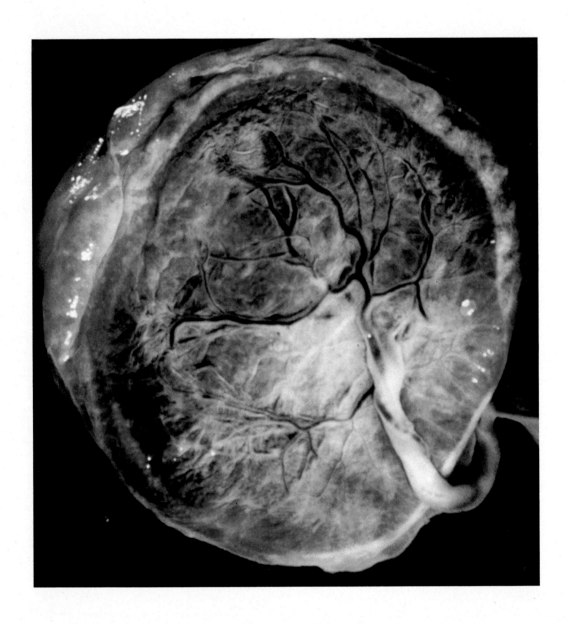

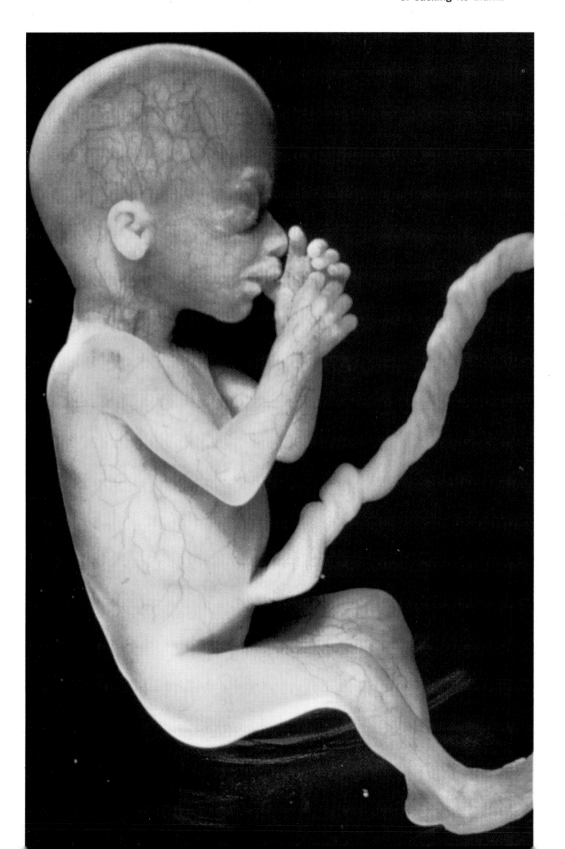

Seventeen-week-old human
fetus showing it in the act
of sucking its thumb

Fraternal twins with two placentae

the third month:
an active human fetus

In the first two months of development the burgeoning fetus appears to be no more "alive" than a growing corn stalk. But in the third month one of the real marvels of development is enacted. By now not only have the organs, the muscles, and the nervous system differentiated, they have also started to become interconnected and integrated. Now when the brain signals, the muscles respond and the fetus begins to kick, turn its feet, and curl its toes. Its delicate arm bends at the wrist and elbow, and its tiny hand forms a fist. The massive head atop the puny body pivots slightly on its stumpy neck. The face, with its sealed-shut eyes, squints, frowns, purses its lips, and opens its mouth.

The fetus has been observed to swallow some amniotic fluid accidentally, and its primitive, empty lungs expand and contract as though rehearsing for the day of birth, when air will be forced into them. These breathing movements bring some of the swallowed amniotic fluid into the lungs, but it is doubtful that the fetus derives any oxygen from it—all of its needs are satisfied by the mother's bloodstream at this stage.

The first reflexes of the fetus are "total," that is, the whole body reacts equally to any and every type of stimulus. By a gradual process this gross overreaction is narrowed down to the stimulated area alone. By the end of the third month, for instance, stroking of its lips causes the fetus to respond by sucking; if its eyelids are stroked the fetus squints instead of jerking its entire body back, as it did earlier.

The third month has been called the month of initial activity. It could also be called the month of sexual emergence because the shadowy, ill-defined structures of both sexes begin to take recognizable shape. A month earlier an examination of the external genital organs of the fetus would not reveal the prospective sex because there is much more similarity than difference. It is hard to say at the time whether the lump known as the genital tubercle will become the penis of the male or the clitoris of the female. Both sexes have a urethral slit or opening for passing urine. The swellings in either sex which later on become the scrotum or the labia have similar origins, and all of these landmarks are in the same position relative to the anus. It is toward the end of the third month that the penis and scrotal sac become so enlarged that they appear to be growing out from the body. At this time the testes, although formed, do not generate sperm-producing cells and do not descend from the body cavity into the scrotum (this will happen closer to the day of birth). In addition, the prostate glands begin to form.

These changes in the reproductive system are accompanied by changes in the related urinary system. As described in the preceding chapter, the fetus undergoes a metamorphosis in which three successive pairs of kidneys are produced. Only the last (metanephric) pair, which stems from the lower ends of the paired ducts of the second (mesonephric) kidneys, actually functions, since this is the permanent set that must last a lifetime.

There are interesting differences between the development of the male's urogenital system and that of the female. In the female, remnants of the first and most primitve (pronephric) kidneys become the ostium (the ciliated opening of each oviduct that captures ova liberated by the ovaries); the ducts of the pronephros become the oviducts (Fallopian tubes). But in the male the pronephric kidneys vanish completely. On the other hand, the ducts of the intermediate (mesonephric) kidneys, which actually attempt to function before the metanephric kidneys take over, are transformed into two of the most important sperm-carrying ducts in the male, the vas deferens and the epididymis. Of course, since the female develops oviducts instead of sperm ducts, the mesonephric kidneys degenerate completely in the female fetus. This is but one more illustration of how the fetus uses seemingly superfluous or vestigial structures to derive parts of permanent structures.

It is well known that a girl matures sexually sooner than a boy, but in the fetal stage the male takes precedence: the female's secondary sexual organs do not become distinct until the fourth month, although the primary structures in both sexes, the testes and the ovaries, form at the same time.

Now that we have seen the role of the fetal kidneys in laying ductwork for the reproductive system, let us look at their more conventional role, namely, that of preparing for their duties in the newborn infant.

In the third month the metanephric kidneys begin to form urine from the uric acid accumulated in the fetal bloodstream, secrete it, and convey some of it to the bladder, from which it passes into the amniotic fluid surrounding the fetus. This "urination" accounts for only a fraction of the waste excreted by the fetus, since most of the urine is eliminated by the mother's own urinary system after it passes through the umbilical cord and placenta and into the mother's circulation.

Water comprises 60 per cent of the adult human body (about 11 gallons), and the mature kidneys must strain about 15 gallons of recirculating fluid every day. Of this total, only about one or two quarts are eliminated, but the outflow contains solids as well as liquids—mostly salts, uric acid, and nitrogen (in the form of ammonia, hence the characteristic odor of urine). To deal with such waste products the kidneys must be complex structures. It is estimated that the mature kidneys are made up of 30 million cells and that they contain 2 million microscopic filters to hold back solid wastes. These filters must be formed before birth and be ready to leap into action almost as soon as the baby draws its first breath. When the baby is born the mother's kidneys are suddenly relieved of a load, but the kidneys of the infant must begin immediately to rid its own body of wastes that would otherwise poison its bloodstream. The speed of this response is attested to by the fact that a newborn baby will often urinate as soon as the umbilical cord is cut.

The perfection of the fetal kidneys, functional as well as structural, is matched by other developments which take place in the third month. The eyes, for example, are formed on the sides of the head and are ready for connection to the optic nerves growing out independently from the brain. The forces that ensure this integration have thus far not been discovered, but they must be formidable indeed, since more than one million optic nerve fibers must mesh with each eye. Think for a moment about what is considered to be a feat of human engineering: the drilling of tunnels from both sides of the Alps that must somehow meet precisely and merge into one continuous highway. Yet any one of thousands of things the fetus must do as part of the routine of development is far more wondrous.

Let us examine some of these changes week by week.

nine weeks

The human fetus at 9 weeks measures 1½ inches in sitting height (crown-rump length) and weighs about one-seventh of an ounce. The most noticeable external change is in its posture: the large head is no longer bent forward on the chest, the back is straighter, and the abdomen is less prominent than it was a week before. The fingernails and toenails and the hair follicles of the skin are forming, and the skin thickens and becomes less transparent. Nerve cells fill the tubular neural canal along which the spinal cord is forming. The eyes appear to be developed, and both the iris diaphragm and the eyelids are formed. When the eyelids or the palms of the hands are touched, they both respond by closing. This indicates that both nerves and muscles are functioning. The eyes are now sealed shut by lids for the next three months. The ears are still abnormally low on the sides of the head. Teeth are beginning to form, and there is evidence that the enamel and dentine-forming organs are developing for the first or temporary (baby) teeth. The intestines bulge less because as the body becomes more erect the hernia tends to retreat. One could now hear a fetal pulse through a stethoscope. The skeleton and all the muscles are rapidly forming, giving the body a more definite and human-like contour. Parts of the urinary and kidney system are beginning to degenerate, while other parts (already described) remain to function later as part of the reproductive system. The male fetus is now quite easily distinguished by its external penis. The female fetus begins to form a uterus, vagina, and bladder associated with the rapidly forming third level or permanent kidney that will be found functioning at birth. This kidney shortly begins to function even in the fetus, secreting small amounts of urine into the surrounding amniotic fluid, to be picked up and eliminated by the mother.

ten weeks

At ten weeks the fetus has grown considerably. It measures 2⅛ inches in a sitting position and weighs about a quarter of an ounce. The head has grown less rapidly than the rest of the body during the week, but it continues to be disproportionately large. The face appears to be more human because the ears are now higher on the head and the eyes have moved forward. The basic divisions of the brain have been formed, and except for refinements, the brain is much as it will be at birth. During this week the connections between muscles and nerves increase three-fold over the previous week, and if the forehead is touched, the fetus will turn its head away. This is a new achievement. The sensation of touch may be found all over the skin except for the sides, back, and top of the head. The face is particularly sensitive. The upper part of the mouth, the palate, forms by the coming together of two bony plates. (In rare cases the plates don't meet and the infant may be born with a harelip or cleft palate.) The thyroid gland is now complete, as is the pancreas (the gland that secretes digestive enzymes and insulin). The lungs are also complete, and the gall bladder actually secretes bile, even though there is no fatty food to digest. The muscles of the digestive tract are developed, so that later they can move food along by peristaltic action. Bones are forming in many places, even in the fingers and toes. Blood, which was formed in the first month by blood islands outside the body of the embryo, and in the spleen and liver during the second month, is now beginning to form in the bone marrow, where it will continue to form throughout life. The blood vessels are better formed, and the secondary sexual characters of both sexes are further refined externally.

eleventh week

During the eleventh week the fetus measures 2½ inches and may weigh one-third of an ounce. The tooth buds appear for all of the twenty temporary milk or baby teeth, and sockets for these teeth develop in the ossifying jawbones. These jaws are formed from cartilage remnants of the gill arches that in themselves are vestiges of our aquatic ancestors. Twenty tooth germs form, ten in each jaw, each of which has the capacity to form the dentine core and the enamel surface of a tooth. It is therefore important for the mother to provide an adequate supply of calcium and other minerals at this time if the fetus is to have

properly formed teeth. Baby teeth normally do not erupt
through the gums until the baby is from 6 to 24 months of age,
although there have been cases of newborn babies with exposed
baby teeth. The vocal cords of the larynx begin to form, but of
course the fetus cannot use this "voice box" without access to
air. The digestive system, which begins with the first opening of
the mouth at about 4 weeks, donates some of its lining to the
formation of the thyroid and the thymus glands (which also
form from parts of the rudimentary gills). Farther down the
digestive tube the trachea, lungs, stomach, liver, pancreas, and
intestines are all actively developing into their final and functional states. The liver starts to pour bile into the intestines,
even though there is no fat to digest. Temporarily, the liver is
the major producer of blood, since there is not enough bone
marrow. While the fetal blood transports nutriments, protects
against disease, and scavenges debris, it performs those functions less critically than the blood of the newborn, since the
mother's blood does most of this for her fetus. Ductless glands
within the pancreas (known as the islets of Langerhans) begin
to form insulin, a chemical that burns excess sugar and starch in
the body. The lining of the intestines begins to form microscopic
folds and thereby multiplies the surface area available for digestion and absorption. Each fold ultimately is lined with more
than 3,000 cells, and the adult intestines will grow to about 32
feet in length. Food is not in the same form as human protoplasm; thus, all of it must be broken down physically, digested
with enzymes supplied by the stomach and intestines, diffused
into the bloodstream of the fetal placenta, and resynthesized
into human fetal protoplasm. The intestines form a mucus
which helps to propel food through them. While the mother
supplies nutrients in a form that can be assimilated and resynthesized by the fetus, the fetus forms its own digestive
system in order to be fully prepared to take over these functions
at birth. It will have about 20 million glands to secrete all the
digestive enzymes it needs.

twelfth week

By the twelfth week the fetus measures about 3 inches in body
length and weighs about half an ounce. Its thumb can now be
opposed to the forefinger (a characteristic of all the primates).
This represents great progress in dexterity because it allows us to
pick up objects, hold a pencil or paintbrush, or manipulate a
dial on a spaceship panelboard. The swallowing and sucking

reflexes of the fetus are better developed now, but its general reactions are still primarily to avoid an annoyance rather than to respond positively to any particular stimulus. However, the quality of some responses is beginning to be altered. The motions of breathing, eating, and various body movements become more purposeful. Fetuses of the same age begin to show individual variations, based in all probability on behavioral patterns inherited from the parents. This is sometimes particularly evident in the facial expressions. The digestive glands are complete and could be functional, but they still have nothing to digest. The eyes have moved closer together on both sides of the narrowing bridge of the nose. The taste buds are numerous, and the salivary glands form. Ribs and vertebrae form by ossification of cartilage, and the vocal cords are completed. Both sexes now have milk glands which are capable of secreting a milky substance. Sometimes the mammary glands of the fetus become engorged with milk in response to the hormone released by the mother to stimulate her own breasts to lactate.

Physicians commonly divide the period of gestation into three subunits or trimesters, each lasting three months. By the end of the first trimester the fetus has developed all of its major systems and is virtually a functioning organism—almost, but not quite, for it is still unable to survive independently. During the next trimester no new organs begin to form. Rather, the ones that have already been laid down become more and more like what they will be in the newborn infant. Some of the changes to be noted in succeeding months will be detectable only at the microsocopic level, but the net effect will be a marked deviation from the generalized pattern of all species of anthropoids.

the second trimester: rapid growth and activity

If the first three months of life in the uterus are the period of rapid development, the second trimester is the period of growth. By three months the fetus has fairly well-developed organs, but it is still a homunculus—a manikin 3½ inches long from crown to rump and weighing only 1 ounce. During the fourth month the fetus shoots up to almost 6 inches in crown-rump length and 4 ounces in weight. No other month of this pregnancy will witness comparable growth.

Most of the elongation takes place in the body, and the top-heavy appearance imparted by the oversized head becomes far less noticeable. At two months the fetal head represents 50 per cent of the total length; from three to five months it is 33 per cent of the whole body; by birth it will be 25 per cent, and in the adult approximately 10 per cent. But as the head becomes relatively smaller it also becomes more important.

The obverse of this happens with the legs. At two months the legs account for only about 25 per cent of the total length of the fetus; at five months they are 33 per cent; at birth 40 per cent, and in the adult about 50 per cent. The trunk and arms

**Human bony skeleton at 15
weeks' gestation**

tend to retain their relative proportions as the balance swings
from the head to the legs.

The posture of the fetus becomes more erect with growth.
In the embryonic stage there was nothing to keep the head from
drooping on the trunk, but at four months the neck muscles
have formed, the back is supplied with more muscles than previously, and a bony skeleton is developing, all of which are
needed to hold the head in an upright position. Now the face
may be seen more clearly, and certain refinements become
evident: lips have formed on the mouth, and the vertical groove
seen in the upper lip of the adult human is developing between
the nose and the slightly overhanging upper lip.

The skin at this stage is thin, loose, and wrinkled, and it
appears pink or red because of the underlying blood vessels.
The tips of the fingers and toes develop "touch pads," which
also appear on the palms and soles. The ridges, whorls, and
lines in these areas, such as the fingerprints, remain the same
throughout life and are unique for each individual. They are so
distinctive that they may be used forever after to identify the
individual. The "heart," "head," and "life" lines are actually
formed a month or two earlier, but they are not completely
defined.[1]

It is clear that the fetus responds to touch at this stage—
usually by a "startled" reflex action—and spontaneously
stretches and exercises its arms and legs. But all of this may not
be perceptible to the mother.

Now is the time for the female fetus to catch up to the
male in the development of its sexual organs. Oöcytes arise in
great numbers from primitive germ cells lodged in the outer
covering (cortex) of the ovaries. The oöcytes form clusters
known as nests. Most of these oöcytes are destined to nourish
and protect the few among them that are selected for full development. There seems to be no doubt that every ovum which
will ever mature comes from an ancestral primitive germ cell
originating in the yolk sac (as described in Chapter 1). All
potential ova are present in the female child at birth; if they are
not there then, they will never develop.

The accessory sexual organs of the female are also developing, perhaps because of the influence of the hormones. The
paired Fallopian tubes (or oviducts) are fashioned from ducts
left behind by the degenerating first (pronephric) pair of kid-

1. Recent findings by Drs. Menser and Purvis-Smith in Australia
suggest that the palm lines of fetuses may indicate Mongolism, prenatal
rubella (German measles), and possibly leukemia and chromosomal
abnormalities.

neys. The two Fallopian tubes merge to form a single uterus, which in turn empties through a cervical canal into the birth chamber, the vagina. At this time the vagina is temporarily filled by a mass of cells which will be eliminated during the fifth month.

There are also external sexual organs in the female which at this stage resemble those of the male. The genital tubercle, which in the male becomes the penis, in the female becomes the much smaller but similarly sensitive and erectile clitoris. The urethral groove, which runs down the center of the penis and is shared by both sperm and urine in the male, remains a shallow open chamber in the female. This vestibule has lips known as labia, and it is partially covered by a membrane known as the hymen.

By the fourth month the fetal heart is recirculating about 25 quarts of blood through the body per day. The heart muscle is now strong and its contractions are regular, as one might expect from this remarkable organ, which in an average 24-hour day pumps more than 72,000 quarts of blood through more than 100,000 miles of vessels of an adult. If the mother is small and if her abdominal wall is thin, the obstetrician may be able to treat the father to the sound of the fetal heartbeat through a special stethoscope. This heart pulsates from 120 to 160 times a minute—about twice the rate of the mother's own heart. The two pumps are completely unrelated and therefore are in no way synchronized.

While listening for fetal heart sounds the obstetrician may also hear sounds that are collectively called a "funic soufflé" or others that are called the "uterine soufflé." The first of these sounds come from the umbilical blood vessels as blood rushes through them, and the second come from the blood vessels of the placenta. Murmuring or whistling would be a more accurate description of these soufflés than beating or throbbing.

The lungs, which in the newborn infant will work as the heart's partner, are now collapsed and inactive. But except for the alveoli (the air sacs with which they are honeycombed, and which will not be completed until after birth), the lungs are already structurally formed.

The surface of the brain is now much convoluted (full of folds and wrinkles), and the forepart overlaps the rest. The front and top of the human brain, the cerebrum is the seat of intelligence and memory as well as control over motor activity; if an electrical current were applied to the so-called motor strip of the cortex (the covering of the brain), it would cause an arm or

leg to twitch. The eyes would be sensitive to any light that
reached them (the eyelids are sealed at this time), but sounds
would not produce any impression on the four-month-old fetus.
The smaller, underlying structures of the brain are the seats of
emotion, hunger, sexual drive, and other basic impulses. The
cerebellum, the hindmost part of the brain, which acts as a
balance center for the body, is distinguishable in the four-month-
old fetus, but it does not reach structural completion until some
weeks after birth. The basal metabolic rate shows a progressive
increase beginning at this time, increasing by 16 per cent at the
end of pregnancy.

fifth month

At five months the development of its organs appears to be so
well advanced that one may even wonder whether the fetus
could live outside the uterus. However, it is a forlorn hope. A
five-month-old premature or aborted fetus will invariably die
(the youngest infant known to have survived was about 25
weeks old and weighed a pound and a half). Prior to six months
the lungs, the skin, and the digestive organs of the fetus are
unprepared for independent existence; there is no provision at
this time, among other things, for regulation of body temperature.

The fetus at this stage still exhibits some interesting vestiges that resemble structures found in the embryos of other
species. For example, it has many more taste buds than it will
need at birth. The buds are located all over the surface of the
tongue, on the roof and walls of the mouth, and even in the
throat. This suggests that some prehistoric or prehuman ancestor had much more need of a keen sense of taste than does
modern man.

The fetus also has a firm hand grip, denoting a high degree
of muscular strength, coordination, and reflex action. Why? The
newborn baby surely does not need them. But it may have been
useful in some simian ancestor (if indeed man is descended
from simians), when the infant may have had to cling to the fur
of its highly mobile mother.

From all this it would appear that some parts of fetal
development are wasted effort, since the structures or capabilities are either discarded or barely used. However, we have
learned that this waste is minimal, and that almost every vestige
that has been retained is somehow associated with another,
more essential, organ, structure, or function. This fifth month

turns out to be a sort of threshold, in which the fetus begins to jettison its inherited but no longer needed structures and shows greater efficiency and selectivity in its further developments.

Even the adult human undergoes a dynamic process of change, namely, the continual replacement of cells. This applies to most of the soft tissues and organs, but not to the central nervous system (lost brain cells or nerve cells lying completely within the spinal cord never regenerate) and very little of the skeleton. It has been said that every person is made up of atoms not present seven years earlier, the original ones having all been replaced. No one has ever gone to the trouble of systematically charting the history of large numbers of living human cells, but it is undoubtedly true that cells of the kidneys, stomach, intestines, and skin—and probably of many other organs—wear out and are replaced by daughter cells. This is even truer of the blood cells, some of which are short-lived. Thus a cycle of tissue loss and replacement is begun even in the fetus which will continue through life.

The process of exchanging new cells for old begins in the fifth month, particularly in the skin, where the sebaceous (oil) glands secrete a fatty substance which mixes with loosened dead cells on the surface of the skin to form a cheeselike paste known as vernix caseosa. This coating acts as a protective layer for the tender and delicate new skin of the fetus, which is exposed constantly to the mineralized water of the amniotic sac. The sweat glands, which are believed to number about 2 million in the skin of the adult, are now forming close to the base of hair follicles, but they do not open to the outside until the seventh month. After birth they help in maintaining the correct body temperature by the cooling effects of evaporation. So the skin, while enclosing and protecting the fetus (as well as housing sense receptors), is constantly losing and replacing its constituent cells even as it expands to ensheath the enlarging fetus.

During this fifth month the fetus grows to about 8 inches in length from crown to rump, and it weighs about half a pound. It is suspended in a quart of amniotic fluid that recirculates at the rate of 6 gallons per day; thus it is used over and over again and cannot become stagnant. It is estimated that one-third of the amniotic fluid is replaced every hour by water from the maternal plasma. This means complete replacement every 3 hours. Not only does the amniotic fluid cushion the fetus against shock, it helps to control the body temperature. Possibly as another aid in the control of body temperature, the fetus develops a fine, hairy covering known as lanugo, and baby hair is seen on the head and eyebrows. The growth of a faint fringe of eyelashes gives the fetus the look of an old man. In another month the hair on the head might be long enough to cut, if it were accessible.

The fetus has all the necessary apparatus to breathe at five months, and would try to do so if it were delivered, but it could not succeed. The fetal heart sounds are now louder and more easily distinguished from the soufflé sounds previously mentioned. The father may be able to hear the heart sounds even without a stethoscope if the fetus happens to lie close to the abdominal wall of the mother. Twins can sometimes be identified by the separate heart sounds at this time, especially if their heartbeats differ in rate by more than 10 beats per minute.

Both sexes develop pale pink nipples over the mammary glands, which are equipped with milk ducts. As explained earlier, these developments are under control of the female hormones secreted by the mother. Therefore, further development will take place only in the female after birth. Much of the skeleton is now bony hard, and nails are forming, first on the fingers and shortly thereafter on the toes. These nails sometimes grow so long that they have to be trimmed at birth.

Fetal movements may now be recognized as kicking or turning. Sometimes an elbow, a foot, a head, or the buttocks may be identified through the abdominal wall. Occasionally the fetus will hiccup, causing rhythmic jarring of the mother's abdomen every 2 to 4 seconds. Of course there is no intake of air, but it involves the same sort of muscular reaction as that of an air-breathing child. Such hiccuping movements generally subside within half an hour and should please rather than frighten the mother, since they are naturally associated with the increased movements of the fetus. Periods of drowsiness and sleep alternate with periods of activity, much as in the newborn infant. Sleeping habits begin to appear. The mother can sometimes detect and anticipate them, and even determine when the fetus awakens and stretches. Sometimes it may seem to the mother that the fetus is seeking a more comfortable position in its watery chamber. Movement in the water of the amniotic sac is free, as though the fetus had achieved weightlessness. The fetus has been likened to a gracefully swimming seal, liberated from gravity by the buoyant fluid. The mother can even awaken the fetus, if she wants, by tapping on her abdomen or by making a jarring movement. Even a loud noise or music can stir the fetus, though the mother probably thinks she is soundproofed!

During this fifth month the mother may notice some

changes that she should discuss with her obstetrician. If she seems to fatigue more readily than in the past, if she appears pale and has spells of nausea different from those at two and three months, she should be examined for anemia of pregnancy. Such anemia is not surprising or unusual, since she has been increasing the burden on her heart by supplying increased circulation to the placenta, even though the fetus is developing its own circulatory system. This condition can be remedied easily under the direction of the obstetrician. Also, the mother must avoid overfatigue, since the rapid growth of the fetus during this month compounds the burden on her heart, lungs, and kidneys.

sixth month

During the sixth month the mother may gain as much as a pound a week, and she must be careful not to gain more rapidly than this. She may find a dark line on her abdomen running from the navel to the pubic region, a sure sign of pregnancy (as if she didn't know it anyway!). Her pelvic joints begin to relax as the upper part (fundus) of the uterus is pushed upward until it lies just above the navel. Because the fetus is growing so actively the mother needs and stores more protein at this time than at any other.

The fetus grows to an average crown-rump length of 10 to 12 inches and weighs about 1½ pounds at six months. It is now a miniature human being. It has more nearly the proper body proportions and is erect—straighter even than in adult life. This assumption of an erect posture is related to the need to accommodate the enlarging visceral organs, particularly the liver and heart. The intestines, which at one time bulged from the body, are now retracted; they have found a new, relatively vacant region in which to be housed, namely, the pelvic basin. This descent enables the heart, liver, diaphragm, and lungs to take up positions lower down than previously. But the nerves that developed in conjunction with these structures must adapt, either by growing longer or by being stretched, if they are to retain their connections. This helps to explain the surprising length of certain nerves that extend from the brain or upper spinal cord to the lower abdomen.

Prior to the sixth month, when the fetal head was bent forward and the abdomen was bulging, the enlarging internal organs were closely packed. As the fetus changes its posture, the amount of surface to be covered increases, and therefore the skin takes on added significance. At this time the skin is reddish and wrinkled, with little or no fatty deposits underneath. This is one of the reasons that a premature or aborted fetus at six months requires continued incubation. Since it cannot regulate its own temperature or protect itself against cold, it rarely survives more than a few hours. But the skin develops special means of protection in the remaining three months before birth. Each square inch of skin ultimately will have 700 sweat glands, 100 sebaceous or oil glands, and 21,000 cells sensitive to heat, pressure, or pain. The skin will contain more than 500,000 hair follicles, which first form during this period. These follicles are so strongly embedded in the scalp that an adult's hair can sustain a load of 5,000 pounds. The hair is growing long by the sixth month, and by birth may have to be cut; thereafter scalp hair will grow at the rate of about 4.6 inches per year.

During fetal life at six months the vernix caseosa (cheesy coating of the skin) is abundant and seems to be glued to the skin (a layer may be as thick as one-eighth inch at birth). As the fetus becomes more and more active this coating protects the delicate skin from abrasions and keeps it from hardening, which would result because of constant submersion in the mineralized amniotic fluid. The hands develop a very strong grip, and the feet bend downward when tickled. In the male the testes approach the scrotum, but do not descend into it yet. A pasty, green mass of dead cells and bile, known as meconium, accumulates in the intestine at this time and may remain there until birth.

Earlier, at about 22 days after conception, the eyes began to develop as two outward bulges from the most primitive brain-plate tissue. These two eyecups, or vesicles, evaginated (grew outward) and eventually reached the surface on the sides of the head, where contact caused the skin to invaginate (grow inward) to form a lens for each eye. In the meantime the eyecup from the brain inverted as if it were a rubber ball with one side pushed in to form a double-layered cup, the inner layer or the retina, the light-sensitive part of the eye, while the skin again closed over the eyes to form the cornea, the transparent coating over the front part of the eyeball. Optic nerves to each eyecup extended along an inverted channel to make connections with the retina to form the optic nerve. By the sixth month each eye is structurally complete. But, as pointed out earlier, during the third month the eyelids form and close shut, only to reopen during the sixth month. By the next month the eyes will be sensitive to various levels of light and darkness, though not to objects.

Man is a vertebrate, but the early human fetus is cartilaginous (having tough, elastic tissue like a shark rather than
hard bone). The first true bone formation occurs early in the
sixth month—in the breastbone. Cartilage has been present
throughout the body of the fetus from the second month, and
the replacement of some of it by bone has begun, but now this
process of ossification is advanced and the bone contains
enough calcium so that X-ray pictures will reveal a true skeleton. Ossification (changing of cartilage to bone, or else the
direct formation of bone, as in the skull) will occur continually
until after birth. Paradoxically, bone contains both bone-
forming and bone-destroying cells; the former are especially
active in the fetus of six to nine months, the latter in aged
persons. Bones are tough and strong. For example, the seemingly fragile adult human shinbone can sustain a weight of 2
tons. Such adult bones are 90 per cent calcium, while the same
bone in the six-month-old fetus may contain as little as 12 per
cent calcium as it is forming and is therefore less strong. If the
mineral content is inadequate, bones may turn brittle and break
easily. This is one reason the pregnant woman is advised to
increase her calcium intake.

The human spine is made up of 33 rings, 150 joints, and
1,000 ligaments which are used to support the body weight. All
begin to form at six months. A total of 222 bones is needed by
the fetus for adequate support of the soft parts of its body,
especially in the vertical position. (While the bony skeleton of
the fetus can be seen in X-ray pictures, such radiographs are not
usually taken because of the particular sensitivity of developing
tissues to radiation, as pointed out in Chapter 10.)

the third trimester: the emergence of intelligence and personality

The final stages of embryonic development occur during months seven, eight, and nine. There is one significant difference even from the sixth month: the fetus now has a fighting chance for life outside the uterus, and the probability of survival gets better and better every day it stays in the uterus (that is, until a total of about 280 days).

During the third trimester the mother's weekly weight gain should taper off to ¾ pound, and then to ½ pound, and she should gain a total of not more than 25 pounds, of which about 7½ will be the fetus itself. Her pelvic joints progressively relax. Painless muscular spasms known as Braxton Hicks contractions become more frequent. These contractions expand the uterus to accommodate the enlarging fetus; sometimes they are feared by the mother to be early labor contractions. Breathing during the last two months may be a bit labored, but this shortness of breath eases as the time of delivery approaches. Now the enlarging fetus finds it increasingly difficult to move about in the confines of its watery chamber. No longer is it capable of its former weightless acrobatics or swimming motions.

During this trimester the fetus gains about 5 pounds (it almost doubles its weight during the last six weeks of confinement), but only about 7 inches in length (from head to toe), for a total of approximately 20 inches. The fetus assiduously absorbs and stores calcium for its developing skeleton, iron for its red blood cells, and protein for its growth. The skin, which at six months is as wrinkled as that of a very old man, gradually smooths out, and the body becomes almost rotund by comparison with its former elongated shape.

seventh month

For the first time the fetus could survive if it were born prematurely. If labor occurred now, there would be at least a 10 per cent probability of survival, depending largely on the care given to the "preemie." Such an infant is still not self-sufficient and would require supplemental care as a substitute for its mother's body. Why is survival more likely now? The main thing is that the nervous system, particularly the brain, has developed to the point where it can direct rhythmic breathing movements if air becomes available, control swallowing movements if food is put into the mouth, and regulate body temperature. While these functions aren't carried out well enough to sustain the premature infant, oxygen can be administered to the immature alveoli (tiny air sacs) in the collapsed lungs, food given frequently and in small amounts, and the preemie kept in an incubator with controlled artificial heat. The baby would be able to cry.

The seven-month-old fetus typically measures about 12 inches in sitting height (body or crown-rump length) and weighs between 2 and 3 pounds. The downy lanugo, which a month earlier covered the entire skin, is now limited to the back and shoulders. Hair continues to grow on the head and becomes quite long on some fetuses. During this month the fetus has been known to suck its thumb; some babies are reported to have been born with calluses on one thumb! In the seventh month the fetus would respond to sweet, sour, or acrid substances placed on its tongue by changing its facial expression. This hypersensitivity to flavors is accounted for by the fact that the fetus still has an excessive number of functioning taste buds; many of these will be lost before birth. The fetus is quite active, but its activity is not purposeful. As birth approaches, these random movements decrease markedly, the fetus is usually relaxed and passive, and the uterus and the bearing down of the mother, rather than the fetus, take care of the ultimate ejection process.

Man's advance over other animals depends primarily on the size and refinement of his brain. As stated in the second chapter, the central nervous system begins to develop as early as 19 days after conception. Many of the nerves originate in the brain and branch out through the spinal cord, joining with other nerve fibers and ultimately connecting with and stimulating a muscle, a gland, or some other organ, which then responds in its characteristic fashion. Some nerves function long before birth, and the fetus responds to stimuli that reach it even in the seclusion of the uterus. Other nerves are not normally developed until some weeks before birth, but eventually every minute part of the baby's body will enter into two-way communication with the brain, the ultimate control center. Each nerve fiber consists of many individual nerve cells (neurons), and each neuron is protected by other encasing cells (glial cells). All of these cells are descended from the fertilized egg, hence all are basically alike in their inherited potential. But during development each nerve is assigned a particular function.

The brain is not only the foremost part of the body, but also the first to begin development. This is in part responsible for the seemingly exaggerated dimensions of the head early in fetal development. At first the brain is tubular, but gradually it fills with nerve cells, leaving only a small central canal that joins with a matching canal in the spinal cord. The result is a fluid-filled cavity that passes through every major part of the brain and spinal cord. In rare cases the brain cells do not multiply sufficiently. This permits an excess of fluid to collect in the cavity, which tends to enlarge. In this way a hydrocephalic child (said to have "water on the brain") develops. The condition is congenital rather than hereditary, and it is most likely to occur if, during the early stages of development, the brain is damaged by drugs, disease, or radiation.

In the seventh month the brain makes enormous strides. The forepart enlarges so much that its two hemispheres cover almost all of the other brain structures. Its surfaces develop groovelike depressions known as clefts or fissures which increase the surface area of cortical nerves. Every normal human brain has these fissures in exactly the same place, to the same depth, and connected in the same way to other fissures. Thus, neurophysiologists and neurosurgeons have been able to map those areas on the cortex of the cerebrum which act as the centers for hearing, sight, smell, speech, walking, and so forth. It is during the seventh month that this localization of the functional areas of the brain really begins. Until this time the cerebral cortex was relatively unwrinkled, more like the brains of lower animals. (The dolphin, which is considered to be intelligent, has a large, convoluted brain, too.) If the cerebrum fails to develop properly, the individual may have low potential—he exists, but with reduced faculties of memory, imagination, and reasoning power. The "motor strips" of the cerebrum are also important because they coordinate all voluntary muscular movements, gross or refined, athletic or artistic.

The development of the brain and nervous system and its role in the integration of all other systems remains one of the most profound mysteries of embryology. Where did all of those more than 10 billion cell units (neurons) come from? Above all, how do they interconnect with other neurons to form a network extending from the brain throughout the body? It would be relatively easy to understand if the neurons were connected to one another and thereby formed straight lines that radiated from the brain like spokes of a wheel, but they are not. Most of these neurons are connected to a great many other neurons; one estimate is that on the average each neuron is cross-connected to about 1,000 others. This means a total of ten trillion (10,000,000,000,000) connections. A complete wiring diagram for this network would stagger the imagination. All of the telephone cables of the world would comprise no more than a small fraction of it.

The neuron, like any other cell of the human body, contains a nucleus in which lie chromosomes that are identical to those in the original fertilized egg. Thus the nucleus of each neuron contains a catalog of potentialities inherited from both mother and father. How can a collection of genes possibly account for the multifarious connections between neurons in the human nervous system? Or for the relationship between neurons and the muscles and organs of the body? There are only some 40,000 genes in all the chromosomes—seemingly not enough to encode instructions for forming 10 trillion connections.

But if every last interconnection isn't spelled out in the chromosomes, then how *do* the neurons get connected? Do they just reach out for one another haphazardly? Obviously not, since all neurons fulfill definite, specialized functions, not random ones. Connections between the nerves associated with hearing and those controlling, say, the biceps muscles wouldn't be logical or effective, and above all the nervous system effectively coordinates whatever the person does or thinks.

The answer would seem, then, to be somewhere between these two extremes: a completely wired nervous system present at birth on the one hand, and a network that is completed largely after birth on the other. Neurons (like other cells) are capable of recognizing those proteins they should accept and those they should reject. This "memory" is also a mystery. As experiments on animals have established, a definite pattern of permanent neuron wiring is formed during the fetal stage. These connections ensure that certain neurons are correctly interwired, so that the ability to see or hear or smell or feel or taste does not have to be learned on a hit-or-miss basis. On the other hand, there is still substantial room for making new neural connections based on learning or experience.

The development of intelligence or personality cannot be studied under the microscope. Instead it gradually unfolds as the child grows. It is during the seventh month that fetuses begin to diverge in personality, based upon the structure and function of their nervous systems. Heredity very definitely plays a part in this development. In the seventh month after conception much of the physical basis of personality is already present, for in the two remaining months of pregnancy and the first few weeks after birth additional nerve tracts develop, so that there is still room for change. Even after the entire network comprising thousands of nerve tracts is laid down, these nerves must still be used if the child is ever to realize the potentialities inherited from its parents. Depriving an infant of sensory stimuli would be one sure way of retarding it. History shows that the gift of intelligence may lie dormant for generations if the opportunities for exercising the mental faculties do not exist. In addition, there is some evidence that proper diet (particularly protein) during pregnancy is essential for maximum development of the central nervous system, especially during the final two months.

NERVOUS RESPONSES

From the third or fourth month on, the average pregnant woman may notice movement on the part of the fetus—mostly in response to some kind of stimulation. Still later, when the limbs and other parts of the fetus can be felt through the abdominal wall, it is possible for the physician to pinch or otherwise stimulate the fetus into reaction. This indicates that the nervous and muscular systems are well developed, and that the fetus is sensitive to tactile stimuli as well as to the mother's movements. During the last two months of pregnancy the fetus can be taught to respond by association with certain stimuli. The reflexes so evident at birth no doubt develop very early and include:

Sucking reflex: When the lips are touched, there is a vigorous sucking movement.

Rooting reflex: When the cheek is touched, the body nuzzles the head around so that the face is turned toward the side that was touched, in search of a source of food.

Moro reflex: This is an embracing or startling reflex caused by any sudden change in the body position or by sound waves. If one taps the table on which the baby is placed it will throw out its arms, open its hands, and spread its fingers. Then the arms make embracing or encircling movements, the legs are drawn up, and the baby cries and appears to be frightened.

Grasp reflex: The fingers firmly grasp any object placed in the hands. If the sole is tickled, the toes flex in a grasping movement (plantar reflex).

Step reflex: When the baby is held upright with the feet on the table or floor, it will try to take a step. This reflex disappears shortly after birth.

It is very likely that most of these reflexes are present at an early age in the fetus, and most assuredly by seven months in the preemie.

We know the fetus can feel pain. For example, blood can be transfused directly into the abdominal cavity of the fetus by means of a long, thin hypodermic needle. Of course, the obstetrician can see the fetus under the fluoroscope and easily insert the needle without injury to lungs, liver, or heart. Nevertheless, the upper portion of the hypodermic needle, which still protrudes from the mother's abdomen, can be seen moving about, indicating that the fetus is trying to escape this slightly painful object. Some fetuses appear to be more reactive than others, partly because the contact may be made in a more sensitive region. It is doubtful that pain is localized, since the whole body reacts. (Even the newborn continues to do this.)

The seventh month also represents a milestone in sexual development. While male and female fetuses are initially so much alike that one cannot distinguish them at, say, two or three months, the testes are now descending into the scrotal sac of the vast majority of male fetuses at this time. (Nothing comparable happens in the female.) It is believed that spermatozoa cannot survive for long at 98.6 degrees Fahrenheit, the normal body temperature of the adult human male. The reason for having a scrotum, then, is to keep the testes in an external chamber cooled by the outside temperature. Males with undescended testes are usually sterile. Curiously, the body heat of the female fetus or adult does not affect the ova, which are found in the internal ovaries. If the testes fail to descend at seven months, it is not crucial, for permanent damage is not likely to result. They may descend in the eighth or ninth month, or they may be surgically assisted in their descent. The paired testes move into the scrotal sac through a small passage called the inguinal canal, aided by a pair of ligaments which are also found in the female, only in the same position relative to the ovaries rather than the testes. After the testes descend, the inguinal canal closes off, and therefore the testes do not ordinarily return to the body. However, many men could gently force their testes back into the body through the canal if they tried, and in cases of extreme exertion involving the abdominal muscles, the intestines may be forced out through the same canal. This sort of hernia occurs occasionally in male infants.

eighth month

During the eighth month the rate of gain in weight slows down for both fetus and mother. On the average the mother will weigh about 22 pounds more than she did before she became pregnant. The fetus will weigh 4 or 5 pounds in this month, and will measure an average of 13 inches in sitting height. Most of its weight gain this month consists of fat deposited under the skin. This fatty layer tends to smooth out the wrinkles seen during the sixth and seventh months, and causes the arms and legs to appear chubby. The dull red skin turns to luminescent pink, and even among dark-pigmented races the skin at eight months is usually quite light. If the infant were delivered suddenly, the accumulating fat would help in controlling body temperature. The probability of survival rises to 70 per cent (from that of 10 per cent the preceding month) because now the fetus is almost a newborn infant. Breathing would still be a problem, but no longer because the respiratory center of the brain malfunctions. Rather it is because the alveoli—those tiny air pockets honeycombing the interior surface of the lungs—have to be prepared to inflate with air and to exchange oxygen for carbon dioxide with the bloodstream. The eight-month premature infant must usually be given supplemental oxygen. Thus respiration ranks second only to temperature control. A lesser problem is that of nutrition. All babies tend to lose weight in the first few days after birth, partly because of dehydration (evaporation of water from the tissues) but also because the newborn infant is not fully prepared for or accustomed to procuring and using its own food. The eight-month preemie is likely to lose even more

weight at first than the baby delivered at full term because its
digestive tract (the stomach, liver, pancreas, intestines) is still
too immature to satisfy all the requirements of an independent
organism. As a sort of safety mechanism, therefore, the eight-
month fetus stores nutrition taken from its mother against the
possibility of early birth. The eight-month preemie is also more
vulnerable to infection than it would have been had it remained
in the uterus for another month, since it has not yet acquired all
of the substances from the mother that grant it temporary
immunity.

Aside from the foregoing there is little to distinguish the
eight-month fetus from the newborn infant. For example, it is
sensitive to sound (mechanical vibrations in the range of human
hearing), whether from an orchestra, a piano, a voice, the
vibration of a washing machine, or tapping on the bathtub its
mother is sitting in.

ninth month

During the ninth and last calendar month of its stay in the
uterus the fetus seems to be less active than previously, but only
because it is so large that it fills much of the available space. At
36 weeks it measures about 14 or 15 inches from the top of the
head to the buttocks (in a sitting position) and about 19 to 20
inches in over-all length. It typically weighs between 6 and 8
pounds (it is not unusual for a boy to weigh a bit more). The
final weight is partially affected by the mother's recent eating
habits. Giving birth to a large baby is not a desirable end in
itself. Therefore, the mother must exercise her body and curb
her appetite, not only for the sake of her appearance but also to
avoid unnecessary problems before and during delivery. However, she may not be able to control her weight gain as much as
would be desirable if she is hereditarily disposed toward excessive weight.

The fetus almost always assumes an upside-down position
shortly before delivery, with the head down in the pelvic basin.
This is the most comfortable position for the fetus as well as the
easiest and safest from the standpoint of delivery. Body movement is the chief factor in this optimal reorientation of the fetus
to the uterine shape, but gravity may also play a role, since the
fetal head is still the heaviest part. Despite this turnabout, the
movements of the fetus are much more restricted than previously—and therefore not as perceptible to the mother. The
fetus may kick and flail its arms vigorously as a form of expres-

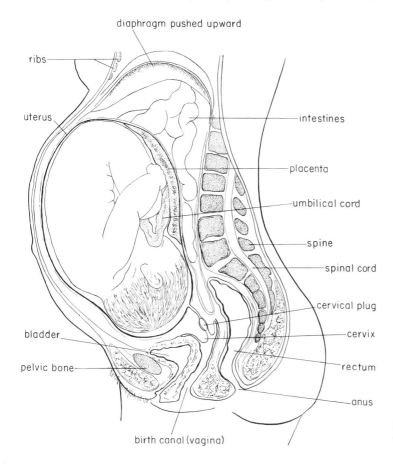

diaphragm pushed upward

ribs

uterus

intestines

placenta

umbilical cord

spine

spinal cord

cervical plug

bladder

cervix

pelvic bone

rectum

anus

birth canal (vagina)

Position of baby at about one month before birth

sion. When it moves, the mother should be able to identify the appendages—the arms and legs—but may confuse the head with the buttocks through the stretched skin of her abdomen. This distension should not concern her at all, since the smooth muscles of her uterus and abdomen, through growth and stretching, are capable of being increased to 60 times their size before pregnancy, yet will return almost to their original size by 6 weeks after delivery.

Although the fetus could be delivered at any time during the ninth calendar month, at the start of that month it could hardly be said to have all the finishing touches. The vernix caseosa, that cheesy covering of dead epithelial (skin) cells and fat, becomes dislodged, so that now only the back is coated. The amniotic fluid surrounding the fetus is muddied with vernix that has fallen off. The intestines accumulate considerable meconium, a dark-green, viscous mass of cells and debris from the fetal liver, pancreas, and gall bladder. The peristaltic contractions of the small intestines push the mass into the large intestines, from which it will be eliminated shortly after birth (or beforehand, if that event is too long delayed). While this may not sound very pleasant, it is all perfectly normal.

During this final month the baby usually acquires antibodies—disease-resisting proteins—from its mother's blood. These will grant it temporary immunity against certain diseases that could prove disastrous to the newborn. Antibodies are formed by the mother against diseases incurred before—or even during—her pregnancy. The temporary immunities a mother could transmit through the placenta might protect against such diseases as measles, German measles, mumps, whooping cough, scarlet fever, some strains of streptococci, and even colds and influenza (see Chapter 10 on drugs, diseases, and radiation). In addition, if the mother is vaccinated against poliomyelitis late in pregnancy, it will be of some benefit to her unborn child. Some antibodies are administered later—through the colostrum of the mammary glands at birth, or through the milk that follows. Immunities acquired in this way from the mother generally protect the child against infection and disease for the crucial first six months of independent life, and then this protection gradually wears off. But in the meantime the baby begins to develop its own immune reaction to mild infections. For example, gamma globulin, which comes from the placenta as well as the mother, helps both mother and infant to combat such virus diseases as hepatitis. In fact, the newborn infant may be even more resistant than the mother.

Late in the ninth month the baby's fingernails and toenails might have grown so long that they require trimming at birth (lest the child scratch himself). The gums are ridged at nine months and might even give the false impression of erupting teeth. In fetuses of both sexes the wee breasts are firm and protruding, under the influence of the same hormone from the placenta that stimulates the mother's own breasts to prepare for the arrival of a hungry child. The eyes are usually blue at this time, regardless of the final color they will assume, because the pigmentation has not fully formed. (This generally requires a few weeks of exposure to light.)

The picture that has been presented up to now is that of a fetus preparing to face the world, and every added day spent in the uterus—up to a point—prepares it all the better to assume an independent role.

The date of birth is calculated as roughly 266 days after conception, or 280 days after the beginning of the last regular menstrual period. About 75 per cent of all children arrive within 10 or 15 days of the scheduled date (the first child rarely arrives exactly on time). Early arrival—known as prematurity—may be due to poor nutrition, to excessive physical or emotional stress, or to excessive smoking on the part of the mother.

About ten to fourteen days before birth the uterus descends into the pelvic basin. The change of fetal position is called "lightening," since it involves a new sensation of relief and comfort for the mother. Her breathing becomes easier because the pressure on her diaphragm and lungs is reduced. At about the same time a highly sensitive mother may feel slight uterine contractions—a sensation of inner tension—similar to those of labor. These contractions are considered by many obstetricians to be a prelude to the more vigorous contractions of true labor, a sort of "tuning up" of the uterine muscles. They also help in placing the baby's body into a deliverable position. The movements are beyond the mother's control, but since she is generally aware of them they are unlike the involuntary and peristaltic movements of the viscera. The contractions, which last only a few seconds, are noticeable, although usually not painful.

About two or three weeks before delivery the growth pattern of the fetus changes—in fact, it seems to be arrested—largely because the placenta regresses rather than develops further. The placenta becomes tough and fibrous (instead of spongy) as its surface cells degenerate. Blood clots and calcified patches appear, which indicate that the placental blood vessels have degenerated, thereby preventing the mother's blood from reaching the fetal capillaries. The expectant mother may normally lose a few pounds in weight near the end of her pregnancy. All of this bodes impending failure of the placental function and mandates that the fetus take care of its own respiration, digestion, and excretion. The onset of labor is imminent.

This slowdown of growth in the uterus and baby in the final month is inevitable and even fortunate: if the newborn infant's growth rate were equal to that of the eight-month fetus, it would weigh close to 200 pounds by its first birthday, and if the child continued to grow unabated it would be two stories tall and weigh millions of tons by its twentieth birthday.

What are the biological controls that enable a fertilized ovum, a mere speck, to reach a weight of seven pounds by parasitically drawing on its mother's bloodstream, and then compel it to give up its willing host for the rigors of independent existence? What makes it possible for the child to continue its growth outside the uterus until it is about five and a half or six feet tall and then stop growing altogether? This continues to be one of the most perplexing biological riddles.

preparations by the baby for its advent into the world

Birth is only an event in life, not the beginning of it. But birth marks a radical adjustment from a sheltered, parasitic existence to a physiologically independent one. No longer will the mother supply the fetus with oxygen and predigested food, eliminate its wastes, afford the stimulation it needs for development and testing of its nerves and muscles, and protect it against shocks, changes in temperature, and the prevalent infections of the outer world. For the fetus the moment of truth is here at last.

Since the baby, as opposed to the fetus, is a self-supporting organism, its various systems, both singly and in conjunction, must be ready to take over from the mother's body. Let's see how these systems prepare for such an abrupt transition.

digestive system

As we have seen, the gastrointestinal system starts to develop during the first month after conception and is structurally completed long before the baby is born. By the fourth month the

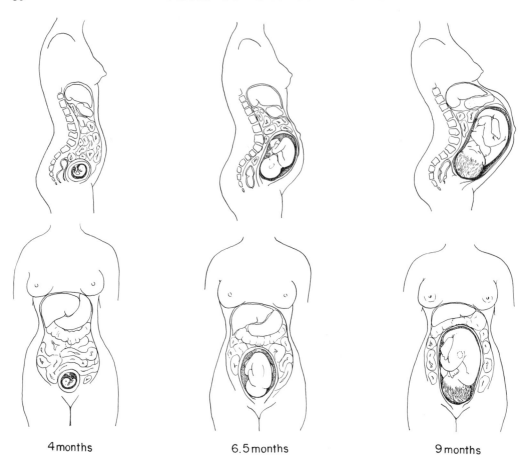

4 months   6.5 months   9 months

Views of relative size and different positions of fetus in mother's abdomen from 4 months to term

fetus is able to suck[1] and to swallow some of the surrounding amniotic fluid; by the eighth or ninth month it may swallow as much as 6 to 8 pints of recirculated fluids a day. Since the fluid usually contains proteins and sugars it has some nutritive value, although it does not compare as a source of food to the rich infusion from the mother's bloodstream. If the amniotic fluid were artificially sweetened the fetus would swallow more of it than usual. This seems to prove that numerous taste buds are functional—in fact, the number will actually decline after birth.

The ability of the fetus to swallow is sometimes used as a diagnostic tool by the obstetrician. First he takes an X-ray picture to silhouette the fetal organs against an opaque background. Next he injects a radio-opaque fluid (a harmless dye)

1. X-ray pictures have shown fetuses with a thumb or hand in the mouth, in a sucking posture, and babies have occasionally been born with calluses on their thumbs. It has been conjectured that this indicates hunger and discontent as well as an ability to obtain solace. Continued thumb or hand sucking will not alter the shape of the mouth, but it may affect the shape of the thumb or the hand.

into the amniotic fluid. When the fetus ingests fluid, some of the dye will lodge in its stomach and intestines. Now, just as with adults, X radiation or fluoroscopy can reveal both the structure and the function of the gastrointestinal tract. (Although the amount of exposure to radiation is minimal in this procedure, X-ray pictures of the fetus are not taken except in diagnosing conditions that are potentially serious and that are otherwise difficult to study. See Chapter 10.) Some of the radio-opaque dyes are excreted by way of the umbilical cord and placenta and are eliminated through the mother's kidneys. Other dyes are retained in the digestive tract until after birth, since the bowels are not usually evacuated until then. The radio-opaque dye technique is one of the most recent advances in the diagnosis of abnormal conditions that are correctable before or immediately after birth. It has proven particularly valuable in diagnosing Rh incompatibility (see Chapter 13) or fetal anemia, either of which might require blood transfusions before birth if the baby's life is to be saved.

respiration

The respiratory apparatus must be fairly well developed at least two months before birth, since babies delivered prematurely at seven months are able to breathe and to cry, although not with the same vigor and regularity as at nine months. A full-term baby can breathe about 45 times a minute for the first two weeks if he is exposed to air, then this rate is gradually reduced to the normal range of about 18 to 25 a minute for the rest of his life.

The normal mechanism by which the baby draws his first breath is now well understood. During its confinement in the uterus the fetus depends entirely upon its mother (via the placenta and the blood vessels of the umbilical cord) for oxygen and for the elimination of carbon dioxide. Its own lungs are either collapsed or partially filled with amniotic fluid, which must be removed at birth. The rate of exchange between mother and fetus is determined by the needs of the fetus. At birth the umbilical cord is tied and cut—usually after a brief delay to allow one final surge of blood from the placenta to reach the still-attached newborn. This will be its last blood ration from the placental reservoir—an oxygen and iron bonus—since with the cutting of the cord the mother ceases to supply oxygen to her baby. But circulation continues within the baby's own body, and the concentration of carbon dioxide in the bloodstream increases to a level that chemically stimulates the respiratory center in a portion of the brain known as the medulla oblongata (the lowest portion of the brain stem, which connects with the spinal cord). The respiratory center signals the muscles of the diaphragm and rib cage. The muscles contract, expanding the rib cage and pulling the diaphragm downward. There is now room for the lungs to fill like balloons. Of course, drawing a great big breath for the first time is a frightening sensation for the newborn. At any rate this unusually deep inhalation (the lungs contained no air) prompts the baby to exhale vigorously, and in so doing he naturally cries.

The first cry is a welcome and exhilarating sound to both mother and obstetrician. It is possibly the most critical moment in human life and certainly the most important positive sign of successful adjustment to extrauterine existence. The failure of "preemies" to survive is often due to respiratory inadequacy. If the infant doesn't cry immediately the obstetrician spanks his buttocks or rubs his feet or back; this usually initiates crying, which requires inhalation of air. (The spanking is never applied to the back for fear of damage to the kidneys.) But if the newborn doesn't begin to breathe within 30 seconds of delivery, the physicians will take such resuscitative measures as:

Clearing the air passages by mild suction catheterization, and holding the baby upside down by the ankles.

Continuing to stimulate the baby by mild back massage or buttocks spanking.

Keeping the body warm, since cooling has an adverse effect on respiration.

Administering oxygen by mask if breathing doesn't start within 90 seconds.

Giving mouth-to-mouth artificial respiration through gauze (if oxygen apparatus is not available), combined with alternate mild pressure and release on the chest.

Premature babies delivered by Caesarean section may be prone to hyaline membrane disease, which is characterized by a sticky exudate in the alveoli (tiny air sacs) of the lungs. When a newborn infant shows respiratory distress with dyspnea (lack of sufficient air) and cyanosis (bluing), he should be placed in an incubator of controlled temperature, high humidity, and oxygen and be given antibiotics. This is rarely needed, however.

circulatory system

With the first inhalation the circulatory system of the newborn baby must make radical changes. Some of these changes take

The circulatory system of a 30-week-old female fetus which has been injected via the umbilical artery with a micropaque solution, shown in a radiograph.

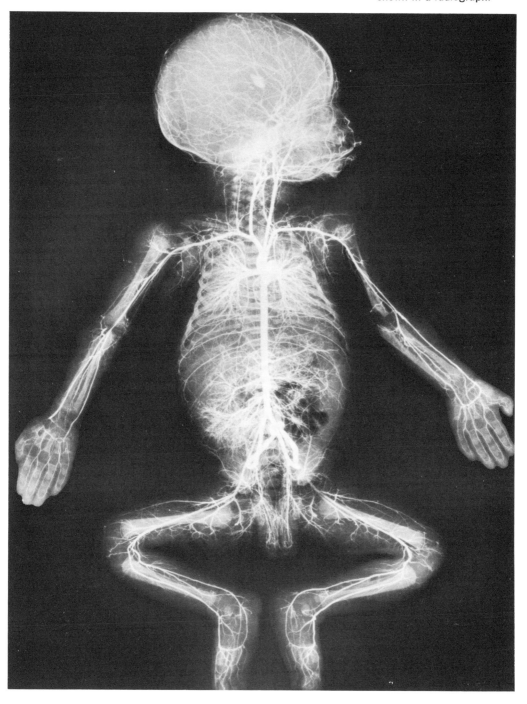

place immediately, within hours, and others within weeks. The main adaptations are as follows:

The opening between the two auricles of the heart, known as the foramen ovale (oval opening), closes. In the fetus blood is diverted from the right to the left side of its heart instead of being sent to the lungs for oxygenation, since the mother takes care of that requirement. At the moment of birth this passage begins to close, so that the baby's blood is shunted to his lungs for the first time. When the blood flow is unequal in the two auricles, two flaps of heart tissue fold together over this opening to form a septum (partition) which fuses permanently. In the newborn these two flaps may not effectively separate the two auricles and there may be brief periods of cyanosis (bluing of the skin) because pure and impure blood can mix. In the fetus there is a blood vessel that connects the vein and arteries associated with the nonfunctioning lungs. Now that the lungs have begun to function, this connection is shut off by contraction of muscles in the wall of the temporary vessel, but it is usually not totally and irreversibly sealed for about three months. Incomplete closure of this vessel (the ductus arteriosus) may also produce a temporary "blue baby." Only in very rare cases does closure fail, requiring surgery.

There is a fetal blood vessel that connects the umbilical vein directly with the heart. It forces any remaining umbilical blood directly into the fetal liver, and from there to the heart. With the cutting off of the umbilical vessel all visceral blood of the fetus goes directly to the fetal heart via the inferior vena cava. This shift in blood flow occurs within minutes of birth, but may not be complete for a week or two, and all vestiges of the original ductus venosus should be gone by the eighth week after birth.

At birth about 10 per cent of the body weight of the baby is accounted for by its blood (similar to that of the adult). This ratio may vary with the time at which the umbilical cord is clamped off; the later this tying is done, the greater the amount of placental blood that will return to the baby's circulation.

The newborn's heart has one burden removed, since its circuit now lies exclusively within the body of the baby and it does not have to pump blood into and out of the placenta. However, the baby's increased muscular activity, plus the exposure of his body surface to the cooler outside environment, will soon call on the heart to work many times harder than the adult heart relative to its body weight. The baby's pulse at birth is 125 to 130 per minute, but it may go as high as 180 following excitation. A greater independent need for oxygen stimulates an increase in the production of red blood cells and hemoglobin. This increase lasts for a few days and then settles at a level comparable to that of a normal adult. Hemoglobin content at birth is about 20 grams per 100 cubic centimeters of blood. This concentration is high, but it declines within 7 to 10 days to a normal level of about 12 to 14 grams. The white cell count is very high—sometimes as much as 45,000 per cubic millimeter compared with a normal count of about 7,000—but this declines rapidly by the seventh day. Clotting time of the blood tends to lengthen after birth, and occasionally vitamin K is given to prevent hemorrhage of the newborn owing to imbalance of the prothrombin level. Bile pigment in the newborn baby's blood is usually under the control of the liver, but this organ is not fully prepared to take on such a duty at birth, and a temporary jaundice results in as many as 50 per cent of newborns by the third or fourth day after birth. The percentage is likely to be even higher among the premature infants (see discussion of Rh blood factor in Chapter 13).

excretion

The baby's kidneys are completely formed and able to function long before birth, but they are still immature. They do virtually nothing for the fetus, since metabolic waste products are eliminated via the placenta and the kidneys of the mother. However, urine has been found in the bladder of a four-month-old fetus, and some has been found in the amniotic fluid of many fetuses. Occasionally an excess of amniotic fluid is formed (called polyhydramnios). Swallowing some of this fluid reduces the congestion and therefore tends to relieve the outside fluid pressure. Much of the amniotic fluid comes directly from the fetus—from its lungs and skin as well as from its kidneys. At birth there may be as much as 50 cubic centimeters (more than one ounce) of urine in the baby's bladder.

The functions of the kidneys include maintaining water balance in the tissues and organs. The fact that occasionally a newborn child is found to be edematous (swollen with fluids) indicates that its kidneys are not yet functioning properly. Relative to the adult, the newborn's tissues may hold as much as 10 per cent more water. The main edematous regions are the hands, feet, legs, face, and pubic area. Apparently the fetus doesn't excrete salt and other minerals efficiently, and this compounds the failure to control the water balance. Excessive

ammonia evident in the diaper of the newborn suggests inadequate hydration. During the first few days after birth there is
almost invariably a considerable weight loss caused by dehydration and low water intake. The loss may continue until rectified
by consumption of milk.

One of the difficulties with prematurely delivered infants is
a weight loss greater than that of normally delivered babies
owing to excessive dehydration, and water balance may be very
critical. The newborn's kidneys, while apparently structurally
complete, are not functionally adequate, and may not be fully
so for a year or two. Uncertainties about kidney function at
birth generally indicate that it is better not to give the newborn
any water for at least 6 to 8 hours, during which time the
physicians monitor for signs of edema. The child is first given 5
per cent sugar water.

temperature control

The body heat of the fetus (and later of the newborn) is regulated by a thermostat-like control center in the brain. However,
food intake is essential as a source of caloric heat. The thermal
control center functions imperfectly in the newborn, and heat
production is about 30 per cent less (relative to weight) than in
the adult. This is one reason that premature babies must be
provided with supplemental heat in incubators.

During the final month in the uterus the baby develops a
layer of fatty tissue beneath its skin to insulate its body against
the relatively cold outer world. The original insulation was the
fluid environment, but this is taken away at birth. The baby
must rely solely upon his subcutaneous layer of fat until his
circulation and thermostatic controls are working properly.

The birth temperature of the baby is determined by that of
his mother, in whose body he has been "incubated." This
temperature drops about 2 to 5 degrees Fahrenheit immediately
after delivery but rises again in a few hours until it is close to
that of the normal adult—if the baby is kept warm in the
meantime. Since the source of heat energy is food, intake must
be regulated according to the baby's needs and his ability to
digest food. As the fat reserve is used up the baby must con-
sume digestible food for his caloric needs. (The best food is his
mother's milk.) Generally the baby can survive well on his own
reserves for a few days, but very active babies burn up this
reserve rapidly.

Occasionally, when labor is to be induced, it is necessary

to insert a catheter via the vagina into the cervix in order to record uterine contractions and the fetal pulse. To avoid infections, the region is sometimes flushed with a cold antibiotic solution. The reduction in temperature elicits avoiding movements from the fetus and produces an accelerated heartbeat. Within its amniotic fluid the fetus has been kept in a well-regulated, constant-temperature bath, so any drop in temperature is an effective physical stimulus.

sensitivity

We have already mentioned that sound (mechanical vibrations) can be transmitted through the mother's abdominal wall. There is some evidence of general sensitivity to light, inasmuch as the eyes are structurally well developed. However, visual acuity is low and must be actively improved after birth.

labor, delivery, and afterbirth

In most large cities, maternity centers hold classes for prospective parents. The classes usually focus on information that is basic to all pregnancies: the best ages for childbearing (twenty to thirty years for the woman), the normal physiology of childbearing, maternal hygiene, diet and exercise, recreation, labor and delivery, the adjustment of the infant to his new environment, and items for the layette and nursery. Some classes may instruct the prospective mother in regular exercises she should take in preparation for the purely physical aspects of delivery, postnatal control, and recuperation.

The physical preparations for labor and delivery are inevitably in the hands of nature. As the time of delivery approaches, the placenta begins to reduce its functions and to degenerate, forcing the baby to function more and more for itself. That marvelous exchange device is soon no longer adequate for the baby, who must then emerge and fend for itself.

The process of expelling the fetus is divided into labor and delivery and afterbirth. In the first stage, the contractions of the uterus stretch the opening at its lower end, the cervix, so the baby can pass out into the birth canal (vagina). In the second, the baby passes through the birth canal and out through the vaginal opening (which also stretches to let the infant get by). In the third, the placenta and membranes (the afterbirth) are loosened and delivered.

labor

The labor stage lasts on the average of from 7 to 12 hours; for the firstborn it may be more like 16 to 18 hours. Labor begins with the shortening and widening of the cervix and cervical canal; the opening, which normally has a diameter of one-half centimeter, ultimately dilates to about 10 centimeters in diameter. For the duration of the pregnancy the fibro-muscular cervix has held the baby firmly within the confines of the uterus.[1] Now, it gives in to the baby by relaxing without any conscious control by the expectant mother. The opening is stretched by the baby's head. Some hormone secreted by the ovary relaxes the cervix, making it softer and more pliable as pregnancy advances. The vagina secretes abundant glycogen (a complex carbohydrate). This metabolizes in turn to glucose and then to lactic acid, a bactericidal agent, so that infection of the area is either pre-

1. When the cervix is "incompetent" (0.3 per cent of pregnancies) and might allow spontaneous abortion, it can be closed with a surgical suture to help retain the baby.

Listening for the fetal heart

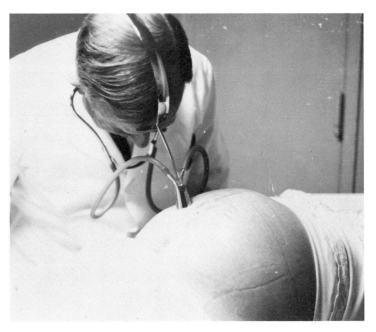

vented or limited. During this early dilation of the cervix the first true involuntary contractions of the uterus begin. These contractions give notice of the impending birth.

At first the contractions are usually mild and last only 15 to 25 seconds each; they occur about 10 to 15 minutes apart. Some women hardly notice them. The initial discomfort may seem to lie in the small of the back, rather than the muscular walls of the uterus, where the contractions actually occur. As the contractions occur more frequently (3 to 5 minutes apart) they also become stronger and longer-lasting. This is no cause for alarm. If the woman is still at home she can even go about her minor household chores. She should, however, be alert to the moment when at last she must go to the hospital. She should certainly call her obstetrician.

birth

The birth stage can last from 30 minutes to 2 hours. It tends to be shorter for subsequent births. Birth begins as soon as the baby's head passes through the cervix. At this time the contractions have a duration of about one minute and occur every two or three minutes. Usually the amniotic sac ruptures early in this stage; with this the baby's marine life is terminated. It must be remembered that the amniotic fluid has protected the baby, kept it at a regulated temperature, and prevented adhesions for almost nine months, and now it is suddenly removed. Upon rupture the fluid gushes from the vagina. The obstetrician may plan to hasten the delivery and can, under aseptic conditions, rupture the amnion surgically.

During this phase the mother bears down hard with her abdominal muscles and tries to expel the contents of the uterus. Usually the head of the baby is well down in the pelvic basin. It passes through the fully dilated cervix and appears as the opening of the vulva spreads wide. Between contractions the head may recede, only to emerge farther with the next contraction. As the head becomes increasingly visible, and the contractions almost continuous, there comes a moment when the head stretches the vulva to its maximum opening. Now the obstetrician is able to grip the baby's head as it fully appears ("crowning") and assist it in its emergence into the air. The bones of the baby's head are not firmly knit together before birth, so that the shape of the head can change slightly to accommodate passage through the birth canal.

In 95 per cent of all human births the baby descends in the

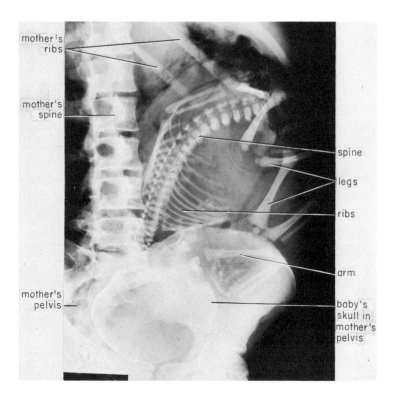

mother's ribs

mother's spine

spine

legs

ribs

arm

mother's pelvis

baby's skull in mother's pelvis

X ray of human fetus at term (in position for delivery)

head-down position, in only 3.5 per cent in the buttocks-down or breech position. The remainder may lie in a transverse (crosswise) or compound position, and this may be troublesome. The head-down position may be due in part to the pear shape of the uterus and in part to gravity (the head is heavier than the feet).

In labor involuntary uterine contractions started the delivery. During the second phase voluntary abdominal contractions on the part of the mother aid the action of her uterus. Now all the prenatal exercises the mother has taken to strengthen her abdominal muscles pay off, for she can effectively help. (If the mother is given a general anesthetic she is unable to help.) The uterine contractions alone may not be sufficient for delivery, and her bearing down helps to expel the baby from the uterus. Nevertheless a baby can be delivered from a totally unconscious woman, even from one in a coma. Once the head is through the vaginal chamber the rest of the body follows readily. The position of the baby before birth, and particularly that part which is first to emerge, will determine to some extent the ease of the process. The most natural position is head down, with the back of the baby's head toward the front of the mother. As the baby is emerging its body changes its position and contours so that even the widest portions (where the appendages are) will assume the smallest possible diameter in order to ease the process. The mother's expression typically becomes serious and she accepts the inevitable stress and strain. It is no wonder the mother needs time for her body to recuperate from the physical exertion, and for her mind to adjust to her newly acquired role in life.

While she is still on the delivery table, the mother is often given her child to hold, after he is cleaned, dried, and checked. For many, this is one of life's most satisfying moments.

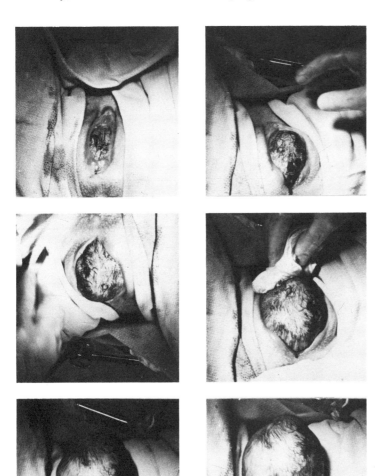

"Head Start" The second stage of labor, when the baby's head first emerges, is called "crowning." It is still attached to the placenta by the umbilical cord and is therefore not yet physiologically independent of its mother.

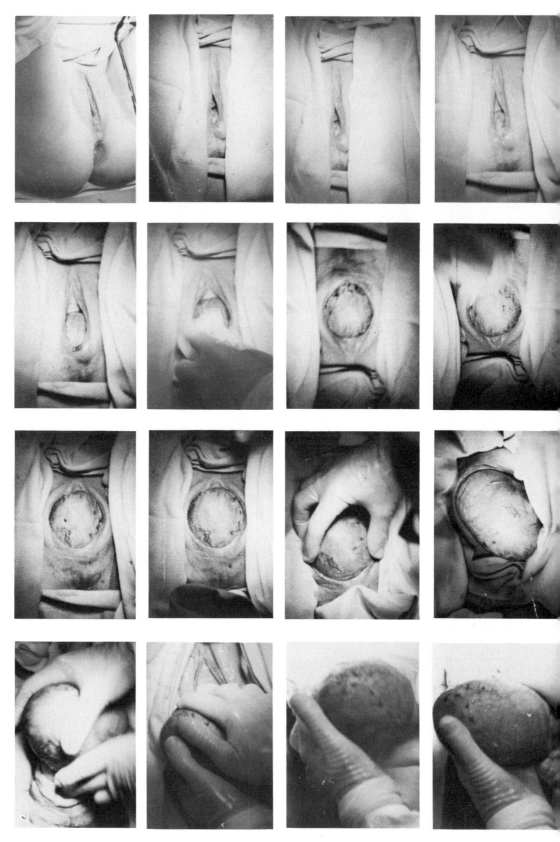

Normal delivery of a child

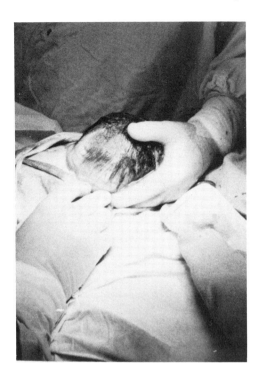

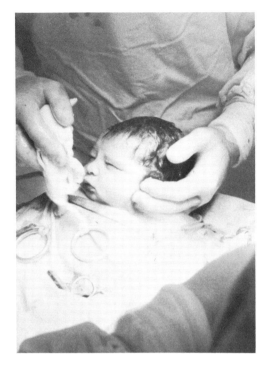

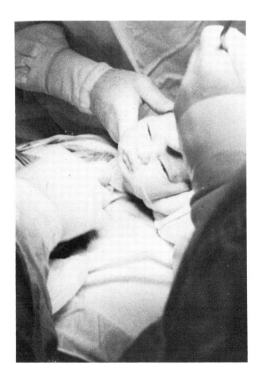

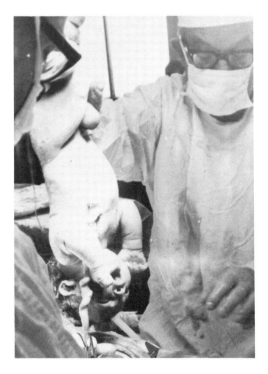

Delivery by Caesarean section

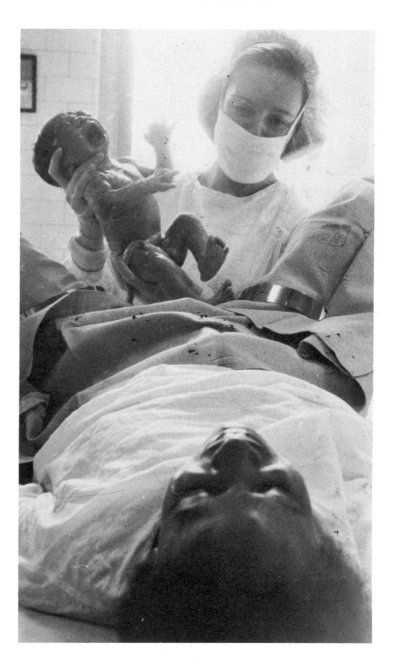

Relief and exhilaration

afterbirth

The placenta follows the baby, usually within 5 minutes after delivery, in a process lasting up to half an hour. This is followed by a resumption of the normal shape of the uterus, upward displacement of the uterus from its position in the pelvic basin, and further emergence of the umbilical cord, accompanied by a free flow of blood from the vagina.

Separation of the placenta from the uterus is automatic, but the expulsion can be aided by the same downward (kneading-like) contractions of the uterus and abdominal muscles that were used to expel the baby itself. Manual pressure may be applied gently by the nurse or obstetrician. Uterine contractions after delivery help to expel the placenta, but they also retard or even stop the hemorrhage caused by the tearing away of the

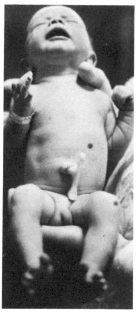

Newborn boy at two minutes of age, held by doctor

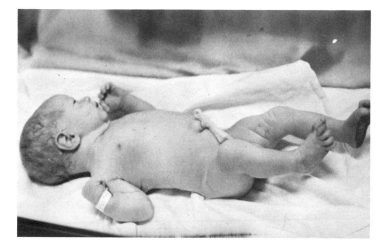

Newborn boy Apgar rating-8

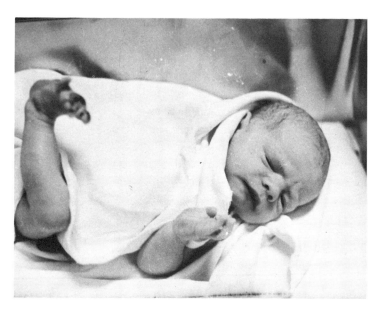

Newborn baby all ready for his mother ten minutes after delivery: umbilical cord tied; baby cleaned and dried; wrist labeled; footprint taken; drops in eyes; head measurements taken; heart and lungs checked.

placenta from the uterus. The uterine muscles actually clamp the many small blood vessels within them. Normally there may be a loss of 200 to 300 cubic centimeters of blood at this time.

With first babies (primagravida) the mother may sometimes experience what is known as false labor. True labor can always be identified by the following signs:

1. Contractions occurring regularly with shortening intervals and greater intensity. Pain is felt first in the lower back. Both pain and contractions are increased with walking.

2. An unnatural discharge of blood, rupture of the fluid membrane from the vagina, or both.

3. Dilation of the cervix to more than its relaxed 1-centimeter diameter.

The contractions in false labor occur irregularly without decreasing intervals or increasing intensity. They are usually abdominal rather than uterine. Walking tends to relieve rather than accentuate the pain—a dead giveaway. There is no evidence of bleeding or discharge of mucus from the vagina, and the cervix is undilated.

caesarean section

A Caesarean section is a major operation and is performed under anesthesia. It involves removing the infant from the uterus by way of an incision in the abdominal wall and the uterus. It may be done prior to the onset of labor, but generally only when the baby is judged to be ready for delivery. It is medically prescribed when normal delivery might prove difficult or even hazardous for the child or the mother. Situations in which a Caesarean operation is indicated include: unusually large size of the infant with respect to the mother's pelvis and birth canal; severe toxemia related to the pregnancy; a scar in the uterus left by a previous Caesarean (which might be ruptured with the straining of labor); hemorrhage or the threat of hemorrhage; and fetal distress.

When it is elected, Caesarean section can be scheduled for a specific time. (Spontaneous natural deliveries, on the other hand, frequently occur at night.) Successive children can be delivered by Caesarean section; the number is governed by the wishes of the parents and the integrity of the previous operative scar. Four successive Caesarean sections are not uncommon. Since this is a major operation, full recuperation is likely to take longer than for a normal delivery.

health of the newborn

It is possible to evaluate within one to five minutes after birth how well the new baby can be expected to function in his new world. His chances for leading a normal, healthy life can be gauged by means of the Apgar Scoring System. This system, named after Dr. Virginia Apgar, who directs research on congenital defects at the National Foundation in New York City, consists of five tests; rating of 0, 1, and 2 are made of the baby's heart rate, respiratory effort, muscle tone, reflex irritability, and color. (Where the natural skin color of the newborn is nonwhite, alternative tests are applied. These relate to the mucous membranes of the conjunctiva and mouth, color of the lips, palms of the hands, and soles of the feet.) The system is reliable when the scoring is objective. A perfect score is therefore five times two, or ten. A score of seven or above is considered good, four to six only fair, and below three so poor that the physicians have to apply resuscitative measures. Apgar scoring is as follows:

	0	1	2
PULSE	Absent	Less than 100	More than 100
BREATHING	Absent	Slow, irregular	Good cry
MUSCLE TONE	Flaccid	Some flexion of extremities	Active motion
REFLEX IRRITABILITY	No response	Grimace	Vigorous cry
COLOR (See above comment)	Blue or pale	Body pink Extremities blue	Pink all over

further adjustment

We have described the nine months of intrauterine development and noted in the previous chapter those critical changes the fetus must go through at the time of delivery. We now move on to those physical conditions commonly noted in the newborn baby. We do not intend to enter the province of the pediatrician, but rather to acquaint prospective parents with what is happening as their child develops, and what to expect when they first see their offspring. Now that the baby has completed his existence in the uterus we will merely summarize certain situations.

Prenatal development normally takes up to about 40 weeks. The average newborn child weighs about 6 to 8 pounds and has a body length of about 20 inches. Premature infants

Routine check of newborn baby: injection of vitamin K for hemorrhage control, prophylactic eye drops of silver nitrate, listening to the heart, checking the lungs, inking the sole, and taking identification footprint.

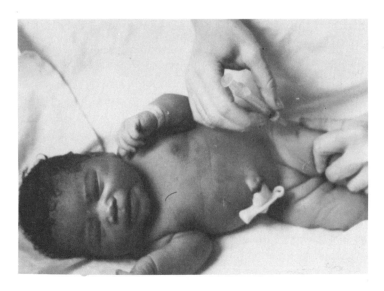

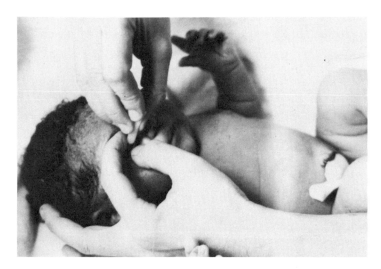

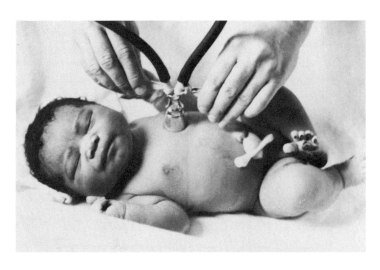

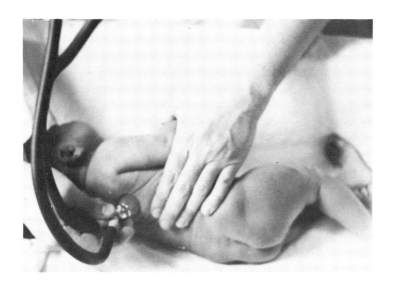

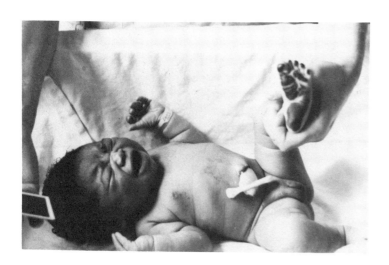

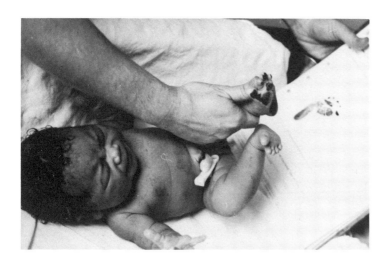

(those weighing less than 5½ pounds) require special attention, since they are not equipped with proper fatty insulation, their thermostatic control is still inadequate, their circulatory systems do not function well enough to cope with the sudden independence, and their kidneys and digestive systems are not yet ready for full duty. Boys tend to weigh a bit more than girls do at birth, Caucasian babies more than non-Caucasian, and second and subsequent babies more than the first-born. The ratio of boys to girls among the first-born is statistically almost one to one, contrary to a general impression that girls predominate among first-born children. The general birth ratio is 106 boys to 100 girls.

For some time after birth the baby will continue to assume the body posture he had in the confines of the uterus. The arms are usually extended and the legs bowed. The neck is usually short, as though telescoped in, and the skin may bunch in folds. The baby is able to lift his head backward but not forward. A cheesy white covering may persist on the skin, but is soon rubbed off (if it is yellow in color this suggests erythroblastosis, a blood condition, which must be treated). The healthy skin of a white baby is pinkish; it may temporarily become redder. There may be some shedding, especially on the soles and palms. The outermost layer of skin seems loose, and water may accumulate (edema), especially on the hands, feet, legs, and face. However, the skin will tighten up and the edema will disappear quickly. Since the newborn baby cannot yet perspire, the glands of his skin may become filled with a whitish material which disappears in 10 days or 2 weeks. If the baby is premature, his body may be covered by persistent lanugo, a downlike fine hair (mostly on the forehead, cheeks, shoulders, and back). The scalp sometimes has light-brown crusty patches where the oil (sebaceous) glands are overactive, accumulate dust, and give a mild appearance of uncleanliness. This can be gently shampooed away.

The breasts of newborn babies of either sex tend to be engorged for several days, probably because the hormone that stimulates the mother's breasts to produce milk is still present. This hormone can pass through the placenta to the late fetus. A whitish secretion in the baby's breasts, called "witch's milk," may persist for several months.

Sometimes cyanotic (bluish) areas may appear on the skin. This means that the circulation is still inefficient and that pure and impure blood are mixing. Cyanosis generally clears up within several days.

The human skull is extremely strong once it is fully formed. However, at birth the baby's brain is protected by headbones that are partially calcified but loosely knit rather than fused. In delivery the head is somewhat compressed by its passage through the 6-inch stretched cervical canal, and it may appear to be misshapen after birth. This so-called molding may involve mild overlapping of some of the cranial bone plates—a minor distortion that is readily adjusted after the baby is free of its confinement in the uterus. If the birth is assisted by instruments, the bony plates may be so displaced as to give the newborn a "pin" or "peaked" head. This, too, usually corrects itself in a few days. The skullbones begin to interlock, but they do not fuse firmly for about 18 months in order to permit growth. On the top of the head (at the junction of the frontal and parietal bones) there is left a diamond-shaped soft spot (the fontanelle) through which a pulse may be detected. Ultimately the bones will interlock to provide a continuous hard skull, and every part of the brain will be well protected.

Sometimes the newborn may develop an edema (swelling) of the scalp (possibly caused by manipulation of the head through the birth canal), but this usually disappears within a few hours as the excess fluid is absorbed. Sometimes there is a bluish discoloration owing to minor (and harmless) local bleeding called hematoma.

The newborn baby's personality began to develop during its stay in the uterus. By the time of birth no two babies will react in the same manner to similar stimuli, since they differ not only genetically but also in exposure to their environment. All normal newborn babies react to light, but they surely cannot see in the sense of distinguishing figures or faces. They react to sound, even as they did in the uterus (Moro reflex), and have other reflexes as well.

It must be remembered that the skin and the mucous membranes of the newborn's mouth are very sensitive and may be injured easily. The newborn may even have mouth ("thrush") or eye infections, acquired at birth, which can easily be treated by the physician. Many states require that the physician treat the eyes immediately with silver nitrate to take care of any possible infection.

The region of future tooth development may actually have a few teeth, but more frequently there is only a scalloped edge where the milk teeth are later to appear. Sometimes the tongue is fastened to the floor of the mouth by a membrane. This membrane usually tears spontaneously or, if it persists, it may be cut by the surgeon. In these cases the baby is literally "tongue-tied," but this does not seem to impede his crying abilities. Breathing is abdominal and diaphragmatic rather than coming from the chest. It appears to require considerable effort at first, especially since the untried chest muscles are not fully prepared to inflate the lungs by negative pressure. On the other hand, the baby is capable of producing loud sounds precisely because he uses his abdominal muscles and diaphragm—a technique that is acquired with effort by the adult operatic singer. Breathing is rapid at first—about 45 times per minute—and irregular, with variations between 20 and 100. The pulse also is high—about 125 beats per minute, and with stimulation going up to 180 per minute. The abdomen is usually firm and smooth, except that crying causes some abdominal distension. The umbilical stump usually dries and sloughs off in a few days.

In some boy babies the testes may not yet have descended through the inguinal canal into the scrotum, but they should do so within a few weeks. If not, they should then be assisted by the physician in their descent. The foreskin of the penis should be loose and retractable so that the baby can urinate properly and the penis can be cleaned. Orthodox Jewish parents require circumcision of all boys on the eighth day. Otherwise, obstetricians circumcize boys in the delivery room or on the second or third day. Circumcision is deemed a healthy practice (irrespective of ethnic origins). It is believed to result in a lowered incidence of cancer among men and in fewer infections and less cancer of the cervix in women who become their wives.

In girl babies the lips of the vagina (the vulva) may be widely separated and the clitoris prominent. If there is a mucus-like discharge from the vagina, with a tinge of blood on the third or fourth day, this is no cause for concern. It is believed to be due to the withdrawal of estrogenic hormones derived from the mother which were passed through the placenta just prior to birth.

From the time the baby leaves the hospital he depends on the treatment he receives from his parents. In order for the baby to have the best possible care, we urge the new mother to select a pediatrician in whom she has utter confidence. Her choice should be at least as careful as it was when she found an obstetrician for herself. After all, the infant is hardly in a position to volunteer information about his symptoms.

PART 2

awakening to pregnancy and prenatal care

When a married woman misses her menstrual period she naturally wonders whether she is pregnant. However, failure to menstruate in itself is not proof of pregnancy, since the onset of menstrual bleeding may be temporarily delayed, or even missed altogether, for several reasons. Illness is one; physical or emotional upset and fatigue are others. For example, airline stewardesses who fly on jetliners often complain that their cycles are disturbed, nursing mothers can again become pregnant without having undergone a prior menstruation (even though lactation tends to inhibit ovulation), and adolescent girls have been known to conceive before their first menstruation. On the other hand some pregnant women may be deceived into thinking they are not pregnant because they see a small amount of blood for the first few months of a pregnancy at the very time they expect their period.

If the woman is pregnant she will eventually find out in other ways. Her breasts soon become enlarged and tender. She may feel the need to urinate frequently. She may develop morning nausea. If these symptoms appear in conjunction with her missed period she should consult an obstetrician. The first visit should be arranged as early as possible—no later than the second missed period (without delay if there is a history of miscarriage or abnormal births)—so that he can plan for the delivery and advise her on prenatal care. This is a necessary precaution. The likelihood of miscarriage or infant mortality is always much higher without professional help, and many mothers as well as their babies may be lost in the process. Unfortunately, too many women wait until they are far along in their pregnancy before they see a physician, with the result that avoidable complications have had time to develop. Today only about one pregnant woman out of six consults her obstetrician during the first month. Some women—as many as one in eleven—wait until they are in their ninth month, either because they do not have the money or because they are frightened. This is inexcusable in a modern society. At the very least the knowledge that she is in competent hands early in the game should give the average woman peace of mind, a decided plus factor in the months to come.

what the obstetrician does

How do you find an obstetrician? The obvious thing to do is to ask your family doctor. If you do not have one and are otherwise unfamiliar with medical services in your community, you might inquire at the local hospital or medical society. From the list of specialists you should choose a well-qualified man, one whose training and experience are thorough. An important consideration is the hospital he is associated with—you should lean toward someone on the staff of the best hospital within reach of your home.

To find out about low-cost care, ask either your local health department or a public health nurse. It is not uncommon even for a private specialist to lower his fees for those who cannot afford them. No woman should be deprived of the essential medical advice and care she needs at this time.

At the first prenatal visit, it is a good idea for your husband to go along. The obstetrician will take your complete history: your age, occupation, general health, previous illnesses or injuries, your mother's experiences with pregnancy, and so forth. He will also ask about your husband's health and about tendencies toward such conditions as diabetes in either family. At this time it's wise to bring up any matter that's troubling you,

Drs. Alan and Manfred Guttmacher, identical twins at age six months with their sister Dorothy. Dr. Alan Guttmacher is now Director of the Planned Parenthood Society.

These twins had the identical blood group (MN, B, and Rh+); their hair whorls and palm prints were opposite as one would expect, one was right handed and the other left handed. In all the tests made at Johns Hopkins by Dr. Adolph Schultz they were found to have arisen from the same zygote, hence were identical in every detail.

such as a history of mental retardation on either side or some disturbing hereditary situation in either's background. Of course, you should realize that it is advisable to consult an obstetrician *before you become pregnant.* Your own previous pregnancies, if any, are significant. How many were there? How long did they last? How were the infants delivered? How large were they? Were there any complications? Is there any evidence of twinning in either your line or your husband's? These are but a few of the many queries the obstetrician will ask. Some of the questions may embarrass you: How often did you have sexual relations? Do you ordinarily use contraceptives? Did you or your husband ever have syphilis? The doctor raises them merely to get the most comprehensive profile of the woman's pregnancy experience so that he can be on the alert for any problem that may arise for either mother or baby.

Next the obstetrician concentrates on details of the current pregnancy. He asks about any nausea, swelling of hands or feet, headaches, blurred vision, constipation, cramps, abdominal discomforts, breathing problems, vaginal discharges, and other symptoms.

The interview is followed by a thorough physical examination, the first part of which is similar to any general medical examination. Attention is paid to your height, weight, blood

Fraternal (nonidentical) twins at one year

pressure, heart and lungs, teeth and throat, breasts and nipples. Samples of your urine and blood will be taken. The urinalysis will help detect albumin (an animal protein that may be found in the urine during pregnancy and that may signify a toxic condition) and sugar (an indication of diabetes). Blood tests will determine your blood type (in the event a transfusion is needed at delivery), Rh factor and hemoglobin level, and will also check for syphilis. Your husband's blood type and Rh factor should also be noted, particularly if you are Rh negative (see Chapter 13). Hemoglobin is a protein present in the red blood cells. Its role is to transport oxygen from the lungs to the body tissues. When the blood has insufficient hemoglobin content the person is said to be anemic. The blood-forming activity of the fetus during pregnancy may cause anemia in the mother, so it is important to determine the woman's hemoglobin level at this time.

The general examination is followed by a specific obstetrical examination, which consists of palpation of the abdomen, measurements of the bony configuration of the pelvis, and an internal inspection.

Further conferences with the obstetrician are arranged, usually monthly to the seventh month, biweekly through the eighth month, and weekly in the ninth month. Of course, he will see you as often as is required if there are any complications. *Make sure that the obstetrician can be reached by telephone at any time or else have him arrange for a qualified substitute to stand by.*

At the end of the first conference the obstetrician will generally urge you to take note of such matters as diet, the amount of sleep and rest you get, the nature and effect of daily exercise, the regularity of your daily elimination, your method of daily bathing, the proper fit of clothing, and the presence of dental problems. These may seem routine, but since you are responsible for the welfare of your developing child, any irregularity takes on added significance.

prenatal care

We will make some very general suggestions that we believe will aid you in getting through your pregnancy without misfortune to your child or to yourself. *This is in no way intended as a substitute for conferences with and supervision by a qualified obstetrician.* There are differences of opinion concerning the regimen to be observed during pregnancy, and in every case your own obstetrician presumably is the best qualified to advise you. To assist you, we have compiled a glossary (at end of book), and we recommend that you consult it whenever you are in doubt about the meaning of a term used by your obstetrician.

Prenatal care is basically common sense. It is based upon wide experience, and it takes into consideration both fetus and mother. There will come a day when it includes routine examinations made *before* marriage or conception to determine fitness for pregnancy, but in most cases today pregnancy has been achieved before prenatal care begins. However, the prospective parents must still anticipate a great many situations without, of course, becoming hypochondriacal about them.

weight gain

Virtually all pregnant women gain weight, but how much heavier should they be? A net gain of 15 to 20 pounds from conception to delivery is normal. Of this the fetus may weigh 7 to 8 pounds and the placenta and amniotic fluid 2½ pounds; the rest represents accumulations of fats and fluids in the tissues of the mother. The fetus puts on 90 per cent of its weight after the fifth month, 50 per cent in the last two months. Since the fetus and its accessories don't fluctuate in any given pregnancy, the variable quantity is the weight of the mother herself. Therefore, it is easy to see that a gain of 30 to 50 pounds is unnecessary.

Excessive weight gain affects your circulation, blood pressure, and heart, it makes breathing difficult, it makes you awkward and prone to accident, it gives you aches and pains, and it mars your appearance. A gain of even 10 pounds is said to increase the length of the capillaries through which your heart must pump blood by about 6 miles, and that is a below-average gain. Even more important than the net gain is the rate at which you put on weight. In the beginning you may actually lose weight because your appetite is robbed by nausea, but by three to four months you should register a gain of perhaps 4 or 5 pounds. Thereafter you should expect to gain substantially more. However, if you ever find yourself putting on 2 pounds in a single week, tell your obstetrician immediately, since this is considered abnormal. Excessive gain in weight is difficult to discard after delivery.

diet

Every day the nonpregnant woman of average size, weight, and activity requires an average of 2,300 calories of energy in the form of food. Let us assume you are that average woman. When you become pregnant you require not more, but less, food for yourself because your activity is reduced. On the other hand, your fetus needs more and more food for growth and development, particularly in the later stages of pregnancy. The combined needs work out to only about 2,600 calories daily, or 300 more than normal. Therefore the saying that the pregnant woman should "eat enough for two" is obviously untrue, since it would lead to a gross overweight condition. As may be seen from the following summary,[1] your daily nutritional requirements late in pregnancy are not so radically different from your normal needs. The chief differences are a greater emphasis on proteins, vitamins, and minerals.

	NONPREGNANT WOMAN	LATE-PREGNANT WOMAN
Total calories	2,300	2,600
Protein (grams)	58	78
Calcium (grams)	0.8	1.5
Iron (milligrams)	12	15
Vitamin A (international units)	5,000	6,000
Thiamine (milligrams)	1.2	1.3
Riboflavin (milligrams)	1.5	2
Niacin (milligrams)	17	20
Ascorbic acid (milligrams)	70	100
Vitamin D (international units)	?	400

A good and proper diet of the pregnant woman can alter drastically the baby's health during its first six months. It can improve conditions during labor by eight times, shorten the duration of the first stages of labor by two, reduce convalescence to one-third, reduce miscarriages from 7 per cent to zero, reduce stillbirths from 4 per cent to zero, and prematurity from 9 per cent to 2 per cent. Illnesses of the baby can also be reduced: colds to one-fourth the frequency, bronchitis to one-third, pneumonia to one-third, rickets from 5.5 per cent to zero; deaths can almost be eliminated, and dystrophy and anemia reduced. There is no question but that the mother's diet is crucial for her, for her fetus, and for her child during its first year.

The following diet, worked out by the Food and Nutrition Bureau, is said to provide all the nutrients, vitamins, and minerals required by the pregnant woman under normal condi-

1. From National Academy of Science Publication No. 589, 1958.

tions. However, to make sure that you get enough vitamins and minerals, your obstetrician may prescribe prenatal capsules that contain vitamins A, B, C, and D and up to 13 mineral elements, especially calcium, phosphorus, iron, and iodine. Why should this be necessary? Well, for example, the soil, and consequently the leafy vegetables, in certain parts of the country (notably the Midwest) are deficient in iodine; while iodine should be added routinely for everyone in those areas, it is even more important for the growing fetus.

the adequate and balanced diet

1 pint or more of milk—pasteurized or in cooked food

1 good serving of red meat, fish or fowl (to include ¼ pound of liver each week)

1 egg

2 servings of fruit, one citrus (lemon juice, orange, grapefruit, etc.)

2 or 3 servings of vegetables, one of which is raw (carrots, cabbage, lettuce) and one green or yellow

2 or 3 slices of whole-grain or enriched bread or cereals

2 tablespoons of butter or fortified margarine (labeled to include 15,000 units of vitamin A per pound)

400 international units of vitamin D

We suggest that you increase your fluid intake to six to eight 8-ounce glasses daily, and that this include about a quart of milk or milk products. The emphasis on whole milk is not exaggerated. It is the most perfect of foods, and a quart a day will furnish you with about one-fourth of your total energy requirements. Its high calcium and phosphorus content is an aid in the formation of the fetus' bones and teeth. While there are calcium tablets you can take, you can never be sure your system is actually absorbing the calcium from them. Besides, milk is a source of protein and vitamins and it increases your resistance to infections.

Sometimes drinking fluids presents problems. A full bladder may keep you up nights, liquids may add to the queasiness of morning sickness, and your tissues may retain fluids. Suggested remedies are not drinking anything after supper, drinking iced, flavored drinks (fruit juices and sodas) instead of water, and cutting down on your intake of salt. You should not drink less fluids, because your body needs them.

In the middle months of pregnancy you may acquire a ravenous appetite and perhaps a craving for certain foods. Your appetite should not lead you to eat more than you need. As for the craving, it may be either a whim or a sign of some real lack in your diet. Let your obstetrician figure it out.

exercise and rest

All obstetricians seem to agree that a moderate amount of exercise is desirable to prevent muscles of the pregnant woman from getting flabby. What form it may take depends on the physical condition of the patient. Walking is an excellent form of exercise. Light calisthenics, such as squatting and getting down on all fours, strengthen muscles that will later be used in delivery. Golf, swimming, and bicycling are not considered to be too violent. Some pregnant women can tolerate dancing, tennis, climbing, or horseback riding, but these pursuits may be too strenuous for most. What all of them offer is recreational activity to distract the woman from worrying about what is happening inside her. Housework provides exercise, but it is not entirely satisfactory because it can be a chore.

Obstetricians of all shades of opinion, however, believe that it is essential for the pregnant woman not to get overtired. While the mother can recover by resting, physical fatigue produces toxic by-products that are not good for the developing fetus. Fatigue in the pregnant woman causes hyperactivity of the fetus. When you find that you are more than normally irritable, worrisome, restless, or apprehensive you should take heed and change your schedule. Sleep and horizontal body rest will help to prevent fatigue. One of the worst things you can do is to overwork yourself. You are not an invalid, but you have to accept the fact that you will fatigue more easily as your pregnancy progresses. Therefore, break the workday with short rest periods. Half an hour of complete physical relaxation every morning and afternoon will help you to avoid the cumulative effects of fatigue and tension.

It stands to reason that if your heart is assuming the added burden of pumping more blood through more blood vessels because of the growing fetus, it will have to work harder. When you are in a standing position your heart pumps against gravity. Therefore if you lie down with your legs supported at body level, you will not only be relieving your abdominal back muscles of the added weight of pregnancy, but you will also be giving your heart a resting spell. Moreover, if you have been on your feet for a long time it may prove restful to lie on a bed with your legs stretched upward with your heels touching the wall. This should reduce the blood congestion in your legs and is generally beneficial if not carried out for too long. Or try spreading your legs a bit, turn your feet outward, and allow your arms to lie by your side slightly bent. This position is often conducive to immediate sleep. A good motto might be: Never stand when you can sit, never sit when you can lie down.

The first element of exercise is to learn how to relax. Physical, mental, and emotional relaxation are so interrelated that we can hardly have one without the others. On the other hand, some mild physical exercise, such as walking, bicycling, or swimming, may encourage you to relax mentally. This happens partly because the exercise diverts your attention without exhausting you physically. Conversely, it is possible for you to be physically exhausted yet not be able to sleep, or else sleep restlessly, because your mind is not at ease.

Prenatal exercises aim at maintaining muscle tone. They should be started after the first visit to the doctor, between three and four months, and should be faithfully followed during the eighth and ninth months of pregnancy. By following a proper regimen of exercises you can retain your health, maintain or even improve your posture, and prepare physically (and mentally as a corollary) for labor. The fit woman has less need for medication, anesthesia, or other artificial aids in the delivery of her child.

Pregnancy involves an average weight gain of up to 24 pounds. This increase, along with a shift in your weight distribution (and therefore your center of gravity) may dictate that you deliberately practice good posture and bodily movements.

The correct posture for standing is to bring your two feet parallel and close together, with your body weight evenly divided. Your knees should be straight, your abdominal wall drawn in and up, and your buttocks tightened. Your arms should fall naturally at your sides, your head be held erect, and your shoulders be rotated backward. In standing or walking you should act as though a plate is being balanced on your head, with the important variation that you should pull your abdomen inward. A sagging abdomen can portend trouble. This self-consciously erect stance can be maintained even while you are ascending or descending stairs, but it would be wise for you to use the handrail and to place each foot completely flat on each step.

More people develop back troubles by leaning over a washbowl to clean their teeth than by any other movement, simply because their bodies are not kept erect. An erect posture

**Complete relaxation in
sitting position**

**Relaxing positions with or
without a pillow**

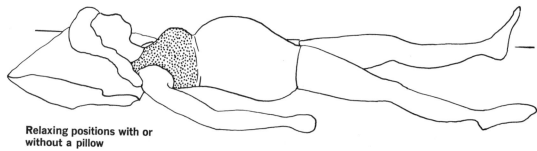

Legs elevated to aid circulation

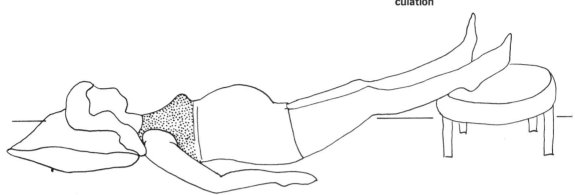

Abdominal breathing
Place pillow under your head while lying flat on the floor, and bend the knees keeping the feet flat on the floor. Place both hands on the abdomen and breathe in through the nose, lifting the abdominal wall. Breathe out through the mouth easily and feel the abdominal wall being lowered. This is done during contractions of labor. Not always easy to do during labor, but helpful.

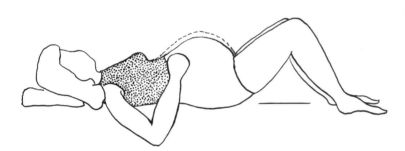

Costal or rib breathing
Place pillow under head while lying flat on the floor, bend your knees keeping your feet flat on the floor. Place your hands at the sides of your rib cage. Breathe through your nose and expand the rib cage, moving your hands sideways as a result. Breathe out easily through your mouth and feel your ribs collapsing inwardly, away from your hands. This is not to be the same as the abdominal breathing. Speed of complete cycle should be about ten per minute. Such breathing exercises are an aid in the first stage of labor as the cervix is dilating.

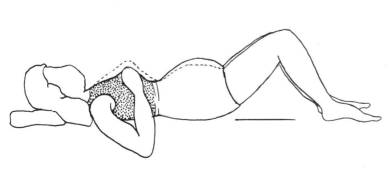

Standing posture

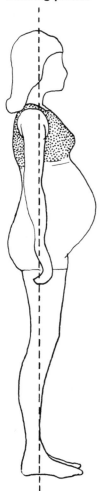

Stooping posture keeping back straight

Carrying objects without loss of posture While carrying any objects the erect posture can and must be maintained. The load should be divided so as to avoid undue strain in one direction. When lifting keep the back straight and bend the knees, using the hands, if necessary, for support and security. These directions apply as well to lifting and stooping. Never bend at the waist, bring any lifted object close to the body, assist in the elevation by bending and then straightening the knees. The pregnant woman already has an added load in her abdomen which will aggravate any forward bending at the waist.

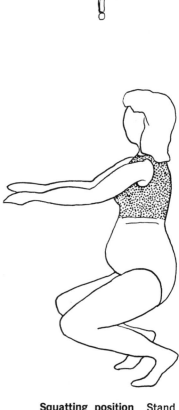

Squatting position Stand upright and practice this squatting position with the back straight and the knees apart. Do this no more than once or twice a day to relax the inner thigh muscles. Always use this position when lifting any object, bending the knees rather than the back. Excellent for pregnant and postpartum women.

Lifting a child without strain

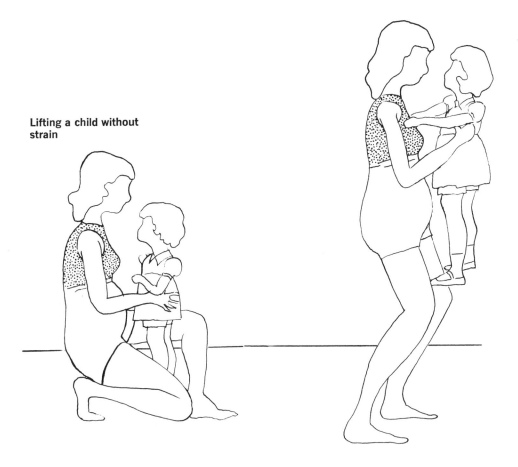

Modified knee-chest position with arms and head on floor This position tends to relieve pelvic pressures, cramps in the thighs and buttocks, pain in the back and legs. It may also reduce the tendency to develop hemorrhoids, or relieve them if present.

The knees should not be too close together, tighten the abdominal muscles, place your arms in front of your face, on the floor. If you keep your back straight, your buttocks and pelvis will be the highest part of your body (the most elevated). Maintain this position for several minutes, then relax completely on the carpeted floor—and repeat.

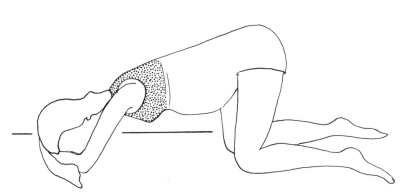

Initial position for pelvic rocking

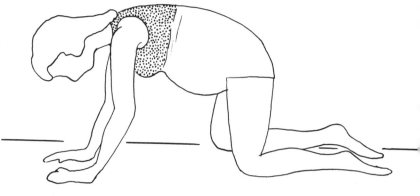

Mild prenatal exercise to help the mother retain her good posture and prevent undue abdominal and back strain. When in kneeling position hump and then hollow the back, pull in the stomach muscles, turn head from side to side as well as up and down. These are very mild but useful exercises. To be done on knees only for a few minutes. Can do this lying on back or side, and used during labor contractions.

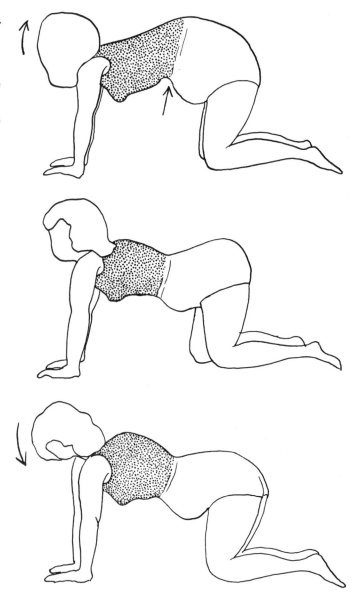

Practice position for delivery On the delivery table there will be stirrups to support the mother's legs and feet, which can all be adjusted for maximum comfort. If the mother can assume this position prior to the delivery so that at delivery she can relax her inner thigh and pelvic floor muscles, she will help greatly in the final stages of the delivery.

Assuming this position, even without a pillow, draw up the knees with the feet flat on the bed. Now contract the thigh and pelvic floor muscles, then relax them and allow the knees to spread apart. Alternate the contraction and relaxation attitudes for a few minutes daily during the last few weeks before expected delivery.

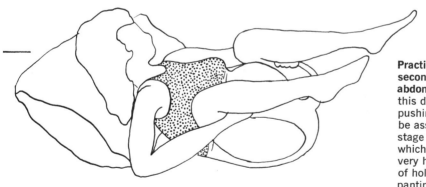

Practice position for second stage of labor: abdominal pushing While this drawing shows the pushing position which will be assumed in the second stage of labor—during which breath control is very helpful—the practice of holding the breath, quick panting, and again holding the breath as will be done during delivery can be done at any time even while sitting in a chair. It would be unwise to assume this position and push vigorously prior to the second stage of labor.

is particularly important when you carry objects of considerable weight. *Never carry heavy objects far without periodic resting.* If possible use handles, divide the weight evenly between your two arms, and bend your knees in lifting—never your back. Your arm muscles are less susceptible to harm. If you use them properly you can keep your body erect, with your shoulders level and your back straight. In a similar way if you lift a child or open a window, do it with a straight back, starting from a squatting position with your feet wide apart. Some find it helpful to place one foot slightly in front of the other, flat on the floor, thus taking the bulk of the weight. Hold the object close to the body and lift by using your leg muscles.

As your pregnancy progresses, finding even a comfortable sitting position may become a problem. You need a chair that you feel comfortable in because it is the right size, texture, and height above the floor. It should be possible for you to rest both feet on the floor or on a stool. The chair seat should support your thighs but at the same time allow your buttocks and back to rest against the back of the chair. It is hard to believe, but it is possible to strain oneself merely in sitting down in a chair. Here, too, your back should be kept straight. Your hands (making use of the arms of the chair) and leg muscles can relieve the body of muscular effort. In rising it is best to slide your buttocks forward first, then, with your hands on the armrests, use your leg muscles to lift yourself to the vertical position without leaning forward. *Remember that the single most important ingredient of posture is a straight back at all times.*

working during pregnancy

Nowadays many women have jobs. Should you continue working during your pregnancy? There is no hard and fast answer. It depends on the nature of the job as well as on how much you need the money and psychological occupation. If the job involves continual physical effort, you will have to have rest periods—more than the usual number—particularly if you stand most of the time. Office work is less taxing than physical work, but since it allows little movement it should be supplemented with mild exercise as well as rest. Strenuous work and exposure to great tension are to be avoided, as are long hours or night shifts. Of course, working in an environment of noxious chemicals, X rays, or isotopes is forbidden. You might inhale or come into contact with some substance that could harm your fetus, even to the extent of causing abnormality or abortion. It is safer to avoid all such contaminants, since the threshold doses or concentrations for ill effects on the fetus have often not been established. Finally, you should stop regular employment a month before expected delivery and not resume it until your physician says it is all right.

travel

It is now believed by most physicians that travel is relatively safe for pregnant women, provided that it is neither too tiring nor too close to confinement time. A long automobile trip is not the wisest thing to undertake unless it is broken up by short but frequent rest periods. And since the pregnant woman supplies oxygen to her fetus, her heart and lungs have to work harder in a rarefied atmosphere. Therefore, the obstetrician may have reservations about your flying or ascending to high altitudes. In any event you should consult him before an extended trip.

sleep

Regular sleeping habits are conducive to full recovery of your energy. During the early months you may feel an increased need for sleep. This is normal and will probably pass. However, you should not force yourself. Most people really do need eight hours of sleep every night.

In the later months sleep may be difficult because you are uncomfortable, for the fetus is active. You may find it helpful to prop your abdomen on a pillow while you lie on your side. But even if you can't fall asleep you shouldn't worry about it. Complete physical relaxation is a reasonable substitute, and you may be able to get some rest during the day, particularly if the fetus is asleep then. Above all, never take any sedative or other drug unless it is specifically prescribed for you by your obstetrician.

marital relations

Marital relations need not be suspended, and if the husband is careful and considerate in order to avoid discomfort to his wife, it is unlikely that the fetus will be injured. Late in pregnancy, however, sexual intercourse may be difficult to achieve, painful to the woman, and disturbing to the fetus. There are many ways in which the married couple can still satisfy each other affectionately and sexually without risk. If you have any questions, ask your obstetrician.

smoking and drinking

Smoking and drinking in moderation during pregnancy may not be particularly harmful, but they certainly don't do the mother or the fetus any good. Pregnant women who smoke have a greater tendency to spontaneous abortion or premature birth than those who do not, and on the average these women give birth to smaller infants. Babies of heavy smokers are more prone to convulsions and fits. While the mechanism that causes these ill effects is not yet fully understood, it appears that nicotine crosses the placental barrier with ease because its molecules are small. Apparently nicotine has a depressive effect on that portion of the fetal nervous system which controls such involuntary functions as respiration and heartbeat. As for drinking, it is known that alcohol readily diffuses through the placenta to the fetus. Alcohol reaches the early fetus less readily than the late fetus. In late pregnancies alcohol concentrates ten times as much in the fetus as in maternal tissues. Alcohol remains in the fetus until all has left the body of the mother. The persistence of alcohol in the pancreas, liver, and brain of the fetus may be damaging. For one thing, it may cause hypoglycemia. Children of heavy-drinking mothers are likely to enter the world in various stages of withdrawal, and yet the condition may not be recognized.

hygiene

Regular habits of elimination are an important facet of prenatal hygiene. You should try to move your bowels at the same time every day, perhaps right after breakfast. Because the pregnant woman usually doesn't get enough exercise she tends to be constipated. Eating leafy vegetables, fruits or fruit juices, and cereals should help. Do not take laxatives unless so directed by your obstetrician.

You should not douche yourself unless your obstetrician approves—and there is a good chance he will not. Cleanliness can be maintained without douching in most cases. The external genitalia should be washed with soap and water when you bathe.

Daily baths are necessary to clean, stimulate, and refresh the skin. This is more important than you may think. The skin is an auxiliary respiratory organ as well as a protective covering. It supplements your kidneys and lungs in eliminating wastes from the fetus as well as from your own bodily processes. Showers or sponge baths may be taken at any time, provided the water is not too cold and you are not exposed to a chill. There is no medical reason for not taking a tub bath, although it once was thought to be a possible source of fetal infection. The main objection to it is that in the later stage of pregnancy, what with the added weight you are carrying, there is a greater possibility of your slipping and falling.

You should pay special attention to your breasts. The main element of breast care is cleanliness. The nipples may ooze colostrum, a greenish-yellow, watery fluid. If the nipples are not washed daily they may become encrusted with the secretions, and this may lead to cracking and unusual tenderness when the baby begins to nurse. Wash the nipples with soap and warm water with a rotary motion, and then move out in circular fashion until the entire breast has been washed. Sometimes the obstetrician will recommend a cream or ointment to soften the nipples shortly before the child arrives.

Some women have inverted nipples (that is, they are turned in instead of out). This will make it difficult for the nursing infant to suckle from them. In such cases, beginning at about the fifth month, the woman should press simultaneously on both sides of the nipple. She should then work her way around the nipple with her thumbs, always keeping them on opposite sides. In this way the nipple is forced outward, where it can be grasped and gently pulled out farther. If this is done to the inverted nipples for a few minutes each day they can be made more erect and prominent. If this simple treatment is unsuccessful the obstetrician should be consulted.

support and clothing

The breasts tend to sag late in pregnancy because they are so large. It is desirable to wear a brassiere that gives added support from underneath. There are two types available: the relatively loose-fitting nursing brassiere, which may be worn during pregnancy and then let out afterward, and the maternity brassiere, which ordinarily cannot serve the nursing mother. However, in either case, you must not wear a brassiere that is too confining just because you are afraid of losing your figure—this won't happen if you have enough support. Because of the oozing colostrum you should wear absorbent pads.

Once your pregnancy shows, after the fifth month, you may want to have some abdominal support, particularly if you normally wear a girdle or corset. An individually fitted maternity girdle or corset is the best support, and it may also help relieve backache or fatigue. It will certainly not conceal your pregnancy, since it supports the uterus from underneath and pushes it upward. You should not lace or strap in the upper part of your abdomen, since that would only make you uncomfortable and interfere with your breathing. A lithe, athletic woman does not need abdominal support, and a girdle or corset would not flatter her vanity.

The same cautions about tightness also apply to any other restrictive garments. Garter belts rather than garter bands should be worn, since the latter impede the flow of blood from the legs to the heart. The increased pressure is likely to cause or aggravate varicose veins.

Shoes, too, should be loose-fitting, preferably of the low-heeled Oxford type. Some pregnant women manage to wear high-heeled shoes. The criterion is whether the shoes cause backache, fatigue, and poor posture. Clothing should be chosen to suit your own tastes, so long as it isn't too confining. If your pregnancy doesn't show until fairly late you can probably use your normal wardrobe. However, even maternity garments are made to look fashionable nowadays, and some women prefer loose-fitting clothing even though they aren't pregnant. The texture of the clothing isn't important, so long as it's comfortable.

dental care

It is important to take good care of your teeth. You should see your dentist early in pregnancy (beforehand if you have the foresight) to have all your cavities filled and your gums treated. The X rays used in dental examinations won't penetrate much beyond your teeth, so you needn't fear that they'll reach the fetus. Your teeth are important because they're the first element in your digestive system—when you masticate properly they break up the food into small enough pieces for your digestive enzymes to break them down further into absorbable nutrients. Also remember that the fetus is competing with you for its share of all the basic nutrients and minerals, particularly calcium. You need calcium mainly for your teeth, and the fetus needs it for its growing skeleton as well, particularly in the second and third months. While the fetus does not remove calcium existing in your teeth, it can deprive you of what you need for replenishment, so be sure your mineral intake is enough for both of you.

common complaints

Every pregnant woman experiences new sensations and symptoms of which she should be aware. Some of the most common minor complaints are discussed here in alphabetical order. Many of them are innocuous, and all of them are treatable. However, you should bring them to the attention of your obstetrician, especially if they persist.

ABDOMINAL SWELLING

This is normally experienced at about four months, although the intestines may feel distended before then. Some women show it more than others, and it seems to be more common after the first pregnancy because the abdominal wall may lose its elasticity. A maternity girdle or corset will give support.

ANGIOMA

Cobweb-like radial lines, probably of congested capillaries, may appear on the shoulders, arms, or face.

BACKACHE

During pregnancy the pelvic joints tend to relax in order to accommodate the growing fetus, and the unaccustomed weight of the fetus may produce low backaches. This may be eased by lying down and by certain exercise already described. Wearing comfortable shoes and an individually fitted maternity girdle or corset may bring relief. Massage may work wonders, especially by a sympathetic husband!

CONSTIPATION

This may be due to sluggishness of the digestive tract. While any pregnant woman may suffer from constipation it is a greater problem for those who normally have irregular bowel movements. Pregnancy aggravates the condition because you get less exercise, the smooth muscles of your body tend to relax, and the growing fetus exerts pressure on the intestines. If constipation is allowed to go unchecked it may lead to hemorrhoids. If you do become constipated, *do not* take purgatives (like castor oil) or any other harsh laxative, but consult your obstetrician. Physicians generally advise you to take some exercise, drink fruit juices, and add roughage to your diet in the form of fruits, vegetables, and cereals. You should make a conscious effort at maintaining a regular toilet schedule. Don't strain. It isn't necessary for you to have a bowel movement every single day.

FAINTNESS OR DIZZINESS

The extra burden on the pregnant woman's heart and blood supply may cause periods of faintness associated with a sort of anemia. Rarely, however, does she lose consciousness. You may be able to remedy this by lowering your head between your knees or else lying down. If it occurs frequently, carry a vial of smelling salts.

FLATULENCE

The stomach and intestines may be loaded with gas, giving rise to a bloated feeling. In a pregnant woman physical congestion of the abdomen because of uterine pressure aggravates this situation. Certain foods, such as cabbage, raw vegetables, and beans, should be avoided for a while, as they produce gas.

FREQUENT URINATION

Pressure on the bladder by the enlarging uterus during the early months causes the pregnant woman to urinate more frequently, or at least to feel she has to. This pressure should ease midway through pregnancy as the uterus shifts, only to reappear late in pregnancy, when the baby moves down again. Another cause is the increased activity of the pregnant woman's kidneys. The number of nocturnal visits to the bathroom may be reduced by limiting the amount of fluids taken during the evening. If voiding is accompanied by a painful or burning sensation you should consult the obstetrician.

GROWING PAINS

Lower abdominal discomfort may be secondary to ligament and uterine enlargement, causing stretching.

HEARTBURN

Heartburn is a form of indigestion caused by sluggishness of the stomach and the regurgitation of gastric juices, which are acidic. Some common commercial antacids may be used (but check with your obstetrician anyway). *Do not use sodium bicarbonate,* since sodium is not good for you during pregnancy, partly because it calls for an excess intake of fluids which in turn may affect the blood pressure, through excessive retention of water.

HEMORRHOIDS (PILES)

These are enlarged veins at the opening of the rectum. Like varicosities elsewhere, they are caused by poor circulation, which builds up pressure on the blood vessels. They may protrude from the anus, and then they are accompanied by itching, pain, and even bleeding. They are treated by anesthetic suppositories or ointments prescribed by the physician, rest, and ice packs. Hemorrhoids may be particularly bothersome for a few days after delivery, but they usually shrink by themselves.

INSOMNIA

This is generally caused in the early months by preoccupation with the pregnancy and in the later months by the difficulty of finding a comfortable position or by the activity of the fetus. If you understand the causes you can train yourself to get more sleep. A warm bath may help relax you. *Do not take any sedative* unless the obstetrician prescribes it for you, and never exceed the dosage he advises.

LEG CRAMPS

A sudden "Charley horse" or kink in the calf may be caused by poor circulation or by a calcium shortage in the blood. Drinking some milk should supply the calcium, and rubbing your legs should stop the muscle cramps. Propping up the legs when resting helps you avoid such cramps.

LETHARGY

The feeling of actual or impending fatigue is common in pregnancy and may be of both physical and psychological origin. If you rearrange your schedule to get enough sleep and daytime rest and you acquire the proper perspective of your pregnancy, lethargy need never be a problem.

MOODINESS

Any pregnant woman is subject to emotional ups and downs; her ability to control her moods is a measure of her emotional maturity. You may fluctuate between depression and irritability when you think you are beset by insurmountable problems that only you have to face. Often some attention from your husband is all that is needed to show you that you are exaggerating, but if not you may want to speak with a psychotherapist. Bear in mind that a certain amount of moodiness is natural.

MORNING SICKNESS

Morning sickness occurs mostly during the first three months of pregnancy, and only about half of all pregnant women experience nausea (which may not be limited to the mornings). Eating dry crackers may dispel the nauseous feeling. Having some solid food (but not liquids) in your stomach will make you feel better than going on an empty stomach. Since you are likely to feel queasy shortly after rising, it may be helpful if you delay brushing your teeth until later. You should definitely never try to induce vomiting. Some women actually vomit a little every day, but this should clear up with time. If vomiting persists, and particularly if you lose considerable weight or are unable to hold down solids and fluids, tell your obstetrician. He wants to make sure that you are getting enough nourishment and that your body fluids are at a normal level. In rare cases he may order intravenous feedings.

NOSEBLEEDS

Under the influence of her hormones, all mucous membranes of the pregnant woman, including the lining of her nostrils, become more vascular; that is, they are supplied with more blood vessels. In hot, dry environments (common in the winter in heated houses) the capillaries tend to break and bleed. The usual treatment for nosebleeds, namely, a cold compress applied to the upper lip with pressure, will generally suffice.

QUICKENING

This refers to the first recognizable fetal movement, which may occur during the third month but is not likely to be felt by the mother until the fourth month. It is usually a pleasurable sensation, described as "butterflies fluttering in my stomach." It may be confused with the mother's own intestinal movements, but when the fetus kicks and jabs there can be no mistaking it. One cannot draw inferences from such activity with regard to the sex or physical condition of the fetus. If the activity stops for 48 hours or more it should be brought to the obstetrician's attention.

SHORTNESS OF BREATH

This is most likely to occur at seven months of pregnancy, when the fetus and organs press upward against the diaphragm and crowd the lungs. Propping up your head and shoulders with pillows until you are reclining rather than lying might make it easier for you to sleep. The condition also calls for reduced exertion, particularly lifting or climbing.

SKIN PIGMENTATION

Changes in skin pigmentation (more noticeable in brunettes) may take place on the face, in the area of the nipples, and on the abdomen. They are harmless and will disappear after the delivery.

STRIAE

These are reddish streaks on the breasts, thighs, and abdomen resulting from stretching of the skin. They are most commonly seen during the first pregnancy. After delivery they fade to thin lines with a silvery color.

SWELLING OR TENDERNESS OF THE BREASTS

This sensation, which is felt early in pregnancy, is similar to that experienced by most women just before a regular menstrual period. However, this time it persists and becomes accentuated. The breasts, of course, will remain large throughout pregnancy, but the feeling of tenderness (described as a tingling) subsides in a few months.

VAGINAL DISCHARGE

The mucous membranes of the vagina secrete a clear, thin, odorless fluid late in pregnancy, which usually subsides with delivery. Sometimes a stubborn case of leucorrhea—the "whites"—develops. This is caused by a parasite. Therefore, if the discharge becomes thicker and more copious, if it is accompanied by vaginal itching, see your obstetrician. The condition is not a serious one, but douching should not be attempted.

VARICOSE VEINS

These are due to dilation of the superficial veins of the legs imposed by the excess weight of the pregnancy and the erect posture of modern women. Discomfort can be relieved by lying on your back with your legs extended up the wall so that your feet are higher than your body. If this is impractical, sit with your legs propped up on a pillow or stool. Elastic stockings should help. If the condition persists long after the pregnancy, you may need injections or surgery (procedures which are not to be resorted to during your pregnancy).

alarming symptoms

It is not our intention to inform you about all of the possible danger signals that may arise during your pregnancy; this is up to your obstetrician. However, we mention some of them without comment because you alone would be aware of them if they occurred. Report immediately any of the following:

> Bleeding or escape of fluid from the vagina
> Headaches and blurring of vision or dizziness
> Edema (swelling) of hands and feet or face
> Abdominal pain, with or without vomiting
> Chills, fever, or cold

Your obstetrician is responsible for treating any irregularity, but you can aid his diagnosis and treatment if you tell him of any unusual symptoms. Sometimes symptoms are purely subjective, without a physical cause, but you should not be the judge of that. The worst thing you can do is to treat yourself. Your obstetrician would forbid you to take any drugs without his instructions and permission. No obstetrician can ever forget such tragedies as those which occurred in West Germany when many pregnant women took tranquilizers, particularly Thalidomide, and produced severely deformed children.

drugs, diseases, radiation, and the fetus

The universal fear on the part of the pregnant woman is that her baby may be born abnormal, malformed, or disfigured. The first question a new mother is likely to ask after delivery is, "Is my baby all right?" The second question is, "A boy or a girl?" Perhaps 94 per cent of the time the obstetrician is able to reply that the baby is fine and healthy. But each year about a quarter of a million babies in the United States—700 each day or 1 every two minutes—are born marred by astigmatism, cleft palate, clubfoot, split spine, Mongolism, or a host of other defects, so a mother's anxiety is not entirely unfounded. Today there are approximately 3 million Americans of all ages who are mentally retarded because of birth defects. It has been estimated that up to 15 million living Americans are stigmatized by some birth anomaly.

The 1,375,000 preschool children alive today who were born with defects amass 6 million days in our hospitals—and at least $180 million in care—annually. Ten per cent of the families in this country have had some direct experience with a defective child. About 500,000 fetuses fail to make it to birth each year. Another 18,000 infants die before the first anniversary of their birth because of birth defects. Thirty per cent of the pediatric inpatients are hospitalized for congenital defects. Many defective children live on but succumb at a rate of 60,000 per year at all ages because of an anomaly present at birth. This is a terrible waste of human life, especially since much of the tragedy, expense, and heartache is simply not necessary.

Too many babies come into the world deformed in ways that could have been prevented. *Half of the children treated in our hospitals are there because their parents did not exercise reasonable care during pregnancy.* Fully 50 per cent of all mentally defective children were exposed to an abnormal prenatal environment. More defective children are born to girls under eighteen or women over forty than to women between the ages of twenty and thirty, the recommended childbearing age. Women over forty-two are much more likely to bear Mongoloid children than their juniors in any other age group. These statistics are not pleasant, but perhaps they can help to convince the reader that there is a major problem which has at least a partial remedy: it consists of educating prospective parents in avoiding those situations which are known to affect the unborn child adversely.

In this chapter we must be brutally frank because the well-being of millions of future babies is at stake. One would think that the uterus is the safest place in the world in which to develop—and so it is—but drugs, disease toxins, and radiation can penetrate even there to damage a fetus during its development. At least 1,487 natal abnormalities (mistakes in body formation or function) caused by heredity or induced by drugs, virus disease, or exposure to X rays have been described by medical scientists engaged in the field of teratology, the study of birth defects.

It is true that many defects are not seriously crippling and need not deprive an individual of the ability to earn a living. Almost anyone might be considered defective if we included moles, birthmarks, color blindness, pigeon toes, and left-handedness. However, even such a minor deformity as webbed fingers or an extra digit can exact a severe psychological toll on children or their parents. Superficial and external defects can often be remedied by surgery. But what if the defect is internal and structural (heart, kidneys, liver) or chemical (producing such conditions as diabetes)? Proper diagnosis may be delayed until the child has grown up. Perhaps he or she will suffer chronic and unrecognized discomfort for decades. The frustration and physical pain of the child, the mental anguish of the parents, and the cost to everyone concerned—including society —can be devastating.

Only 20 per cent of all birth defects may be blamed solely on heredity. These tendencies can be traced directly to one or both parents and may be passed on to succeeding generations. Congenital defects, by contrast with hereditary ones, cannot be passed on to the next generation. They are brought on after conception by an unfavorable fetal environment. It is known, for instance, that congenital dislocation of the hip occurs twice as frequently among children born in the winter, and anencephaly (absence of head) is greatest in October and February. When a *congenital* anomaly resembles an *inheritable* anomaly, it is called a phenocopy. However, it is still not inheritable. It is probable that while congenital anomalies are not inheritable, all expressions in development result from the interaction of genetic predispositions and prenatal environment. Congenital anomalies, in contrast with those that are due to some hereditary tendency, are avoidable. It is for this reason that we feel compelled to be very frank and to warn each pregnant woman against those drugs and conditions that could produce abnormal babies. The following are but a few of the more common causes of congenital anomalies in the human:

Infections: German measles (rubella) or influenza A

Physical injuries: Excessive pressure, extreme changes in temperature, ionizing radiations

Hormones: Variations in thyroid activity of the mother, ACTH, cortisone, steroid hormones, insulin, and diabetes mellitus

Nutrition: Deficiencies in almost any of the vitamins, niacin, ascorbic acid, folic acid, proteins, amino acids, unsaturated fatty acids, and potassium

Respiratory: Hypoxia (insufficient oxygen), excess of carbon dioxide, and anesthesia with ether-gas-oxygen

Miscellaneous: Antimetabolites, alkylating agents, quinine, trypan blue, pilocarpine, boric acid, nicotine, sulfonamides, antibiotics, salicylates

Maternal diseases or defects: Uterine tumors, inflammation or malformations, defects in implantation, severe emotional disturbances or stress, and rapid succession of multiple pregnancies

During the first six weeks after conception the fetus is highly vulnerable to external influences, called "insults." Not only is this the period during which its organs are forming; it is also a time when the mother still may not recognize she is pregnant. So the overriding advice to all women of reproductive age is this: *Never prescribe for yourself or act on the advice of a friend. Don't take any drugs unless you are directed to do so by a physician. Stay away from people suffering from an infectious disease, particularly of the virus type. If you require X rays, fluoroscopy, or radiation therapy, advise your radiologist that you may be pregnant.* If all pregnant women followed this advice faithfully, the incidence of abortions, stillbirths, and congenital defects would most certainly be reduced.

No drug or vaccine known can prevent the development of a congenital anomaly. Some defects may be due to heredity and environment acting in conjunction. Birth defects are by no means peculiar to modern living, even though our ancestors did not have X-ray machines or a wide range of synthetically derived drugs. The Babylonians compiled a list of more than 60 birth defects among their own people. Dwarfism, cleft palate, clubfoot, short arms, and hydrocephaly (water on the brain) have been recognized for more than 5,000 years, and traces of some of these defects have been detected in disinterred mummies and even in fossil remains. Such disorders as diabetes, cystic fibrosis, and muscular dystrophy may have existed for a long time.

Most of the 250,000 babies born annually with birth defects (1 in 16 live births) in this country fall into one or more of the following 17 categories:

Birthmarks: These are frequently seen in the form of red or wine-colored patches on the skin. Although not severe, they are unsightly. Those which are not inheritable may be removed by means of plastic surgery or skin grafts. Some birthmarks disappear in time, even without treatment.

Cleft palate (1 in 2,500 births) or *cleft lip* (1 in 1,000): More frequent among the Japanese. Cleft palate may usually be treated surgically during the first weeks of infancy and cleft lip at about 14 months of age. Some plastic surgeons are geniuses when it comes to remodeling a face. The therapy may also involve a dentist, an orthodontist, a speech therapist, and a psychiatrist.

Clubfoot (1 in 250): This rather common defect is one in which a foot is turned inward or outward and remains in a fixed position, as though the child were always walking on tiptoes. The condition sometimes can be treated by means of special shoes or a plaster cast, although surgery may be necessary. It is entirely reparable.

Congenital heart defects (1 in 60): Such defects as a perforated or open septum (wall) of the heart can be caused by rubella (German measles) contracted by the mother during the early stages of pregnancy, as well as by other causes. Open-heart surgery is now so common that many children can be mended early; they may live a normal life and even have children of their own.

Cystic fibrosis (1 in 1,000): Known as fibrocystic disease, it is believed to be hereditary and metabolic and is evident soon after birth. One symptom is abundant perspiration. Death may be associated with lung problems, but chemical treatment is possible. For some reason—presumably genetic—it is rare among Negroes and Orientals.

Erythroblastosis: This involves about 10 per cent of babies whose mother's blood is Rh negative and whose father's is Rh positive. When the baby's blood factor is incompatible with the mother's, the mother develops antibodies which may produce the disease in fetuses of her subsequent pregnancies. There may be anemia owing to dissolution of the red cells of the blood, jaundice, mental retardation, and often stillbirth. Some babies may be saved by transfusions before or shortly after birth, others by a new drug known as Rhogam (see Chapter 13).

Extra or fused fingers or toes (1 in 600): Extra digits occur more frequently (1 in 100) in the Negro population. The condition can be corrected by amputation or surgical separation of the digits.

Galactosemia (1 in 10,000 or less): This hereditary condition is due to the absence of an enzyme which is necessary to digest milk sugar. It causes cataracts and damage to the liver and brain, and it led to many deaths until methods of early diagnosis and treatment were instituted recently.

Genitourinary defects (1 in 250): Abnormalities at birth in the kidneys, ureter, bladder, or related parts, such as the genitalia, are serious, but many lend themselves to surgical correction. One cause may be a potassium deficiency, possibly brought on by the taking of diuretics.

Hydrocephaly (1 in 500): Commonly known as "water on the brain" because fluids gather in and around the brain. This anomaly is easily recognized and diagnosed at birth. It is often due to obstructed circulation of the cerebrospinal fluid and it may be caused by prenatal infection. Techniques have been devised for draining off excess fluid, thus saving the life of the child and preventing mental retardation.

Imperforate anus: Sometimes the anus fails to open, and therefore the bowels cannot be evacuated. This can be corrected by surgery.

Missing limbs: This is rare, but it may involve any or all of the limbs. The cause is unknown. The tranquilizer Thalidomide taken by the mother during the first five weeks of pregnancy caused this defect in many West German children, although there have been cases of hereditary absence of hands and feet. Prosthetic or artificial limbs have been fashioned to help the sufferers.

Mongolism (average of 1 in 600): This anomaly is generally due to the presence of one particular extra chromosome. The person thus afflicted is characteristically short of stature and has slanted eyes (hence the name). Most important, Mongoloids are mentally retarded. Mongolism is incurable, but the sufferer can be trained to some extent. With pregnant women over forty-five years of age the incidence of Mongolism is 1 in 50, while it is only 1 in 2,000 for women twenty-five years of age. This does not mean that normal pregnancies are exceptional toward the end of the reproductive years in the female, just that there is a greater risk of abnormality. One hypothesis is that the ova in an older female have lain dormant for many years and may "go stale."

Phenylketonuria, PKU (1 in 10,000): This is an inheritable chemical imbalance that causes mental retardation. It can be detected during the first week of postnatal life by examination of the urine. The treatment consists of a proper diet, which inhibits further progression.

Pyloric stenosis: This is hereditary and limited to males. It involves a narrowing of the pylorus, the opening from the stomach into the small intestine. One symptom is projectile vomiting soon after delivery. The sphincter muscles of the pylorus, which are capable of closing the opening completely, can be surgically cut to relieve the blockage. The prognosis for survival and the leading of a normal life is excellent.

Sickle cell anemia (10 to 14 per cent of all Negroes anywhere): This is hereditary, and usually fatal if the child receives the genetic factor from both parents.

Split spine, or *spina bifida* (1 in 500): This can result from some infections if they occur at the critical time in pregnancy. In many cases the neurosurgeon can repair and close the opening. This prevents paralysis below the waist, which would affect the child's walking, bowel, and bladder functions, as well as his mental and physical adjustments to society. It is sometimes associated with hydrocephaly.

Modern medicine, modern hospitals, and modern research are all improving the survival prospects of children who are born defective, and even in granting them a normal life expectancy.[1]

drugs

In the United States the consumption of drugs has gotten out of hand and we seem to be a nation of pill-takers. There are those who take pep pills to awaken them in the morning, tranquilizers to help them face the problems of the day, and sleeping pills at bedtime. Since many drugs now on the market and available even without a prescription can harm the embryo (and fetus), the taking of drugs by pregnant women should be limited to situations that seriously threaten their health, and *always under the direction of a physician*. The obstetrician may be regarded as the unborn child's pediatrician, for that is his major concern. Without that concern, how can a fetus ever be entirely safe from its own mother's folly?

Consider these statistics: Pregnant and nonpregnant women alike take aspirin, antibiotics (42 per cent),[2] appetite suppressants (27 per cent), tranquilizers (21 per cent), pep pills, antiemetics (16 per cent), analgesics (65 per cent), laxatives, and nasal decongestants such as antihistamines (26 per cent). The most common reasons given by pregnant women for resorting to drugs are a fear of their pregnancy, restlessness, insomnia, or fatigue. It was for reasons no less plausible than these that thousands of pregnant women in West Germany took the seemingly innocuous tranquilizer Thalidomide in the early 1960's, with the result that many fetuses died or were born defective. There has been no more dramatic example of the potential hazards of drugs to the fetus. Physicians now know of a wide spectrum of teratogenic drugs.

Dr. Virginia Apgar, a nationally recognized authority on birth defects, advises young women in their childbearing years who contemplate taking drugs—"Don't." She advises even against extra vitamins unless prescribed by a physician. It has been estimated that 92 per cent of all pregnant women are directed by their own physicians to take at least one drug, and

1. Consult the National Foundation, 800 Second Avenue, New York City, should you have any unanswered questions about birth defects.

2. The percentages in parentheses are derived from a study of 240 pregnant women examined (Nora 1967, *J. Am. Med. Assn.* 202:1065). All had been exposed to teratogens, and 10.8 per cent had defective children. Those who were given antibiotics took tetracyclines, penicillins, sulfas, and chloramphenicols.

3.9 per cent are given as many as ten different drugs. The average is 5.4 drugs per pregnant woman. *The taking of drugs under medical supervision need not of itself invariably produce defects in the fetus,* and some drugs, to the best of present medical knowledge, are not harmful to the fetus.

Even the Thalidomide tragedy befell only 20 percent of the fetuses of those pregnant women who took that tranquilizer. Perhaps the other 80 per cent went unscathed because their mothers used the drug outside the critical period for the fetus. Nevertheless, no woman or even physician can predict how any particular fetus will react to its mother's drug therapy. The variables that preclude exact knowledge are the stage of fetal development, the amount and concentration of the drug, and the ease of passage through the placenta to the fetus. A single agent (drug) may cause multiple anomalies, but several different agents may cause the same anomaly, strongly suggesting that the developing fetus is responsive to virtually any insult at certain crucial stages. There is one more unknown factor: hereditary differences in resistance or susceptibility among fetuses of the same age. In most cases there is a greater likelihood of gross physical defects if the drug is given during the first eight weeks after conception because this is the period of organ formation. If given later, the same drug may have no effect or else may cause functional defects that might escape immediate detection. For example, mental retardation, unless severe, may go undetected for some time.

We have provided in Appendix B an alphabetical listing of dozens of drugs or medications that have been administered to pregnant women, along with some of the possible consequences of their use. Where a question mark appears in the appendix table, it means that the results are based on experiments with animals which, however suggestive, are not as definitive as human-use data.

To summarize what is believed about drugs and pregnancy:

1. All drug treatment must be held to an absolute minimum during the first three months of pregnancy, and always under the direction of the obstetrician. *Consider any pill, capsule, powder, or liquid medicine as a potential enemy.*

2. Certain drugs can also be passed to the newborn through the milk of the lactating mother.

3. Sex hormone treatments (androgens, etc.) should be withheld during early pregnancy so as not to affect the sexual development of the fetus.

4. The treatment of diabetes in a pregnant woman by tolbutamine is fraught with hazards to the fetus.

5. Anticoagulants given to the pregnant woman in the treatment of thrombophlebitis or venous thrombosis may result in hemorrhage and death for the fetus or newborn. Agents that would affect blood pressure or tend to break down blood cells should never be used unless the mother's own life is in jeopardy.

6. Adrenocorticosteroids (cortisone or ACTH) cause fetal damage, notably cleft palate, and are to be given only when the mother's life is actually in jeopardy.

7. Thyroid and antithyroid treatment of the mother for thyrotoxicosis can cause sporadic congenital goiter. The fetal thyroid begins to function by the 14th week, and it can be damaged thereafter. Complications can arise at birth owing to enlargement of the thyroid, and radioiodine (used in diagnosing the mother's thyroid activity) can damage the thyroid and pituitary glands of the fetus.

8. If the mother is suffering from cancer, it may be necessary to perform a therapeutic abortion because the life of the mother would be endangered by withholding chemotherapy or radiation treatment. Cytotoxic (cell-destroying) and antimetabolic drugs are very likely to abort the fetus anyway, or else cause severe brain damage.

9. Every day babies are born showing the signs or effects of drug addiction—particularly withdrawal symptoms. These cases are imputed entirely to the mother's consumption of narcotics during her pregnancy. In one New York City hospital alone, 133 drug-addicted babies were treated in a 30-month period. Weaning of newborn babies from their maternally derived drug addiction takes from 2 to 6 weeks.

10. Purely involuntarily, each person in the United States inhales an average of half an ounce of pesticides daily. It has been demonstrated that these chemicals can cause the embryos of experimental animals to develop abnormally. Most susceptible is the all-important central nervous system. It remains to be proved that this is also true of humans, but it stands to reason that the constant exposure of pregnant women to noxious pesticides—particularly in certain environments and during peak seasons for their use—isn't doing their fetuses any good.

smoking and alcohol

The effects of smoking during pregnancy are still not fully charted, but it is known that the gaseous materials in cigarette smoke are absorbed by the mucous membranes of the mother's mouth as well as by the lungs. This smoke contains nicotine, carbon monoxide, furfural, pyridine, collidine, hydrocyanic acid, carbonic acid, methyl (wood) alcohol, and alkalis.

It has been established that smoking even one cigarette by the pregnant woman can increase the fetal heartbeat by as much as 39 beats per minute within 8 to 12 minutes after the mother snuffs out the butt. Circulation sometimes slows down perceptibly because the blood vessels contract. This has been demonstrated dramatically by thermograms (infrared pictures) taken through the mother's abdomen. Before the viewer's eyes the thermographic traces grow dim. This means that less heat is given off, which in turn indicates poorer circulation. These cardiovascular effects on the fetus are most acute during the eighth month.

Excessive smoking is believed to cause premature delivery (at 32 to 36 weeks instead of at 38 weeks) as well as stunting of growth. Why is this significant? Because the birth weight of the child is a crucial indicator of its survival probability. Babies weighing 3½ pounds or less at birth account for about 50 per cent of the deaths of newborns. A woman giving birth to a premature child is four times as likely as the next woman to have another premature child. It has been estimated that smoking two packs of cigarettes a day will reduce the baby's weight by about 10 per cent, or 10 to 12 ounces. Moreover, mothers who smoke are also more likely to have spontaneous abortions and babies with fits and convulsions than mothers who do not smoke.

As for drinking, alcohol passes very quickly from mother to fetus. Any condition that is physically harmful to the mother is likely also to be harmful to her fetus. However, an occasional drink during pregnancy would normally be innocuous. There is no evidence that drinking will cause alcoholism in the fetus or newborn, so the mother's own tolerance and weight control are the main factors to consider. Alcohol contains calories, and cocktails are generally richer in calories than straight beverages.

infectious diseases

A pregnant woman can transmit a number of diseases to her fetus, including smallpox, chicken pox, measles, mumps, scarlet fever, erysipelas, tuberculosis, syphilis, influenza Type A, German measles, recurrent fever, toxoplasmosis,[3] malignant mela-

---

3. Toxoplasmosis (produced by a protozoan parasite) in the mother may cause encephalitis, hydrocephaly, hepatitis, heart damage, severe brain damage, or death of the fetus.

noma, and malarial parasites. From what was said earlier about the filtering action of the placenta (see Chapter 2), one wonders how this is possible. It is true that most bacteria are physically too large to cross the barrier (pneumococci, which cause pneumonia, are one exception), but this is not at all true of the smaller viruses. And it is also not true of the toxins produced by bacteria or by the mother's blood in response to viruses. In fact, it is now believed that any toxin or drug of less than 1,000 molecular weight can traverse the placenta. In addition, it is possible for the infant to acquire a disease in the process of birth, for in emerging from the uterus it is exposed directly to the mother's blood and tissues without the protection afforded by the placenta.

Toxic substances transmitted through the placenta may cause defects even late in pregnancy, so that there may be no escape for the fetus, early or late. For instance, the exact time of infection by a viral agent is critical: if it occurs during the first month of pregnancy it is likely to induce cataracts, and during the second month anomalies of the heart. Even a slight fever may produce deafness during the third month. Cardiac defects are caused over a long gestation period. The embryo or fetus is a mosaic of developing organs, and no two organ systems are at the same stage of development at the same time. Thus, the gestation age (developmental stage) of the fetus will determine which organ or organs will manifest the abnormality caused by any insult (drug, disease, or radiation). It so happens that the most important system, the *nervous* (brain, spinal cord, sense organs, etc.) develops from about the 19th day and is not complete until after birth, so that at almost any stage the fetus is vulnerable on that score. However, in the earlier stages it can be more seriously damaged, so that surviving the first 6 or 7 weeks of development without unnecessary insults is critical.

Not only infections but immunity to specific infectious diseases can be passed to the fetus through the placenta. This is generally called "passive immunity" because the child gets it from its mother rather than from an encounter with the disease itself. Antitoxins for diphtheria and tetanus, and those immune bodies which oppose the virus of measles, mumps, poliomyelitis, smallpox, and the common upper respiratory infections, can all cross the placenta. This may protect the fetus for six months after birth. A shorter period of protection would follow the mother's bout with pneumonia, influenza, scarlet fever, either streptococcal or staphylococcal toxins, and typhoid bacillus. No passive immunity to whooping cough is granted. Imposed or injected immune substances have little value for the baby during the first three months after birth, although whooping cough vaccine can be administered at one month, diphtheria toxoid at three months, and tetanus toxoid at six months, with boosters given later.

INFLUENZA

Maternal mortality in 1,350 cases of influenza uncomplicated by pneumonia showed spontaneous abortions, stillbirths, and premature delivery in 26 per cent, but when there was the complication of pneumonia for the mother the incidence of anomalies or death was more than 50 per cent.

RUBELLA

It was not until 1941 that the virus disease known as German measles, a seemingly less serious affliction for the adult than true measles, was recognized as an insidious cause of birth defects. The virus strain was first isolated in 1961. Only within the last five years has it been demonstrated that the effects of maternal rubella can be passed directly to the fetus. Moreover, the fetal infection may persist even after birth, making the infant a carrier who can transmit the infection for as long as six months after birth.

Infection of the mother with rubella during the first month of pregnancy results in a 47 per cent occurrence of defective children, 22 per cent when the infection is incurred during the second month, and only 7 per cent during the third month. Contraction by the mother of rubella during the first 16 weeks of pregnancy carries a substantial risk of fetal loss and infant death, and those fetuses that survive are severely debilitated. The fetal organs most susceptible to damage are the lenses of the eyes (50 per cent[4]), the inner ear (30 per cent), and the brain (10 per cent). Typical defects at birth are enlarged liver and spleen, cataracts, heart lesions, deaf-mutism, and microcephaly (pinhead) with psychomotor retardation.

German measles seems to break out in cycles. The epidemic of 1964 and 1965 is estimated to have ravaged tens of thousands of fetuses. Approximately 20,000 babies were born with serious birth defects, while another 30,000 fetuses died. Perhaps it is fortunate that from 10 to 20 per cent of the pregnancies complicated by rubella result in spontaneous abortions

---

4. Percentage of children with reported damage from infectious diseases.

or stillbirths. Many physicians would recommend therapeutic abortion if the mother contracts the disease in the early stages of pregnancy.

Recently a vaccine against rubella was licensed in the United States, so this disease and the serious congenital anomalies it causes may be eliminated. While in the long run a widespread program of vaccination should sharply reduce the incidence of this disease, pregnant women or women who may shortly become pregnant are not in a position to benefit directly from the vaccine, since a live virus is used and this is potentially dangerous to the fetus. Twenty per cent of all women are susceptible to German measles, and should be vaccinated at least 60 days before any pregnancy. Vaccination is protective in 2 to 3 weeks and lasts at least 3 years. The Public Health Service suggests that all children be inoculated between one and about ten or eleven years of age, since the effects of German measles are mild in prepubescent children. Infected children transmit the disease to pregnant women, who then produce abnormal children.

MUMPS

Spontaneous abortions are frequent when the pregnant woman contracts mumps, and those fetuses that survive may develop cardiac fibroelastosis, a serious heart defect.

CYTOMEGALOVIRUS

This virus disease, like rubella, may persist after birth and may involve various organ systems. As the translation of its name suggests, cytomegalovirus is identified largely by the appearance in the urine of giant cells. It may be carried by unsuspecting women and transmitted at birth, although it is believed to cross the placenta. Cytomegalovirus has been identified for only about a decade. It may be more widespread than previously suspected, sometimes causing mild liver malfunction in otherwise healthy individuals.

SYPHILIS

Infection of the fetus with syphilis can occur after the fifth month. However, infection of the mother is not necessarily followed by fetal infection, provided that the placenta remains intact. But once spirochetes gain access to the fetal circulation, there is apparently nothing that will impede their growth and multiplication. As many as 80 per cent of children born to untreated syphilitic mothers will be infected in the uterus if the fetus is exposed at the onset or in the early stages of the disease. About 25 per cent will die within the uterus. Most of the survivors will arrive prematurely, but 30 per cent will die shortly after birth. Of the infected and untreated children surviving infancy, about 40 per cent will develop symptomatic syphilis during their lifetimes. The fact that syphilis spirochetes have been found in the placenta, umbilical cord, amniotic fluid, and the fetus itself indicates the extent of their invasive power. Obligatory prenatal blood testing usually identifies any presence of syphilis. Proper treatment of the mother with penicillin G prior to the 18th week of pregnancy generally prevents the infection of the fetus. Obviously any case of maternal or fetal syphilis must be reported immediately to the health authorities.

GONORRHEA

This venereal disease may be chronic or it may be acquired by the mother at the time of conception. It is generally confined to her lower genital tract, particularly the vagina and cervix. If the cervical plug has formed before the mother is infected the gonococci may not reach the fetus. Gonorrhea is preferably treated with an adequate dose of penicillin. If the patient is sensitive to penicillin, another antibiotic may be used.

POLIOMYELITIS

This acute infectious disease is a greater threat to pregnant women than to others. Polio may be seasonal and epidemic, and 30 to 60 per cent of all afflicted people become paralyzed. Pregnant women should be inoculated with Sabin (oral) or Salk (injection) vaccine as a preventive measure.

Infectious diseases involving the pregnant woman are all deleterious for the fetus. Such diseases may be acquired by direct contact, by invasion of aerosols (droplets) from sneezing or coughing persons, and even by inhaling agents carried on dust. It behooves the pregnant woman to avoid contact with anyone suffering from an infectious disease.

noninfectious diseases

DIABETES

This disease is not an infection but a hereditary chemical defect, namely, the pancreas doesn't produce enough sugar-metabolizing insulin. Maternal diabetes may be the single most common cause of defects and of survival problems in the newborn. As many as 80 per cent of the pregnancies of diabetic mothers may result in anomalies. Sometimes the mother shows no evidence of the disease until she becomes pregnant, but diabetes should be suspected if the mother, the baby, or both are grossly overweight. About 25 per cent of the population appear to be carriers of this chemical defect, but in people under twenty years of age the incidence is only 1 in 2,500. Above sixty years the incidence is 1 in 50, so age is apparently an aggravating factor. When the mother has diabetes, not only does this indicate that the child may inherit the defect, but it also subjects the fetus to a noxious intrauterine environment. There is a 50 per cent probability that the fetus will be aborted or stillborn because of maternal acidosis if the mother's abnormal insulin requirements are not recognized and met. The pancreas of the fetus of a diabetic mother tends to grow abnormally—it may enlarge to as much as 20 times its normal size. Such a child will appear fat and puffy at birth and show an average excess of about 20 per cent in weight and 3 per cent in length. After birth there may be a sharp decline in weight, accompanied by passage of a great deal of urine. If diagnosed properly, maternal diabetes and its associated complications are treatable. The obstetrician can control the mother's diet, administer insulin cautiously, treat any toxemia, and even deliver the child prematurely to avoid some of the expected hazards.

ANEMIA

This must be corrected in the pregnant woman, for if she doesn't have enough hemoglobin in her blood, the fetus won't get enough oxygen. This, in turn, can critically hamper development—particularly of its brain, which is sensitive to oxygen shortages. The remedy is to supplement the anemic mother's diet with iron. Some of this iron may be stored by the fetus against its first few weeks after birth—a period when its only food is maternal milk, which is normally deficient in iron. The mother—but not the newborn child—can tolerate such iron-rich foods as liver, lean beef, and eggs.

radiation

Ever since 1927, when Dr. Hermann J. Muller discovered that ionizing radiation can speed up the rate of mutations in exposed germ cells, medical scientists have been increasingly aware that various diagnostic and therapeutic techniques involving pregnant women may be adding to the numbers of children born with hereditary or congenital defects. The hereditary effects occur because of induced changes in the sperm and ova before conception, the congenital defects because the developing fetus is particularly sensitive to all kinds of ionizing radiation.

The woman may not realize that she is pregnant and, feeling unwell, may be subjected to diagnostic X rays, fluoroscopy, or radioisotopes. Ironically, the radiologist might find that the suspected tumor, for example, is a living fetus which, as a consequence of its irradiation, develops an abnormality. For this reason, following a practice first adopted in Denmark, many radiologists will not make diagnostic examinations of the female pelvis except during the 9 or 10 days following the onset of menstruation—outside the fertile portion of the cycle. (Of course, this assumes that the health of the woman herself would not be jeopardized by a delay in diagnosis.) If this rule were applied to all women of reproductive age, married or not, radiation-induced congenital anomalies could be all but eliminated.

Modern medicine is not complete without radiological facilities. The mother's teeth require checking, for the fetus may deprive her body of the nutriments it absorbs for its own growth. However, this is a trivial example, since dental X rays are damaging neither to the fetus nor to the germ cells (provided that the apparatus and the patient's abdomen are properly shielded). But in other cases, when proper diagnosis of a medical condition dictates pelvic X rays, the radiologist must weigh the health of the mother against the possible damage to the fetus. And if the mother suffers from an abdominal malignancy, the region of her reproductive organs (including the fetus) may have to be treated with radiation. In these circumstances a therapeutic abortion should be strongly considered when the exposure of the fetus exceeds 10 roentgens (units of radiation) during the first 6 weeks of gestation.

Several general principles have been elucidated about irradiation of pregnant women:

1. There is no one type of ionizing radiation. Some sources generate a single type and some generate a mixture of alpha, beta, X and gamma rays, or neutrons. The different types of radiation have different penetrating powers, but their biological effects are similar. If one molecule of every 10 million in the body were irradiated, it would prove lethal to almost any animal. This would be equivalent to a dose of 1,000 roentgens in the human body. Fortunately, taking a single X-ray film pic-

ture exposes the subject to only about 1/10,000 that dosage.

2. Ionization stops the moment the apparatus is shut off.

3. The physical effect of radiation (such as the formation of an image on a photographic plate or the erythema—sunburn effect—of the skin of the subject) is relatively rapid, but the biological effects may not be discernible for from several hours to several decades later. One example might be the appearance of skin cancer 15 to 35 years after an excessive exposure to X rays.

4. The radiation used in diagnosis is highly penetrating, since it must permit the physician to examine internal organs deep within the human body without the need for exploratory surgery.

5. Despite the depth of penetration, radiation affects only tissues which lie in the path of the rays. There is no effect on remote areas of the body. If the head is filmed by a conical beam of X rays, there will be no effect on the reproductive organs in the pelvis, provided that there is sufficient shielding to prevent the rays from scattering.

6. The effects of radiation on the human body may be cumulative, particularly if the germ cells are involved. Thus, while radiation therapy is usually divided into daily or weekly treatments, the sperm or ova might just as well be exposed in one burst, for the individual doses are additive. This is not true of the somatic (body) cells, which are capable of a certain amount of recuperation from exposure to intermittent radiations.

7. Almost everything already mentioned applies with even greater force to the embryo or fetus. During development cells are constantly dividing and undergoing change (differentiation into specialized cells and tissues). While undergoing these changes the fetal cells are highly sensitive to ionizing radiation—so much so that in general it takes much less exposure to damage a fetus than an adult.

8. The threshold dosage at which radiation effects will take place and the stage of development at which the fetus is most susceptible to radiation have not been determined clearly with respect to the many anomalies that are believed to be caused by irradiation of the fetus. There is, however, abundant suggestive data. Experiments conducted with laboratory animals have shown that the minimum exposure that will possibly affect the fetus is 10 roentgens. Usually, a single X-ray plate requires no more than 0.1 roentgen, or 1 per cent of the threshold dose. Fluoroscopy, on the other hand, can involve a

much higher exposure. In Denmark, if a woman in the early stages of pregnancy is exposed to as much as 10 roentgens of X rays, her physician will recommend abortion, since he has every reason to believe that her child will be abnormal. Eventually this rule of thumb may be adopted universally.

9. The principal structures affected by ionizing radiation are the central nervous system, the brain, and the spinal cord, although all developing systems are susceptible. Since nerve cells and tissues begin to develop at about 19 days after conception and do not reach completion until after birth, they are always vulnerable. Therefore, exposure of the pregnant woman to any ionizing radiation is ill advised unless made to save the mother's life.

10. Radiation attacks the chromosomes within the exposed cells of the fetus—as it does those of the adult. We do not know the minimum dose that can alter a chromosome or cause a mutation (see Chapter 13). Therefore, we cannot speak of a genetically safe dose of radiation. Many geneticists believe that ionization of a single atom (which can be produced by an energy much less than that associated with 1 roentgen) can cause a mutation. It is suggested that more than 99 per cent of all mutations induced in this manner are deleterious rather than beneficial. But radiations do not cause new mutations; they merely accelerate their appearance.

11. A fetus is vastly more vulnerable to radiation when it is in its organ-forming period (about 2 to 6 weeks after conception) than it is, say, in the third trimester (7 to 9 months), when its major organ systems are fully developed. Generally, structural anomalies cannot be produced during the last months of pregnancy, only functional anomalies.

12. While a great many birth anomalies have been ascribed to ionizing radiation during life in the uterus, every single one of them can be produced by other factors. Thus, it is ordinarily not possible to conclude that a particular congenital anomaly is due to radiation at any specific stage of development. After all, 6 per cent of all children are born defective anyway, and in the majority of these cases the mother was never exposed to radiation during pregnancy. Nevertheless, we have learned from experiments with animals that anomalies can be produced with great regularity when radiation of a certain level is applied at certain stages of fetal development. And we have every reason to believe that the human fetus responds like other animals. Therefore, we should—no, we must—avoid radiation which might injure the human fetus.

13. It is not likely that radiation from improperly shielded TV sets could reach and harm the fetus.

14. From studies of children who were developing in the uterus at the time of the atomic attacks on Hiroshima and Nagasaki, we realize that such excessive exposure to ionizing radiations might have caused leukemia, cataracts, microcephaly, stunted growth, and other abnormalities.

abortion and other complications of pregnancy

In conjunction with each of the major categories of hazards to the fetus—drugs, disease, and radiation—abortion, stillbirth, and fetal death have been mentioned. An abortion refers to an interruption of pregnancy before the fetus reaches the state of being able to survive independently. To have even a slim chance of survival the fetus must be more than seven months old and weigh more than 1,000 grams (about 2¼ pounds). Approximately 1 pregnancy in 10 ends in abortion. Of these, 75 per cent occur in the first trimester, so that the woman who has entered a later stage of pregnancy may feel more confident of going all the way.

About 96 per cent of all abortions are spontaneous. They just happen, without any recognizable reason that would necessarily cause the same thing to happen a second time. The remaining 4 per cent are likely to recur with a second or third pregnancy. Since most abortions occur spontaneously, a woman should not be discouraged if she experiences such a loss. Any pregnancy, even an aborted one, is at least proof of fertility. Following a period of recuperation another pregnancy can be planned. A woman who has aborted once has a 66 per cent probability of maintaining her succeeding pregnancies, but if abortions occur three times in succession, her chances drop to a 16 per cent probability of future success. There is always a reason for a succession of abortions, and the competent obstetrician may be able to uncover it. Whether he can correct it depends upon its nature.

Some abortions are not spontaneous. They may be induced with medical and legal sanction or they may be performed criminally. While statistics have been compiled on the former, there is no way to calculate the frequency of criminal abortions, since both the mother and the practitioner are committed to secrecy. It is estimated that in some countries there may be hundreds of thousands of clandestine operations each year.

There are generally signs of an impending miscarriage

(another term for a spontaneous abortion). The mother may experience pain in the lower abdomen with vaginal bleeding. The pain has been likened to menstrual cramps or early labor, and the bleeding may be variable. Once a miscarriage has started, there is little anyone can do to stop it. However, these signs give no assurance that a miscarriage will follow, and in any case the woman should go to bed immediately and have someone call the obstetrician. If tissue is passed from the vagina, it should be saved for the obstetrician to examine.

Therapeutic abortions are now legal in the United States especially if the life of the mother is threatened by the continued pregnancy, and they are legal in Japan for socioeconomic reasons. The decision of the obstetrician must sometimes be approved by a Hospital Therapeutic Abortion Board. This situation may change through legislative action that would permit legal abortions in cases of incest, rape, or likelihood of deformity. (New York state enacted a relatively liberal abortion reform law in 1970, and other states are likely to follow suit.)

Another pregnancy could be initiated several weeks after the abortion. However, it is best to allow a few months for complete recovery of the mother. When a miscarriage (or therapeutic abortion) occurs the obstetrician will make certain that the uterus is cleared of all fetal and placental tissue. If it is not, he will perform curettage, which is a scraping of the inside of the uterus to remove the remaining tissue. Curettage is normally accompanied by some bleeding, but when properly done it involves no more than about one pint of blood, an amount that might be donated routinely to a blood bank. When bungled, however, the operation can result in hemorrhaging, infection, or damage to the reproductive organs. This is one of the tragedies frequently accompanying criminal abortions performed by unqualified persons in less than ideal surroundings. An obstetrician will not attempt curettage to terminate a pregnancy beyond the third month. It is too risky. Instead, he will employ a procedure resembling Caesarean delivery, known as hysterotomy. There has recently been a new procedure, namely, the injection of hypertonic salt (sodium chloride) into the amniotic sac, which causes an abortion shortly thereafter. Recent experience in Japan indicates that this method may be hazardous to the mother. Following an abortion, whether spontaneous or induced, the first menstruation is likely to be quite normal, but may occur between 22 and 71 days later. The time bears no relation to the duration of the pregnancy. Ovarian function usually is normal by the second menstruation, so that it is possible to become pregnant again during the second cycle or there-after. If the pregnancy lasted more than 76 days the ovarian endometrial cycles may not be normal immediately. Variations in recovery are due to the sudden withdrawal of the chorionic gonadotropins (hormones). It does seem that induced abortions are more disruptive of subsequent cycles than are spontaneous abortions.

In most hospitals slightly more male fetuses are aborted than females. This may well suggest some lethal factor either carried by or not neutralized by the nonhomologous portion of the X chromosome (see Chapter 13).

ECTOPIC PREGNANCIES

On rare occasions a fertilized ovum may succeed in im-planting itself and growing in an extraordinary site, such as an oviduct (Fallopian tube), or even in the abdominal cavity if it has escaped the ciliary currents that draw it through the ovi-duct. No place in the body but the uterus is suited for the normal implantation and great expansion of a growing fetus, and therefore ectopic pregnancies must always be terminated by surgery. When they occur they are accompanied by more than the usual amount of pain, vaginal bleeding, and fatigue. The obstetrician can test for an abnormal implantation site. It is believed that there is no hereditary predisposition to ectopic pregnancies; however, they do seem to recur in certain women.

EDEMA, TOXEMIA, AND URINARY INFECTIONS

Edema is a watery swelling of the face, hands, and ankles. It occurs when too great a burden is placed on the kidneys. To reduce the likelihood of edema the pregnant woman should limit her salt intake and avoid getting too heavy. When the edema is accompanied by high blood pressure and detectable albumin in the urine, it indicates a more serious kidney condi-tion known as toxemia, which may eventually threaten the life of both fetus and mother by producing eclampsia (spasticity, convulsions, and eventually coma and malfunction of the liver and kidneys). Delivery of the baby usually clears up the toxemia, but for a while the situation may be precarious. Diabetes or multiple pregnancies will aggravate any kidney problem, thereby bringing on toxemia. This brings us back to the first stage: Edema should always be called to the attention of the obstetrician. Women who are concerned enough to follow the doctor's orders rarely develop toxemia.

Urinary infections may be due to poor hygiene or to infections contracted during sexual intercourse, such as a venereal disease. Since the mother's bladder and kidneys work so hard to rid her body of fetal excretions as well as her own, it is not surprising that inflammations and infections occur. Signs of trouble may be fever, a burning sensation upon voiding, and general discomfort in the region of the bladder.

MULTIPLE PREGNANCIES

Twins occur naturally once in 86 pregnancies, triplets once in 7,500, quadruplets once in 650,000, and quintuplets once in 55 million. With the recent use of drugs to promote fertility, the incidence of multiple births is on the increase. Why is this considered a complication of pregnancy? Because survival is inversely related to the number of offspring in the litter. Quintuplets, for example, rarely survive. The sibling fetuses compete for the available nutrients and oxygen, and all tend to be smaller than normal at birth—in many cases they are considered to be "preemies." By the same token they put an added burden on the heart, lungs, and kidneys of the mother, and thus her health may be affected.

Obstetricians suspect multiple pregnancies when the size of the uterus increases rapidly or the abdomen enlarges unusually fast. There was a time when the obstetrician would order X rays to make a diagnosis, but now he relies on detecting separate fetal heartbeats or on palpating the abdomen.

MATERNAL DEATHS

Maternal mortality in the United States has been reduced to less than 3 for every 10,000 live births, perhaps the lowest rate in the world. About one-third of these deaths may be attributed to preexisting diseases, another third to inadequate obstetrical care, and the remainder to other complications of pregnancy. If the pregnant woman is under proper medical supervision, her probability of dying during pregnancy is lower than the probability of death for the nonpregnant woman leading an ordinary and active life but not getting medical checkups. A pregnant woman can withstand a number of surgical operations, although there is always some risk to her or to the fetus. Among the operable conditions during pregnancy are malignant tumors, benign fibroid tumors, appendicitis, cysts on the ovary, thyroid trouble, or gallstones. Even open-heart surgery may be attempted.

We have tried to caution the pregnant woman about drugs and radiation because there are certain situations for which these must be prescribed; it should further be pointed out that only about 6 per cent of human births carry congenital anomalies, leaving 94 per cent that are considered to be perfectly normal. We have been concentrating on the 6 per cent in this chapter. (See Appendixes B and C.)

the puerperium and the interconceptional period

Probably every new mother thinks about what it would be like to be pregnant again. Because of your recent experience you will forever be a changed woman, and you will not approach any succeeding pregnancy in the same way as your first. But in the meantime you face a time of adjustment in the interconceptional period between pregnancies. First and foremost, your body must recover from the unusual demands of nine months of pregnancy. Second, there is the need to strengthen all of your muscles, some of which may have become weakened, stretched, misshapen, or permitted to lie unused. This is the time to adopt habits of eating and exercise that will allow you to regain your original figure (or even to improve it). Third, since you *can* become pregnant again, even during nursing, you should practice some satisfactory method of birth control so that your second child will not come before it is wanted and planned for. All during this period of readjustment you will be occupied largely with the infant. Yet there are other aspects as well to normal family life.

The second baby for any woman develops in a body quite different from the first baby simply because of the experience of having borne a previous child. In addition to being at least a year older, many of your organs and functions have been permanently, irrevocably changed. Thus, the "interconceptional period," that interim between babies, should be used to build your body up to its maximum level of health. This means Papp smears, annual complete physical checkups, dental checkups, nutritional and health conferences, and counseling on the ideal spacing of children.

physical recovery

The adjustments of the mother to nine months' residence by a growing fetus are total: physical, emotional, psychological, and intellectual. While every woman after childbirth may feel she has accomplished her major mission in life, and find unique satisfaction in it, she must not neglect the need of her body for full and rapid repair and recuperation. The first six weeks after delivery—a period known as the puerperium ("having brought forth a child")—should be set aside as a *minimum* period for physical recuperation. Your uterus and other reproductive organs must return to the nonpregnant state, that is, all but the breasts, which must manufacture milk for the nourishment of the new infant (if you wish to nurse). There are other, less obvious changes, such as loss of excess body fluids. Your blood volume shrinks, and along with it passes the added burden to your kidneys and heart.

Immediately following expulsion of the afterbirth (placenta) the uterus contracts to a hard mass about the size of a grapefruit. Considering that your uterus was distended for almost nine months to encase an entire baby, along with the surrounding membranes and fluids, it is not surprising that it does not return to its original size overnight. Also, the separation of the placental tissues from the inside of the uterus causes bleeding. First the walls of the uterus come together. Its muscles begin to contract and thereby reduce the hemorrhaging. After two days the uterus contracts further. This sometimes causes pain, especially during breast-feeding, which stimulates the contractions.

Immediately after birth your uterus weighs about 2 pounds; by 6 or 7 days it is reduced to about 1 pound; at the end of 2 weeks to about ¾ pound; and by 6 or 7 weeks to about 4 ounces—still a bit larger and heavier than it was before your first pregnancy. Simultaneous with this reduction in size and with muscular contraction, the lining of your uterus reconstitutes itself in anticipation of a subsequent pregnancy. The last region of the uterus to heal and repair itself is the site at which the placenta was attached. During this involution (regression), the uterus normally moves back to its original position lower in the pelvic basin. Sometimes this is done with the aid of the obstetrician or midwife, assisted by mild exercises on your part.

The uterus heals only after it discharges some blood, mucus, parts of the decidua (cast-off lining), and some loose cells collectively known as the lochia. At first this discharge is reddish and thick, then it becomes pink and watery, and finally it changes into a colorless fluid by about 3 to 4 weeks. This is all perfectly natural, and it shows that normal healing is taking place. Any deviations from this sequence should be reported to the obstetrician or gynecologist. There is a parallel healing of other organs involved in the delivery, such as the vagina, vulva, and perineum, especially if there has been an episiotomy. Your abdomen may show streaks for 6 or 7 weeks or even permanently. Its walls may have become so flabby that certain exercises to strengthen the abdominal muscles are called for.

The cervix is usually so stretched during the birth process that it is rendered soft and flabby after delivery; it may even be torn and need surgical repair. By 7 days the cervical opening shrinks so much that it would be difficult even to introduce a straw through it, but it is never again as small and tight as before your pregnancy. The condition of your cervix is permanently altered after your first child passes through the birth canal. It is no longer circular but becomes crescent-shaped.

The breasts, which begin to secrete during late pregnancy, exude a yellowish fluid known as colostrum during the first two days after delivery. Colostrum acts as a laxative to the infant and has little or no nutritive value. However, the initial feeding does stimulate lactation and also gives the infant experience in sucking. By the fourth day your breasts will be larger, firmer, and more tender. By this time true milk appears, thin and bluish-white, and it is highly nutritious.

You may note other physical changes. Your body temperature, while otherwise normal, may rise slightly at the time your breasts become active. There may be temporary "after-pains" owing to the spasmodic contractions of your uterine muscles, accentuated by the first breast-feedings. These should not deter you from feeding your child, who, in turn, is helping you to contract your uterus by stimulating or inhibiting the appropriate hormones. The uterine pains should abate within 48 hours. Your body weight is usually reduced by at least 10 pounds with the eviction of your child and the afterbirth; your weight is further reduced by loss of water.

Your digestion returns to normal after delivery. However, you should remember that while you no longer nourish your child through the placenta, you are now doing it through your breasts. Therefore, a balanced diet and sufficient intake of fluids are just as necessary as ever. You will probably have irregular bowel movements for a few days.

Breast-feeding seems to deter the return of normal menstruation. If you do not breast-feed, your normal cycle may return within two months. However, you must always bear in mind that *whether or not you breast-feed your child you can become pregnant again during lactation.* Every new mother should see her obstetrician about 6 weeks after delivery for a thorough physical examination. He will then be able to determine to what extent she has returned physically to her prepregnant state.

Medical care during the puerperium is provided by the obstetrician for the mother and by the pediatrician for the child. During your 3- to 5-day hospital stay you should be protected against too many visitors; complete rest is almost mandatory. After a few days you will be at home again, only this time with full responsibility for your own child. You will probably be subject to excessive weariness and the "after-the-baby blues." These are neither psychoses nor neuroses, but rather the normal feelings of rejection after a long period of anticipation. A few crying spells will dissipate this feeling and bring you to a more stable acceptance of the inevitable—a new and constant responsibility and a source of pleasure. To make your new regimen more bearable you should rest completely, free from any interruption, from 2 to 4 P.M. every day without exception. Your obstetrician may permit you to take full tub baths at the end of the first day at home, and daily thereafter, even though there may be some persistent bleeding. More frequently, however, he may advise you to substitute showers for tub baths until after your first menstrual period.

A few additional suggestions: You may walk up stairs, but if there are a great many steps you should do it slowly. Stay on the same floor for the better part of your first week at home, but toward the end of that week you should venture outside if the weather permits.[1] After 10 days you can lead an almost normal

---

1. Some obstetricians get their patients out of bed and onto their feet in 2 to 3 days, and put no restrictions on their activity. Some women can tolerate this accelerated recovery, but others can suffer severe and permanent damage. The doctor should be the guide for each patient.

life, one that includes passive entertainment and diversions, such as automobile rides and movies or the theater. You should make a definite appointment with your obstetrician for about 6 weeks after the birth of your child. It is up to you to help him give you a clean bill of health.

lactation

The breasts of the adult female may be described as ample, large, full, moderate, or small; firm, sagging, or pendulous; hemispherical, conical, bowl-shaped, or purse-shaped—yet all have as their function the production of milk for the infant. They are nothing more than sebaceous (oily) glands of the skin which have been modified to secrete milk. Their lobes, ducts, and alveoli are permeated and surrounded by fatty tissue, which gives them their characteristic contours.

Milk forms in the lining cells of the alveoli and is stored in ampullae (milk reservoirs). Some 12 to 25 small ducts leading from the reservoirs empty separately through minute pores in the nipple. The nipple itself is devoid of fat and thinly covered with skin. It is well supplied with sensory nerve endings, capillaries, and erectile tissue and as a result is extremely sensitive to tactile stimulation. This is a distinct advantage, since the nipple can erect and become easier for the baby to seize. The nipple is ringed by a circular area known as the areola, which contains sebaceous glands that lubricate the nipple and prevent oozing milk from caking on it.

The process of lactation is closely coordinated with the menstrual cycle and with the progress of the pregnancy. Hormones that affect the development of the breast are secreted by the cortex of the adrenal glands, the thyroid and parathyroid glands, and the anterior and posterior sections of the pituitary. In addition the uterus, the ovaries, and the placenta play a role. (See page 11.) The anterior lobe of the pituitary acts as the master gland. Immediately after the mother has given birth it doubles its production of prolactin (the hormone that stimulates milk production).

While milk is produced continually by the alveoli, it does not automatically leak from the nipples. On the contrary, the milk must be "let down" into the ducts. What happens is the following:

When the baby suckles it stimulates the nipple, which sends messages through the nervous system to the hypothalamus (a nerve center in the brain adjacent to the pituitary). The

Left human breast

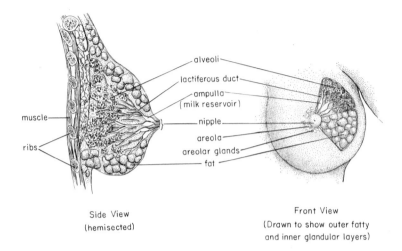

alveoli
lactiferous duct
ampulla
(milk reservoir)
muscle
nipple
areola
ribs
areolar glands
fat

Side View
(hemisected)

Front View
(Drawn to show outer fatty
and inner glandular layers)

hypothalamus signals the posterior lobe of the pituitary to release another hormone, oxytocin, which is transported by the bloodstream to the breasts. The infusion of this hormone induces certain cells surrounding the outer walls of the alveoli to contract, thereby compressing the alveoli. Now milk flows into the ducts. Since the oxytocin reaches both breasts, suckling of either one causes milk to be let down in both.

Mother's milk is rich in milk fat, milk protein (casein), and milk sugar (lactose). Lactose and casein are produced nowhere in nature but in the mammary glands. Cow's milk is chemically similar to human milk and in general is a good substitute, but it contains less lactose and more salts and sometimes has a laxative effect.

During late pregnancy and the first few days after birth the mammary glands secrete a cloudy fluid known as colostrum. Colostrum is not as nutritious as true milk, since it contains less lactose and virtually no fat. Moreover, it is slightly laxative. However, it serves adequately until the appearance of true milk on about the fourth day. But good as milk is, the baby's diet still may have to be supplemented with orange or tomato juice. It appears that the mother's liver retains vitamin C and her milk may not supply enough to the baby.

Milk production continues to increase until about a month and a half after birth, then it stabilizes. Breast-feeding can continue for years (and in some societies it does), but the volume of the milk decreases markedly after nine months. Once the infant is weaned, the breasts dry up and return almost to their former size.

succinct instructions for nursing

The following hints, condensed from various modern sources, are offered for those who wish to breast-feed.

Wash your hands so as to protect your baby from infections. Assume a comfortable position which will allow you to hold the baby so that his head is slightly inclined (a small pillow sometimes helps). Gently squeeze the darker areolar area around the nipple and encourage the baby to take all of it into his mouth. Make sure that your breast does not obstruct his breathing. Use both breasts, in turn, from 5 to 10 minutes each, beginning the feeding at alternate breasts at succeeding meals. Never extract the nipple from the baby's mouth while he is holding on, not only because of the frustrating effect it may have on him but also because the practice may make your nipple sore.

Always accept your baby happily for his nursing, whether at your rest time or in the middle of the night. During the night mother's milk usually flows most readily. As a general practice encourage the baby to burp up any swallowed air. You can do this by gently patting him on the back or holding him over your shoulder. Between feedings allow your breasts maximum exposure to the air so as to avoid excessive tenderness. You may experience uterine spasms as an accompaniment of nursing because of the secretion of oxytocin. These spasms aid the uterus in returning to its prior condition.

At home have confidence in your ability to nurse and to satisfy your baby both nutritionally and emotionally. Human milk appears to have the consistency of skim milk, but is nonetheless the most perfectly balanced food for the infant. Pale urine from the baby indicates that he is getting the milk he needs. You can never completely empty a breast of its milk, but by alternating the breasts you can keep up an adequate supply and persuade the baby to take more food before he falls asleep. Maximum feeding time should never be more than about 20 minutes for both breasts. In general, nurse your baby when he expresses hunger. For some babies this may be several hours during the day and once at night. Babies differ in their metabolic needs, so setting a time schedule for nursing is unreasonable. Occasionally a baby prefers sleep to nursing, but you should encourage him to feed at least every four to five hours, and perhaps even every two hours. Should your baby become quickly satisfied at one breast but obviously has not had enough food, waken him by changing his diaper and then allow him to go to sleep at the second breast. If the baby clamps hard on your nipple with his gums this is a sign to stop the feeding. Nursing stimulates milk production, so more frequent or complete feedings will usually cause the production of more milk. After some weeks your breasts may be reduced in volume, yet should produce adequate milk.

Breast-fed babies are seldom constipated, and it is normal to make diaper changes after each feeding; fluid intake by the mother should be more than usual—at least a glass of milk or water before each feeding. Your milk supply may fluctuate with emotional stress or social activities, so you should get frequent, even though brief, rest periods.

Drugs taken by the mother while nursing can affect the baby directly or indirectly. This applies to tranquilizers, laxatives, alcohol, nicotine, and, of course, to the hallucinogens. Birth control pills should not be taken during nursing—there are other methods for birth control. Very seldom do foods eaten by the mother affect the nursing baby, but a varied and adequate diet with plenty of fluids should be the rule for the mother.

Delay giving your baby solid foods, since they tend to reduce the desire for mother's milk. Bottles may be used for water and formula foods, and for supplementing the breasts, but bottle-feeding weakens the baby's sucking strength. There is every reason to believe that all women can provide adequate food for a baby for the first several weeks and even for months. Sometimes a baby given solid foods is relieved to get back to free-flowing mother's milk. Menstruation should not worsen your milk, although sometimes a baby may appear to be more than usually fussy for a day or so. When there is enforced separation of mother and baby a prescribed formula can be substituted, but the mother's breasts should be pumped free to keep the milk flowing.

Weaning can be made fun by teaching the baby to take food from a cup. If weaning is done gradually, the breasts will recede gradually and painlessly. There is no set age for weaning, but there is a reasonable limit on nursing!

eating and exercise habits

During the period of lactation and breast-feeding the mother must still tailor her eating habits to the nutritional needs of her child as well as her own. *Severe malnutrition during the first months of life can be a factor in producing a mentally retarded child*. The nursing mother should eat essentially the same during the first two months of her child's life as she was directed to eat during pregnancy. A balanced diet should include *extra* proteins, vitamins, fluids, and the essential elements iron and calcium. Such extras can be obtained from the following:

Milk—1 quart or more per day. Cottage cheese for protein.

Meat—lean red meat, poultry, fish, cheese (2 to 3 servings per day), plus at least one egg each day in any form.

Fruit—one or more servings per day, including one of citrus fruits such as lemon, orange, or grapefruit. Melons or strawberries in season and tomatoes or tomato juice are fine.

Vegetables—green or yellow leafy vegetables, but only 1 potato per day. Raw vegetables are good, too, in salads.

Desserts—none except dried or fresh fruits. Avoid cakes, pies, ice cream, and candies.

Breads and cereals—2 servings daily. Best are those with enriched or whole grain; protein or whole wheat. Use enriched margarine unless the doctor prescribes pure butter.

Avoid: oils, animal fats, fried foods, sweets, and pastries. Excess salt generally produces thirst and consequent overloading with fluids. This in turn tends to raise the blood pressure and promote weight gain. The obstetrician can offer a diet program for any situation, and a proper balance is more important than counting calories. A woman, once pregnant, generally remains heavier thereafter, but this extra weight is neither necessary nor desirable.

Maintaining proper posture and exercising are essential if the new mother is to regain her original figure—they can even help her to improve it. As was stated earlier, good posture during pregnancy is necessary to avoid undue strain on certain back muscles. It is true after childbirth, too. The general rule at all times is to try to make yourself as tall as possible, whether walking, standing, sitting, or lying flat on your face or back. Shoes should be comfortable and give you good support.

You should not attempt routine exercises without the prior approval of your attending doctor. This is simply because the conditions of your delivery and puerperium must be considered. While some women might begin mild exercises three days after their child arrives, others should wait a week or ten days, or even longer. In any case, exercises are prescribed to correct flabbiness and to reduce the fat that usually accumulates around the upper thighs, hips, and abdomen during pregnancy.

We have included a series of drawings illustrating some exercises which are safe to execute, and which will help to restore the figure to its prepregnancy state. However, we must

Complete relaxation, face up, without pillow supports The simplest exercises can be done while lying flat on your back on the carpeted floor without any pillows, and with the arms along the sides of the body. To avoid low back strain the small of the back should be placed firmly on the floor. Also good preparation for labor, done with normal rhythm and breathing and feeling of looseness all over.

Stretching exercise Postpartum only. Lie flat on your stomach with legs together and hands clasped in front of your head. Raise head, stretch arms forward as far as possible, tighten the muscles of the buttocks and abdomen, then relax all muscles, and repeat. This is a simple and harmless exercise, and easily executed while lying flat on the carpeted floor. The first day after delivery of the child.

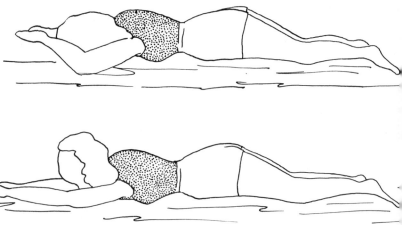

Complete relaxation, face down, with pillow supports Postpartum. The most relaxing position is accomplished while lying face down with pillows under the face, stomach, and ankles. Legs slightly flexed. This position may be assumed for half an hour, then stretch the whole body to maximum length. Repeat. (Pillow under abdomen optional)

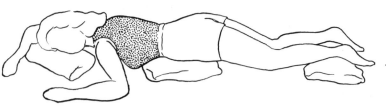

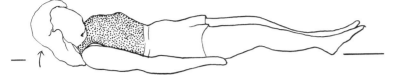

Exercise for neck and abdomen Postpartum. Lying flat on your back on the carpeted floor, raise your head and try to touch your chest with your chin. You will find that this not only involves your neck muscles but also your abdominal muscles. Begin third or fourth day after delivery.

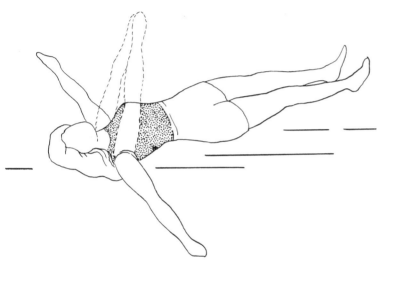

Mild exercise of arms only Postpartum. Lie flat on the floor with the arms outstretched to the sides. Then raise the arms, bringing them together above the body in a vertical position, then lower them again to the starting position. This is a good starter for exercises after returning home, it strengthens the breast.

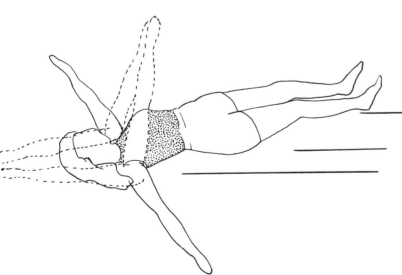

Exercises to shape the breasts Exercises for the breast to be tried **after** breast feeding has been discontinued. With thighs and knees flexed and the back in contact with the floor, breathe naturally and exercise slowly. To increase the effect of these arm exercises hold a book in each hand and bring them together as noted.

Exercise for neck, arms, and abdomen Lying on your back on the carpeted floor, and with hips and knees flat on the floor, raise your head until it touches your chest and then gradually lift your shoulders and upper part of your body from the floor, at the same time lifting your arms to meet above your head. Do not try to achieve a sitting position until you feel equal to it, not before the fifth or sixth day after returning home for some women, and for a few not for six weeks. Strenuous.

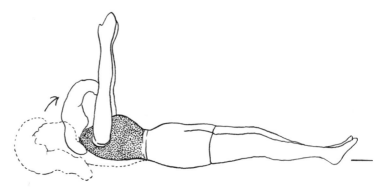

Strengthening the abdominal muscles Postpartum. Starting with the prone position on the carpeted floor, with the hips and knees flexed, raise one leg at a time while straightening the knee. Keep the leg straight if possible. Do the same with the other leg. When stronger, try to raise both legs simultaneously, beginning by first lifting the heels just off the floor. This will greatly strengthen the abdominal muscles.

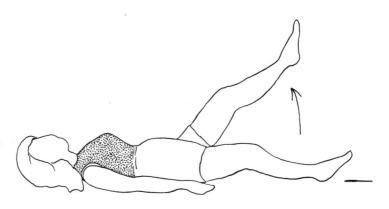

Exercise for legs and abdomen Lying flat on your back on the carpeted floor, bend one knee as far as possible, lifting it toward your head and bringing the heel close to the thigh. Alternate. Flex one leg sharply so that the thigh touches the abdomen, bringing the foot toward the buttocks. Then straighten out the leg and slowly lower it to the floor. Good for the abdomen.

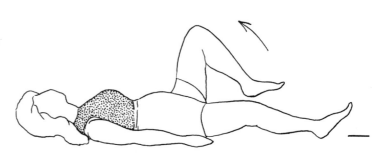

The twist for making body supple Several weeks after delivery, and from the relaxed position flat on the floor, bend the left knee, raise the left leg, and then straighten out the leg lifting the foot toward the ceiling. Twist the lower part of your body toward the right, bringing the left leg over until your foot touches the floor, then try to touch your right hand to your left foot. Straighten the body and repeat to the other side. This will lend flexibility to the whole body.

General body exercises for muscle tone Postpartum. These exercises are for most of the major muscles of the body, and believed by some doctors to help the uterus to return to proper position. **1.** Kneel on the bed or floor with the arms apart and the thighs, knees, and feet together. Move head and hips to opposite sides, assuming a snakelike undulation. **2.** Rest the elbows on the floor, bringing the head down between the arms until the chin meets the chest. Flatten the abdomen, squeezing the buttocks and thighs together. **3.** Bring buttocks back to rest on the heels, and your forehead to touch the floor in front of your knees. Let the arms stretch out easily in front of your head. Return to original position.

Exercises after six weeks for abdomen and thighs
From a prone position raise the upper part of your torso to a half-sitting position while the elbows and palms are resting on the floor. Slowly bring the right knee to the chest and at the same time lift the left leg about 3 inches off of the floor. Alternate this procedure with the legs about 6 times, stopping to relax and breathe deeply between.

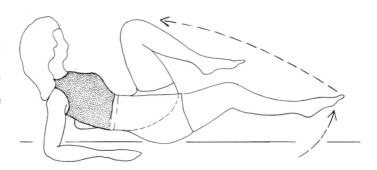

Bicycle exercises for after six weeks   While lying on your back with palms down, rotate legs as though you were pedaling a bicycle. Do this slowly while breathing deeply and easily. Bring the knees as close to the chest as possible, keeping the toes pointed. This exercise will aid conditioning of the abdomen, waist, thighs, lower back, and pelvis.

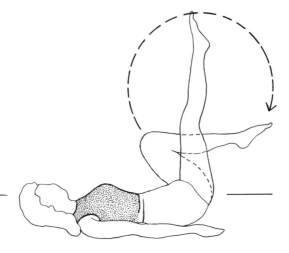

Aid in returning abdominal organs to prepregnancy position   This is the knee-chest position which eases uterine cramps and helps that organ to return to its normal position in the pelvis. It is recommended by some physicians for special conditions. To be held twice daily for 2 minutes each time, after emptying the bladder. Knees may be separated.

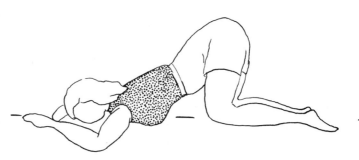

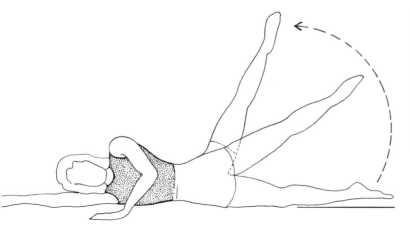

Exercises after six weeks for outer thigh Lying on your right side with the right arm extended and your head resting on your arm and the other palm pressed against the floor, slowly lift the leg inch by inch to the side. Breathe in as you raise the leg and out as you lower it. Change to the other side and repeat.

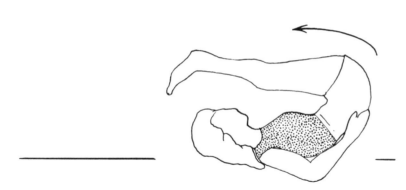

Body bending exercise to reduce abdomen When leg exercises can be done without excess fatigue, then try raising the legs together not only to the perpendicular position but further so that the knees are directly above the head. If your stomach has receded enough you may even be able to touch the floor above your head. Keep the knees straight, and repeat several times. Too strenuous for some women.

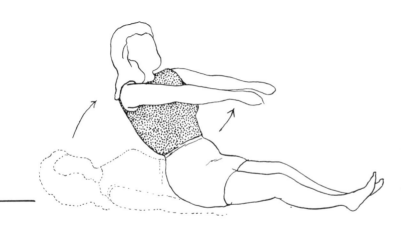

Energetic exercise only with doctor's sanction After 5 to 6 weeks at home you may be able to raise your body from the prone position on the floor to a sitting position. You may either raise the arms, extending them in front of you, or keep the hands locked behind your head or folded across your chest. Do not do this exercise without the express permission of your physician.

Energetic exercise only with doctor's sanction After about 6 weeks place your hands behind your head and from a prone position raise your body with bending at the hips until you achieve a sitting position. Do not move your legs at all. This is strenuous and should be tried only after you have worked up to it. (This exercise may not be recommended by your doctor.)

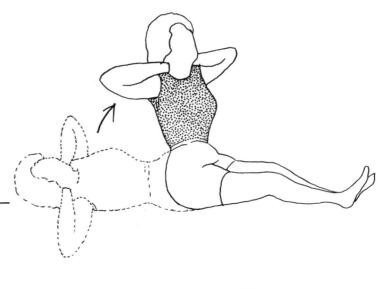

Hip exercises After 6 weeks, and lying on your back on the carpeted floor, draw your knees up keeping the soles of the feet flat on the floor. Put your hands under the buttocks, resting the elbows on the floor. Raise the buttocks above the floor, keeping the thighs together and contracting the muscles of the abdomen and buttocks. Relax and repeat.

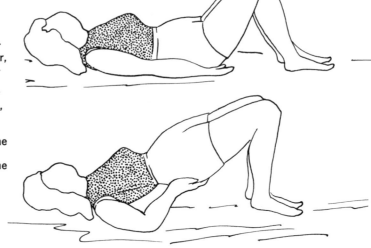

Arching to strengthen the back muscles From the prone position on the carpeted floor, and while keeping the head, shoulders, and feet on the floor, try raising the rest of the body, steadying with the arms. Do this once or twice at first and, as it becomes easier, increase the number to five. This strengthens the back muscles. (Possibly too strenuous for some women, check with your doctor.)

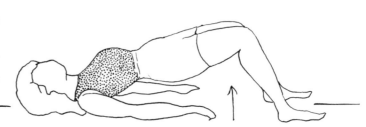

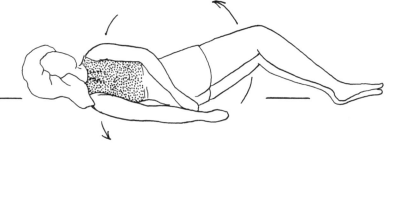

Corkscrew exercise to keep body flexibility Starting in the prone position flat on your back with knees bent, feet flat on the floor, abdomen taut, and shoulders close to the floor, roll both knees to one side and return. Alternate sides. When you feel strong enough, reach one arm across the body in the direction opposite from the knees, assuming a corkscrew position. Return to prone position, and rest. Repeat to the other side. This may be done increasingly, up to 6 times, twice daily.

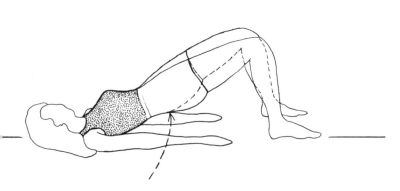

Exercises after six weeks for back and pelvis. Lying on your back with arms to the side, knees bent, and feet flat on the floor, push your hips up off of the floor as high as possible, trying to attain a 45° angle. The weight should be on the head and shoulders. You should feel a stretching at the waist and across the pelvis. Lower the body slowly, beginning at the neck and gradually sink toward the waist.

emphasize that after nine months of relative inactivity a woman should begin this program slowly and easily, without any feeling of compulsion or extreme exertion, and then gradually build up her capabilities until she can do them all. After a few weeks she can perform the program all at once in about 15 minutes, but she could also divide it into two or more sessions. Since not all women react to childbirth in exactly the same manner, it would be advisable for each mother to have her physician plan a routine for her. Her aim should be to have a healthy, beautiful body.

The simplest of exercises can be done while you are lying flat on your back, on the carpeted floor, without pillows and with your arms at your sides. In this position you can rest completely between exertions, yet you can exercise your arms, legs, head—and, with breathing movements, your abdomen and chest as well. You should delay sitting-up exercises and those executed in the prone position (on your stomach) until your physical recovery is complete. At first you should simply try to follow the instructions once, or twice. On succeeding days you may do each exercise three, four, or five times before resting. You should find your strength and vigor returning rapidly. Eventually each exercise may be performed 10 or even 15 times each day. How long should this continue? For as long as you desire to have a good figure.

family planning

Before the pill and IUD's (intrauterine devices) it was estimated that the world population was increasing daily by a number equal to the total population of Rochester, New York, or Toledo, Ohio. By the end of this century there could be 7 billion people in the world. Aside from the ultimate threat to survival of mankind posed by the problems of inadequate space, food, etc., already too many children are born into unwelcome environments of home and society right here in the affluent United States in the 1970's. The population explosion argument for family planning has little meaning to individuals unaware of social, economic, and ecological realities, but almost any intelligent couple can be persuaded that their children should be planned for and spaced with regard to the health of the mother, to the economic status of the family, and to the psychological effects of the increasing numbers in the family as a unit. *Every child born into this world should be wanted, cared for, and given the proper start in life.* No doubt social ills produce some of the maladjusted adults, the delinquent adolescents, and the chronic malcontents we see about us. Many unfortunates were

brought unasked into an environment in which they were rejected. Anthropologist Margaret Mead says, "Above all, we
must recognize that the time to limit the size of our families is
now, if future generations are to be born into a livable world."

More than 90 per cent of American couples now practice
some form of birth control. These people are aware of the
hazards of a "baby every year" to the stability and physical and
mental health of the members of any family, and are beginning
to recognize that quality is more important than quantity. The
average life span in the United States was thirty-nine years in
1850, and now is seventy years, which reflects the advances in
preventative and curative medicine as well as in the general
standards of living. Society will come to condemn irresponsible
conception because all faiths now agree to the importance of
family planning. When a new child arrives in this world he has a
better chance now of arriving to an enthusiastic welcome, which
will help give that child psychological stability. It is hoped that
every educated and intelligent couple will have a child only if
they can assure him of food, clothing, shelter, medical and
health care, education, and proper guidance into the most fruit-
ful avenues of activity.

In many large cities, and always affiliated with some hospital, there is a nurse-midwifery program. This makes available at
little or no charge a thoroughly trained and experienced nurse to
supplement the part played by the very busy obstetrician. There
simply are not enough obstetricians to care for all of the pregnant women and those in need of family planning, so the nurse-
midwife is becoming again a most important adjunct to this
medical need. She has had, in addition to her regular training,
18 months' experience in all of the problems relating to the
prenatal and postnatal care of the mother and the care of the
newborn child immediately upon delivery.

Every good nurse-midwife adds to the *quality* of the next
generation by giving each mother individualized care and instruction which the obstetrician cannot adequately do because
he is so busy with the population explosion. This help is usually
given through groups, classes, lectures, and films, often in or
associated with a hospital, always within the framework of an
approved maternity service. The nurse-midwife, in this country,
is never an independent practitioner but has quick access to the
best available medical supervision. Often the woman in late
pregnancy can allay some of her apprehensions by asking questions of the nurse-midwife which she might be reluctant to ask

of her physician. The nurse-midwife is in a position to discuss a patient's emotional, social, and physical needs and to advise her.

contraception

Attempts at contraception are listed as far back as recorded history. One thousand years ago an Islamic physician wrote: "Occasionally it is very important that the semen should not enter the womb, as for instance when there is danger to the woman in pregnancy, or if it has entered, that it should come out again. There are several ways of preventing its entrance. The first is that at the time of ejaculation the man withdraw from the woman so that the semen does not approach the os uteri (cervix). The second way is to prevent ejaculation, a method practiced by some. A third method is to apply to the os uteri before introgression some drug which blocks the uterine aperture or which expels the semen and prevents conception, such as pills, or pessaries of cabbage, colocyth pulp, bryony, iron scoria, tamarisk dew, pitch, ox gall, inner skin of a pomegranate, animal ear wax, part of a mulberry bush, elephant's dung, scammony, or whitewash. These may be used alone or in combination."[1] More than 60 plants and herbs have been listed in the literature as effective in controlling human fertility.

While contraceptive devices have been used for centuries, only recently have really effective methods been developed. Now parents can have children only when they want them, and are in a better position to give them the love, care, and security they need. Even the lot of the childless may be improved. For the one out of five couples who have not needed contraceptives because they seemed to be sterile, there are now antisterility pills. These pills, which are really hormone additives, not only help many women to overcome some kinds of biological sterility but also seem to increase the likelihood of multiple births. Some long-sterile women, treated with these ovulation-stimulating hormones, have borne twins, triplets, or even quintuplets.

The birth-control method chosen by any couple must: (1) be easy to use, not involving frequent visits to the physician or requiring special elaborate equipment; (2) not interfere with the sex act by interruption or discomfort; (3) be private and yet be convenient and aesthetic; (4) be effective, approaching 100

1. N. E. Himes, *Medical History of Contraception* (Williams & Wilkins, 1936).

per cent; (5) be relatively inexpensive over an extended period; (6) be safe. There will be questions about the safety of either major method (the pill or IUD's), particularly for the woman, for some years to come. Deaths from their use are in the neighborhood of 1 in 50,000 for women who take the pill, and even less for users of IUD's.

There is only one method of birth control that is 100 per cent effective: total abstinence. This is the one most appropriate during the 6 weeks' convalescence from pregnancy. In all cultures and all history abstinence has been the practice during the woman's menstruation. In some societies it is also practiced during lactation; or until the new child can first sit up by himself; or until a child reaches his second birthday or takes his first step. Chastity belts were used even in the late nineteenth century in France, and in accordance with their beliefs Indians never indulged in coitus during sunset. Thus some societies have spaced their children for reasons other than those advanced by modern civilized society.

Coitus interruptus—withdrawal before ejaculation—has probably been the most universal contraceptive practice. (As recently as 1960 it was the most common method used in England.) It may continue to be so until other more satisfactory and reliable methods become available to all peoples. Another common practice has been the douche with hot or cold sea water, lemon juice, or other acid solutions. As recently as 1930 douching was the most common method of contraception used in the United States.

In various cultures women have placed such items as pads, bark cloth, feathers, grass, leaves, or rags in the vagina; even a glass plug has been slipped into the cervical opening before coitus. As early as 1850 B.C. Egyptians made a paste of crocodile dung and used it as a pessary (diaphragm). Other writers have reported plugging of the vagina with honey and sodium carbonate, or a sponge of hacked wool (used by early Hebrews). Records from 1550 B.C. suggest that about 35 centuries ago the Hebrews used lint tampons with acacia triturated with honey, or else shrub acacia (which contains gum arabic that becomes fermented and liberates lactic acid). This combination of occlusion (blockage) plus a drug or chemical (to attack sperm) is similar in principle to the contraceptive jellies and pessary of recent usage. The spermicidal property of acids was realized by Casanova, who in the eighteenth century recommended cutting a lemon in half, extracting most of its juice and then using the rind as a cervical cap with adherent acid juice as the spermicidal agent. Aristotle referred to painting the cervical region with cedar oil, lead ointment, or frankincense mixed with olive oil. Other items recommended for local application in the vagina have been rock salt, pepper, exotic items like elephant dung, and occlusive suppository-like substances such as myrrh, opopanax, rue, and hellebore kneaded with ox gall. Vaginal pessaries were sold in Mecca a hundred years ago. Many drugs were recommended for application to the penis, such as tar, rock salt, balm oil, white lead, sweet oil, juice of onions, oil of balsam or sesame. Condoms have been used since the time of Fallopius (1523–62), not only for protection against infection but as contraceptive devices. Vulcanization of rubber in 1839 reduced the price of the condom and made it more durable and reliable. A decade or so ago this method was used by 51 per cent of Protestant college graduates in the United States. Man's efforts to prevent conception have a long history showing a wide range of imagination, ingenuity, and failure.

After centuries of experimentation, and with the modern knowledge and methods of scientific research, there is no longer any excuse for men and women of any stratum of society to be ignorant of methods of contraception, or not to overcome some of the reasons for sterility. The hassle about abortions will gradually become meaningless except for those who are reckless, or who do not rigidly follow the instructions relating to birth control. It will also be used in cases of rape, incest, and inheritable malformations such as feeble-mindedness, and for early exposure to virus diseases such as German measles. Twenty per cent of all white women in the United States reaching age forty-five have had at least one induced abortion. Since the minority were not for therapeutic reasons, this statistic will surely be reduced with the new refinements in contraception.

modern contraceptive methods

METHODS REQUIRING CONSULTATION WITH THE PHYSICIAN

Rhythm method (74 per cent effective[2]): This method depends upon total abstinence during the woman's fertile period, which lasts about 3 days during a normal 28-day cycle, leaving 25 days of infertility. The single pertinent question, the answer to which varies with almost every woman, is: "When is my safe

---

2. The effective percentages given are the range reported per 100 years of contraceptive exposure. The lower extreme of the range usually applies before the first pregnancy, and the upper extreme before subsequent pregnancies.

period?" The woman whose menstruation falls within the average range will have a 28-day (or lunar) cycle, with 5 days of menstruation followed by ovulation about day 14 after the onset of the menstruation. A more accurate but difficult fact to determine is that, no matter how long the cycle, ovulation occurs about 14 (12 to 16) days *before* the onset of menstruation. But even though a particular woman might have a regular 28-day cycle this month, her next cycle could be 10 days shorter or longer, and consequently her ovulation time altered. Something like 99 per cent of women do not have a regular cycle; thus the rhythm method restricts intercourse to about one truly safe week in each lunar month. If it were possible through electrical methods or body temperature records to ascertain exactly when ovulation occurs, one could then calculate the three days during which fertilization might occur, leaving the other 25 days as "safe." It is believed that the woman's body temperature rises when she ovulates. If the *basal body temperature* is taken by mouth early every morning with a thermometer accurately calibrated in units of 0.1 degrees Fahrenheit, and a daily record is kept beginning with the onset of menstruation, the woman will find that at about mid-cycle this temperature will drop briefly and then rise about 0.5 to 0.75 degrees Fahrenheit above her average. It will remain this much higher than the usual temperature for a number of days. But temperatures do fluctuate during the day and with activity. Therefore, in order to obtain a true basal body temperature, the woman must take it before she sits up, moves, drinks anything, or even speaks to her husband!

Some hypersensitive women believe they can "feel" the rupture of an ovum from one ovary, which of course would be the actual moment of ovulation. Since sperm can live and fertilize for about 48 hours, and there is a 24-hour life for the ovum, there is a total fertile period of about 72 hours or 3 days during each lunar month. But it is questionable whether a woman can really detect ovulation, and certainly the onset of ovulation cannot be predicted. Thus, only a woman who is invariably regular in her cycle can be "reasonably" certain of her "safe period." The usual program for such a woman is to assume days 12 through 16 to include her ovulation, and since sperm can survive in her reproductive tract for 48 hours, her "susceptible" period is extended to days 10 to 17 after the onset of menstruation, if the cycle is consistently 28 days. The rhythm method cannot be used reliably by those women whose intermenstrual cycle varies as much as 10 days during a one-year period of recording the variations. Considering the uncertainty and the need for vigilance—to say nothing of a gift for computation—this method is recommended only for those who for religious or other reasons prefer not to use contraceptives. The physician can explain this with a calendar, but in any case to be truly "safe" the periods of total abstinence in any lunar month are much longer than required by any other method, hence less satisfactory to the couple.

Also, the rhythm method should *not* be relied upon by those who have been subjected to unexpected or unusual physical or emotional disturbances, travel or vacations, changes in altitude without atmospheric pressure adjustments, anxieties, tensions, or illnesses, any of which could alter ovulation time and hence the menstrual cycle.

The cervical cap   (88 per cent effective with jelly): This is a small and deep cup which can be placed over the cervix to block the entrance of sperm which are placed in the vagina during coitus. Rubber caps may be worn for only a 24-hour period, but metal or plastic ones may be left in for the duration of the intermenstrual period. Such cups are generally fitted by the physician and used with a contraceptive jelly or cream. Cups are not extensively used, but they are as effective as diaphragms when properly used.

Diaphragm   (86 to 87 per cent effective with jelly): This is a rather large hemispherical, thin rubber, domelike cap stretched over a collapsible metal ring. It fits over the cervix to block the passage of sperm. It should always be used with a cream or contraceptive jelly. The diaphragm is initially fitted by the physician, but then the woman can insert it herself whenever she wants. The size and shape of the diaphragm are determined by the physician after he examines the birth canal. Generally the contraceptive jelly, cream, or foam is placed on the rim of the diaphragm, which is then pinched together and inserted, to lie snugly over the cervix. It must be left in place for at least 6 hours after intercourse (but may be left in place for up to 24 hours), then removed, washed, powdered, and stored. It must be refitted by the physician after each pregnancy, and it should be checked every two years. As a contraceptive it was most popular before the advent of the pill and IUD's, and it is highly effective unless the woman is careless about its placement. Some 13 to 14 pregnancies per 100 women per year can be expected when this combination method is used.

The birth-control pill—oral contraception[3] (believed to be 99.7 per cent effective): The pill was introduced in 1960 and is now taken regularly by more than 10 million American women, and by a greater number outside the United States. The principle of the oral contraceptive is that it provides a synthesis of two natural hormones, estrogen and progesterone, which mimic the action of the body's own hormones. These pills "regularize" a woman's monthly cycle, causing her period to occur every 26 to 28 days, however regular or erratic her previous history has been. Such pills are therefore biologically normalizing.

There are two types of pills, one of which is a combination of the two hormones and is known as the "combination balanced estrogen-progesterone." The other is known as the "sequential method." The combination method is generally considered the more reliable in preventing conception. Each pill contains both synthetic hormones which together effectively prevent ovulation or release of any ovum from either ovary during the time the pills are taken. Since no ovum is available to be fertilized, pregnancy cannot be achieved. This is probably the single most reliable contraceptive known to man (100 per cent effective when taken properly).

One schedule would be to start on the fifth day after the beginning of menstruation, which is day 1, and take one combination pill each day at the same time for 20 days. Five days after the woman stops taking the pill, menstruation will begin. This again is day 1 for the next cycle of pill taking—beginning, as usual, on day 5, regardless of the bleeding situation. During the first several menstrual cycles a user of this method may experience mild side effects such as nausea; gastrointestinal distress; spotting; enlargement, tenderness, or even secretions of the breasts; some edema; and weight gain. When such side effects persist or seem severe the physician should be consulted. While these synthetic hormones have been properly tested, and used by millions of women, it cannot be stated definitively that they are totally without side effects which may develop after long and continuous usage. While cancer of the ovary or uterus has not been demonstrated in women using the pill, as it has in other mammals (rats, mice, rabbits, etc.), we must wait another decade before the pill can be given a clean bill of health in this regard. Cancer-inducing agents act slowly, and thus far the pill (or its constituents) have not caused cancer in monkeys, which

3. Oral contraception goes back to 2700 B.C., when the Chinese took quicksilver fried in oil as a guaranteed contraceptive.

are closely akin to humans. The amounts given to the rodents were relatively far in excess of those taken by women on the pill, so that possibly the 50-microgram limit is close to the threshold of causing deleterious side effects. A modified or improved pill may be discovered. In the meantime users might be cautioned against indefinite use (more than two to three years), hoping for more and valid scientific research. World infant mortality rates in 1967 show the United States to be twenty-third with 22.1 per 1,000 births, which is at the moment a far more serious problem than all the known side effects of the pill on the woman of reproductive age. These pills are so satisfactory in preventing contraception that they deserve full and earnest testing. They are sexually most satisfactory for the participants because there is no mechanical interference, no messy jellies, no need for any sort of adjustment—they permit the quality of spontaneity.

The other oral contraceptive, known as the "sequential method," consists of two pills. The estrogenic hormone is taken daily for the first 14, 15, or 16 days, and this inhibits ovulation. The second pill, colored differently to distinguish it from the first, is a mixture of synthetic estrogen and progestin. It is taken for 5 days to ensure that there will be orderly bleeding within 3 to 5 days after the fifth pill is taken, thus completing the cycle. In this second method the pills are taken for a total of 20 to 21 days consecutively. The fact that there are two kinds of pills, each taken for different periods of time, is too complicated for some women to follow.

As with almost all medications one must weigh the long-term benefits against the possible mild anxiety syndromes so easily aroused in such an important hormonal adjustment. There is no doubt that either pill method affords the married partners the most satisfactory and natural sexual relations without the threat of an unwanted pregnancy. There is now available another contraceptive pill called Ovulen which is taken every day of the year, obviating the problem of calendar check. It can be taken as regularly as the breakfast coffee. Cessation of the regimen is followed almost immediately by a pregnancy, if so desired and planned.

Only a very few women are advised not to use the contraceptive pill. These include women with liver trouble, kidney disorders, high blood pressure, or the tendency to blood congestion or clots. Such women are advised to use other methods, such as IUD's or the combination diaphragm and jelly.

Popular Brands and Dosages of the Pill

Combination Hormones	Color	Progestin (mgm)	Estrogen (mgm)
Enovid-E (Searle)	Pale pink	2.5	0.1
Norinyl (Syntex)	White	2.0	0.1
Norinyl-1 (Syntex)	White	1.0	0.05
Norlestrin (Parke, Davis)	Pink	2.5	0.05
Norlestrin-21, 1 mg. (Parke, Davis)	Yellow	1.0	0.05
Norlestrin-28, 1 mg. (Parke, Davis)	White	1.0	0.05
Ortho-Novum 1 mg. (Ortho)	Yellow	1.0	0.05
Ortho-Novum 2 mg. (Ortho)	White	2.0	0.1
Ovral (Wyeth)	White	0.05	0.05
Ovulen-21 (Searle)	White	1.0	0.1
Provest (Upjohn)	Yellow	10.0	0.5

Sequential Hormones			
C-Quens (Lilly)	White (15)		0.8
	Peach (5)	2.0	0.8
Oracon (Mead Johnson)	White (16)		
	Pink (5)	25.0	0.1
Ortho-Novum SQ (Ortho)	White (14)		0.8
	Blue (6)	2.0	0.8

The above pills have been tested and proven to be effective as contraceptives. However, the exceptions, those women who conceive while taking the pills, have almost invariably missed a day or two, and could become pregnant immediately. If a day is missed, the dose should be doubled for the following day.

Experiments are being conducted on a mini-pill to be taken every day; intramuscular injections once a month; subcutaneous implants lasting a year; and "morning-after" pills, used only when needed. The latter should appeal to those who do not indulge in coitus frequently. Contraceptive pills, drugs, and hormone injections for males are also being investigated.

Intrauterine devices—IUD's (98 per cent effective): Small objects made of plastic, stainless steel, or even gold may be inserted into the uterus by the physician, to remain there indefinitely and to prevent pregnancies so long as they remain in place. Usually such devices are provided with a connecting nylon thread which projects through the cervix. The thread can be detected at any time, and this reassures the woman that the device is still in place. Such devices are designed to obstruct the implantation of the fertilized ovum in the lining of the uterus, not to prevent ovulation or fertilization. The exact mechanism

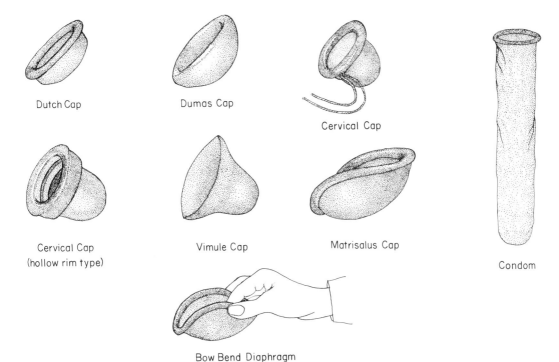

Dutch Cap

Dumas Cap

Cervical Cap

Cervical Cap
(hollow rim type)

Vimule Cap

Matrisalus Cap

Condom

Bow Bend Diaphragm

Some mechanical methods of contraception

is not fully understood. They may so affect the endometrium (lining) of the uterus that it is totally (but temporarily) unsuitable for the implantation of the fertilized ovum. We do know that there must be a delicate balance between the fertilized ovum and the condition of the uterine lining in order to ensure proper implantation.

Such devices have the advantage over the pill in that once in place they may be safely forgotten; no other precautions are necessary to prevent conception. In a few women IUD's tend to wander. However, the woman can always check their presence by locating the attached nylon thread in the cervical canal. The devices can be removed easily by the physician whenever a pregnancy is desired. In a small percentage of cases there may be some slight discomfort at first. There may be some minor bleeding, slightly heavier flow at the usual menstrual period, and occasional complaints of associated cramps or pain. Such devices should not be inserted prior to the first pregnancy, since the cervical canal is narrow and the uterus small. The best time to insert an IUD is immediately after the delivery of the first child. It prevents pregnancy almost as well as the pill, particularly if the woman checks regularly to see that it is still in place. Only about 21 per cent of all women using IUD's become preg-

Intrauterine devices (IUD) now available and in use
BIRNBERG BOW: Radio-opaque plastic can be located by fluoroscopy or radiograph. Two sizes. (Schneller & Co., 250 West 18th St., New York) 92% effective. ZIPPER RING: Handmade roll of nylon thread, designed in Chile. A modified version of thicker nylon tied in several places, designed in Egypt, known as Ragab ring. MARGULIES COIL (GYNFKOLL): Radio-opaque polyethylene plastic, two sizes. (Ortho Research Foundation, Raritan, N.J.) 97% effective. LIPPES LOOP: Radio-opaque polyethylene, made in four sizes identified by color of attached nylon thread. Smallest 25 mm. diameter has blue thread; 27.5 mm. has black thread; 30 mm. yellow thread; 30 mm. thick has white thread. 96% effective. SHAMROCK LOOP: A continuous triple loop somewhat like the Szontagh IUD designed in Hungary. MAJZLIN-SPRING: Finely tempered steel or gold wire spring pressed together for insertion and expands in uterus from wall to wall. (Anka Research, 139–01 Archer Avenue, Jamaica, Queens, New York) HALL-STONE RING: Flexible steel ring, as with all IUD's has a nylon thread attached for removal. (Goshen Instrument Co., P.O. Box 102, Goshen, New York) 90% effective. SAF-T-COIL: Made of radio-opaque polyethylene, supplied packed in its own introducer. (Julius Schmid Pharmaceuticals, 423 West 55th Street, New York) 96% effective.

nant, and when properly checked the effectiveness is 98 per cent. There seem to be fewer possible side effects than with the pill. However, not all possible long-term effects may have been revealed, since the modern versions of these devices have been used for only about a decade under scientific conditions. One thing in their favor is that they in no way alter the normal hormone cycle of the woman. Thus, whatever cycle she has been accustomed to will continue.

METHODS NOT REQUIRING CONSULTATION WITH PHYSICIAN

Coitus interruptus (Male withdrawal—78 to 85 per cent effective): If the man withdraws his penis from the woman's vagina before the ejaculation of semen, there can be no fertilization of the ovum even during the fertile period of the month. This requires practice and self-control on the part of the man. Even so, some sperm may escape before the climax, and only one spermatozoon is required for fertilization, although conception is unlikely unless at least 20 million spermatozoa per cubic centimeter are released. Coitus interruptus, which has been widely practiced, has been held responsible for many failures in birth control. It is generally unacceptable because it does not allow for full sexual expression under natural conditions. It is particularly frustrating for the woman, since she usually comes to climax after the man.

Douche (40 to 66 per cent effective): If the vagina is flushed with a spermicidal solution immediately after intercourse, the spermatozoa may be killed before they can enter the cervical canal and uterus. Since this entrance into the cervical canal can occur within 90 seconds after ejaculation, the woman has to dash for the bathroom immediately. Thus this method, too, involves an interruption of intercourse, at least for the woman, and is rightly judged to be unacceptable.

The condom (83 to 88 per cent effective): Invented by Gabriel Fallopius and in use since the 1500's, this is a rubber sheath which is worn over the penis during intercourse, thus catching all semen and preventing the deposition of sperm within the vagina. It has long been used to prevent contraction of venereal and other infections. If used in conjunction with a vaginal foam, cream, or jelly, and if it is not torn or does not slip off, the condom will prove effective. Aesthetically it does not prove to be satisfactory. Many women complain that their husbands slip out of the condom, leaving it behind in the vagina. Condoms are available at all drugstores without prescription.

Sponge and foam A spermicidal powder or solution is placed on a small sponge, which is then squeezed to develop a foam and placed in the vagina directly over the cervical opening. It must remain in place for at least six hours after intercourse. Oozing of the foam from the vagina is likely to be objectionable.

Chemical methods (80± per cent effective): Any of these chemical methods involve insertion of vaginal suppositories, jellies, or creams into the vagina. This coats the vaginal canal and cervical opening with a spermicidal medium (powerful sperm killer). Protection against conception is provided for only about one hour, since the chemicals may be emitted from the body or absorbed and dissipated. Effectiveness is therefore variable, but is increased tremendously when combined with a diaphragm or cervical cap. The vaginal foams are the most effective, followed by the jellies and creams, probably because the foam expands and fills all crevices and pockets of the vagina. Drainage of the chemicals from the vagina can be objectionable, and the foaming tablets may produce a temporary burning sensation. The vaginal foams are generally inserted with an applicator, the tablets are moistened and inserted, and the conical suppositories are inserted long enough before intercourse to melt and coat the lining of the vagina completely. (Delfen or Emko vaginal foam, Delfen, Koromex-A, Preceptin, Immolin, Lanesta, Cooper, and Veritas creams and jellies are most frequently used.)

The approximate cost per application of the various chemical devices is:

Method	Approximate Cost per Use
Foam liquid plus sponge	3.6¢
Jelly and diaphragm	6.5¢
Aerosol foam	8.0¢
Foam tablets	8.3¢
Jelly or cream alone	10–15¢
The pill	$1.30 per month

sterilization

This method of birth control involves an operation for either man or woman (more easily accomplished for the man). Millions of men in India have been surgically sterilized, and the operation does not lessen one's sexual appetite or alter one's emotions. In most cases the operation is quick, permanent, and no other contraceptive method is ever again necessary.

Sterilization is recommended when a pregnancy would endanger the life of the mother or health of the future child. If serious hereditary defects may be passed on to the children in a particular marriage, sterilization of the parent genetically carrying the tendency is usually advised. If and when a couple have had all the children they care for, or can properly take care of, they sometimes request sterilization.

Sterilization of the man, called vasectomy, is simple and can be done in the doctor's office and under local anesthesia. A small incision is made in the scrotum on each side. The sperm duct (vas deferens) is located, tied, and cut. A stitch closes each incision, recovery is complete in a few days, and the man is totally unaware of any change—but he is functionally sterile.

Sterilization of the woman requires an abdominal operation and a hospital stay of several days. The ducts from the ovary (Fallopian tubes) are tied on each side and cut, thus preventing the descent of any ova toward the uterus. The operation can be performed right after childbirth, better after a Caesarean section. Here too there is no alteration in the emotional or menstrual cycles, but the woman is henceforth sterile. Reversal of these surgical methods of sterilization is theoretically possible but practically difficult.

There remains one more method, and it is irreversible: castration (removal of testes). Moreover, it is one which does alter one's sexual and emotional life and behavior. Historically, castration has been used to produce harem eunuchs and castrati singers. The former were adult slaves altered to serve Oriental despots; the latter were boys delivered by their fathers to papal choirs or to the concert stage.

artificial insemination

Since one of five married couples is biologically sterile, contraception is often not the problem. Such couples often desire children, and when it can be demonstrated that the male partner is sterile, or of low fertility, artificial insemination of his fertile wife can be achieved, either by concentrating samples of his semen until the quantity of viable sperm is adequate or agreeing to the insemination of the wife by an obstetrician who obtains the semen from a donor chosen because of his physical, intellectual, and ethnic suitability—but never revealed to husband or wife. This is being done in thousands of instances in the United States each year, giving the couple a child of at least one of them. By timing the inseminations with respect to ovulation it is possible to sway the pendulum toward the 80 per cent probability of production of male offspring.

what does the child inherit?

In an effort to understand how children inherit inborn characteristics from their parents, scientists in a number of disciplines
have compiled statistics, charted human and animal development through generations, analyzed the chemistries and dynamics of cells, temporarily kept embryos alive in a test tube,
and even synthesized some of the enzymes (special proteins
which are essential to digestion and other metabolic functions)
found in living things. While they are not yet in a position to
answer the direct question: "What does the child inherit?" they
have gained some insight into the interaction of heredity and
environment in the growth and maturation of the fetus.

It never ceases to astonish the scientist that that extraordi-
narily complex creature known as man develops from a single
fertilized egg cell. It has prompted him to search on the molecular scale for the basic mechanisms that enable the seeming
miracle of conception to occur and development and differentiation to unfold. He knows now that each parent contributes to
the fertilized ovum an estimated 24,000 different chemical units
that influence the development of the child. Each unit, called a

gene, is thought to be a giant molecule made up of thousands of atoms. Individual human genes are far too small to be seen under a conventional light microscope, and there are obstacles to their being observed even under an electron microscope. Nevertheless, genes can be detected and exactly located by animal breeding experiments and by the use of viruses that isolate and transport bits of genetic material.

Many genes—a thousand or more—are strung out like a chain on each chromosome. The various chromosomes in any given cell are uniform neither in length nor in shape. Yet there is a regularity and repeatability even in their differences, so that they are identifiable. Every somatic (body) cell normally has exactly the same group of chromosomes as every other cell, and every member of a species tends to have exactly the same number and types of chromosomes. This leads biologists to conclude that each chromosome has its own specialized list of functions in heredity.

There are 46 chromosomes in every human somatic cell— 23 contributed by each parent through his or her germ cells. At certain definite times they line up into 23 pairs, each pair representing the two parents. Many of the paired genes in these chromosomes differ minutely—for example, possibly in the way in which they order the construction of proteins. One gene may be more effective than its partner; it will predominate while the less effective gene will be masked. Thus when we speak of dominant and recessive genes we mean, among other things, that the cell may construct proteins which are, for example, mirror images of each other so that one has preferential expression. Of course, if the paired genes happen to be identical, then neither dominates. And dominance should be understood as a relative factor—one trait may mask another, but it will not wipe out the recessive or masked gene as a genetic potential.

When a newly fertilized ovum divides, all of the constituent genes in its 46 chromosomes must synthesize like genes (that is, construct them out of the available chemicals in such a manner that the original chromosomes are all duplicated). This assures that when the chromosomes split lengthwise during cell division, every resulting daughter cell will contain the same chromosomes and their genes as the parent cell. The most remarkable fact of life is that the gene can copy itself; even a mutated gene is capable of ordering exact copies of itself. If the genes were not so stable, it would be difficult for any species to reproduce itself.

Biologists have discovered that the fundamental ingredient of each gene (and therefore of the chromosomes) is a chemical called deoxyribonucleic acid (DNA). This DNA is a giant molecule comprising five common chemical elements: carbon, hydrogen, oxygen, nitrogen, and phosphorus. Carbohydrates (sugars and starches), however complex, consist of only carbon, hydrogen, and oxygen. Lipids (fats and fatlike substances) sometimes contain other elements, especially phosphorus and nitrogen. Proteins are far more complex than either carbohydrates or starches and contain at least nitrogen and usually phosphorus as well. (One crucial question that must be answered by unmanned or manned probes of Mars is whether its atmosphere contains nitrogen; the absence of that essential element would rule out the existence of even a simple form of life as we know it.) These five elements in the various proteins are arranged in two long chains of alternating sugar and phosphate molecules and nitrogen bases (side chains), all held together by bonds known as cross links.

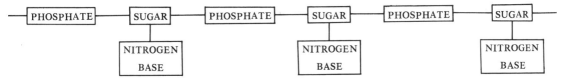

Analysis of the nitrogen bases reveals that there are four in all: adenine (A), thymine (T), guanine (G), and cytosine (C). A single DNA molecule contains thousands of these subunits, in different arrangements. DNA is tightly coiled in a double helix and packed very densely in the cell nuclei. The human body contains enough DNA to reach the moon and return 20,000 times if all of it were laid out in a line.

As a cell is about to divide into two daughter cells which are each identical to it, the DNA double helix in the chromosomes untwines to form two single chains. But each single chain is chemically incomplete by itself, so it seeks appropriate nitrogen bases with which to couple; adenine always joins thymine, and guanine always joins cytosine. In this way each half-chain actually synthesizes its opposite number, forming a complete new double-helical DNA molecule. (Another way of putting it is to say that each chain serves as a template on which the complement of itself is built.) Since the sequence of protein synthesis is stable, the genetic code which transmits hereditary characteristics remains exactly the same. Each DNA molecule has thousands of possible arrangements, however, and this accounts for the differences between the 48,000 genes in each somatic cell. It is conceivable, though unlikely, that no two of the 48,000 genes will be identical. The sequence AGC at some point may have a very different message from GAC, for example.

But how do the chemical units of heredity (genes) determine the ultimate differentiation of cells into numerous types, such as muscle, nerve, and blood? Does each of the specialized somatic cells require its own special arrangement of DNA? Or are they all bearers of the same genetic code? If the latter is true, then why does each cell carry out different instructions? The theory currently in favor is that the master plan for the entire organism is contained in each and every cell. In fact, experiments with lower animals, such as frogs, have shown that a complete animal will develop even if the nucleus of the fertilized ovum is replaced by that of a somatic cell from a somewhat older embryo of the same species. Further proof is that if the cells of the two-cell human embryo could be mechanically separated, twins would be produced who are identical and complete.

If DNA were the only class of nucleic acid, we would still be at a loss to account for the differentiation of cells. After all, DNA molecules never leave the nucleus except during mitosis[1] (division of the cell into two daughter cells), therefore they cannot play a direct role in the construction of proteins. But DNA is capable of collecting additional oxygen atoms and producing another nucleic acid, RNA (ribonucleic acid). RNA, on the other hand, can circulate freely in the cytoplasm and order the specific arrangements of amino acids—and thereby the building blocks of proteins. Because RNA acts as an intermediary between the DNA and the cytoplasm, scientists speak of its "messenger" role. (Actually, the cytoplasm also contains at least two other types of RNA, called transfer RNA and ribosomal RNA.) Since DNA begets RNA and not the reverse, DNA must ultimately control the entire life mechanism. Precise details of the building process are not yet fully understood, but enormous strides have been made in molecular genetics in the last two decades.

Let us return to the relatively gross structure of the 23 pairs of chromosomes found in every human somatic cell. Of these, 22 pairs are concerned primarily with the general physical and mental characteristics of the individual; for this reason

1. Even during mitosis the migration of DNA from the nucleus of the old cell to that of the new is performed not by individual DNA molecules but by entire aggregates (chains) acting as a cohesive unit. These chains are none other than the chromosomes.

they are known as autosomes. The remaining two chromosomes are known as the sex chromosomes, since their presence or absence is related primarily to sexual differences.

For purposes of identification the 22 autosomes are numbered from 1 to 22 (progressing from largest to smallest), but the sex chromosomes are designated merely as X or y, depending on how they appear under the microscope. The normal female, whether infant, child, or mature woman, has in every cell of her body 22 pairs of autosomes plus two large X chromosomes, whereas the normal male has a complement of 22 pairs of autosomes plus an X and a small y that is physically less than one-quarter the size of the X. Obviously, then, the presence of the diminutive y chromosome normally establishes maleness in the sense of both primary and secondary sexual characters—and X-y combination results in a male.[2] It would be grossly unfair for a man to complain that his wife bears him only daughters, since the female produces ova with only X chromosomes; he himself must contribute the necessary y. The spermatozoa decide the sex of the prospective child, and this is fixed at the moment of conception. Whether a sperm carrying an X chromosome or a y fertilizes the ovum is nothing but a grand lottery that hinges on the outcome of the great sperm race, and is therefore pure chance in normal circumstances.

The geneticist can identify the chromosomes in fetal blood cells, in epithelial cells from the lining of its mouth, or even in the few loose cells found in the amniotic fluid surrounding the fetus. Although sex can be determined conclusively through the presence or absence of a y chromosome or the presence of the Barr body[3] in the cell, obstetricians currently feel that it is inadvisable to attempt to discover the sex of every child before birth. Heart rate is not a reliable criterion, and X rays may cause anomalies. There is a technique called amniocentesis, in which amniotic fluid from the sac surrounding the fetus may be sampled by using a hollow needle inserted through the mother's abdomen. This procedure is still too risky for routine determination of sex and is used only when the obstetrician suspects some specific anomaly, such as Mongolism or cystic fibrosis, or when excess fluid is exerting undue pressure (polyhydramnios).

2. There are also so-called mosaics—abnormal combinations of sex chromosomes, and these are discussed later in this chapter.

3. Female cells possess a structure (the Barr body) that can be stained and the resultant color detected under a microscope. If this structure is missing, then the fetus must be a male. This finding is extremely useful to research scientists, because it enables them to study the development of a fetus before there are any telltale external signs of sex.

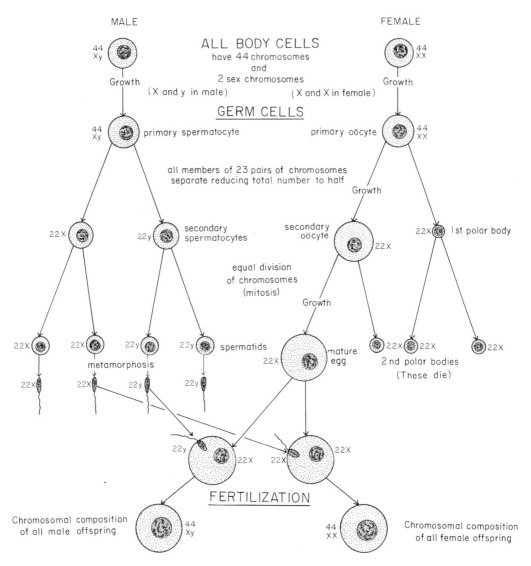

MALE

ALL BODY CELLS
have 44 chromosomes
and
2 sex chromosomes

FEMALE

44
Xy

Growth

(X and y in male)   (X and X in female)

44
XX

Growth

GERM CELLS

44
Xy   primary spermatocyte   primary oöcyte   44
XX

all members of 23 pairs of chromosomes
separate reducing total number to half

Growth

22 X   22y secondary   secondary   22X 1st polar body
              spermatocytes   oöcyte
                                          22X

equal division
of chromosomes
(mitosis)

Growth

22X   22X   22y   22y spermatids   22X 22X   22X
         metamorphosis   22X   mature   2nd polar bodies
                                               egg   (These die)

22X   22X   22y   22y

22y
       22X   22X   22X

FERTILIZATION

Chromosomal composition
of all male offspring

44
Xy

44
XX

Chromosomal composition
of all female offspring

Human sex determination

The production of spermatazoa and eggs can be schematized to show how the two processes are basically the same.

The first stage (spermatagonia and oögonia) is found abundantly from a period long before birth and is represented in the uppermost cells. These cells multiply many times but then grow by accumulating protoplasm. This signals that the maturation stages are to follow since most first-stage cells only multiply. With growth the "primary" cells divide into "secondary" spermatocytes (equal in size) and oöcytes (unequal). In this division process chromosome pairs are separated so that no pair goes into any resulting cell, only one member of each pair. Since the original number is 44 plus the sex chromosomes (XX or Xy), this represents 22 pairs so that the resulting cells have 22 chromosomes plus one or the other of the sex chromosomes (X or y). The original number of chromosomes is restored at fertilization. Another division follows, again unequal in the female, resulting in a still larger egg cell and another discarded polar body. The spermatids metamorphose into spermatozoa by loss of protoplasm and the gaining of a middle piece and a tail. The mature egg is inert but has a food supply (yolk). The mature sperm cell is motile but lacks any food supply.

Chromosomal complexes of the human male and female These chromosomes are found in the nucleus of every cell of the body; those of the females with the XX female sex determining) chromosomes on the left and of the males with the Xy (male sex determining) chromosomes on the right.

The photographs above are of the chromosomes arranged as pairs. Below they are seen randomly distributed as usually found in the cell nucleus.

Why are more boys born each year than girls?[4] After all, the ratio of X chromosomes to y chromosomes is 1 to 1 in the spermatozoa, since these are produced in equal numbers by meiosis in the testes. It has been conjectured that this unbalance occurs because spermatozoa carrying y chromosomes are smaller and lighter than those carrying X chromosomes, and hence can swim slightly faster toward the waiting ovum. This

4. The record for the total population is 106 males to 100 females. There is some slight evidence that as the man grows older his offspring sex ratio more nearly approaches 1 to 1. This may indicate greater survival of the X-bearing spermatozoa. Among 13,372 first births at Columbia Presbyterian Hospital, New York, from 1958 to 1967, 50.6 per cent were males, so the over-all ratio is shifted with subsequent pregnancies.

Barr body

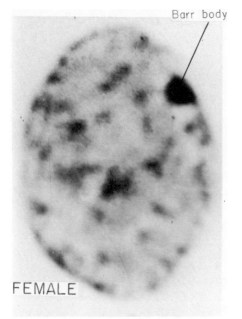

FEMALE

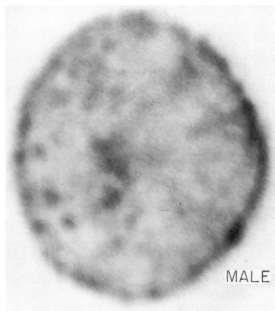

MALE

Nuclei from the amniotic fluid cells of the fetus
The sex of the unborn human child can be determined by examining the nuclei of intermitotic amniotic cells, if and when available, since the cells of a female child invariably show the presence, in these nuclei, of the so-called Barr body, first discovered in 1954. This is a distinct body at the periphery of the nucleus which takes the Feulgen stain, and is best identified when in the intermitotic or non-chromosomal phase.

hypothesis has been applied experimentally to artificial insemination: if the sperm samples are centrifuged, the sperm with the heavier X chromosomes will tend to settle. Sperm ladled off the top, then, should—and do—contain a higher proportion of y chromosomes. Timing of coitus in relation to ovulation can also alter the ratio toward more males.

The X and y chromosomes do more than establish the sex of the individual. Genes associated with these chromosomes also determine, for example, whether that individual is to be color-blind or a hemophiliac (bleeder). These abnormalities are produced by recessive genes attached only to the X chromosome. The y chromosome of the sex pair does not carry these genes. Therefore, the recessive genes in the X chromosome will take over in these cases. This is why few women are color-blind—the other X chromosome in a female usually does not contain another gene for color blindness, so the undesirable but recessive color-blindness genes will be masked by the normal color-sensitive gene. The same is true of hemophilia, but with one crucial difference: if both X chromosomes contain this abnormal gene, the fetus will die. There are no female hemophiliacs, only carriers of hemophilia.

The unique roles played by the X and y chromosomes permit us to speak of sex-linked inheritance. For example, a man can transmit color blindness or hemophilia to his daughters, but not to his sons, since the pertinent genes are never associated with his y chromosomes. But such daughters would be carriers rather than actually be color-blind or hemophilic. There are also hereditary characters, such as baldness, which may be inherited by both sexes, but which are expressed only in the male (although 10 per cent of all women suffer from thinning hair). These are called sex-limited characters, since their expression is (usually) limited to one sex.

Would it be possible to establish which of the genes in any child came from the mother and which from the father? Aside from sex-linked conditions and from certain striking physical traits which are accounted for by a limited number of dominant genes, the genetic profile of an individual is hopelessly clouded by the sheer number of possible combinations of genes—they number in the billions or trillions. To begin with, the 24,000 or so genes contributed by each parent were in turn drawn from a pool of 48,000 that was endlessly reshuffled during the maturation of the germ cells. Next came a halving process that resulted in 23 single chromosomes (with their 24,000 genes) in each spermatozoon or ovum instead of 23 pairs of chromosomes (with 48,000 genes). Finally came the realignment within the fertilized ovum of genes contributed by each parent. *Barring identical twins, it is all but impossible for two biological partners to produce a second offspring identical to their first,* even if they lived to be a thousand and remained active and fertile all the while. And if they would and did procreate to this extent, they would observe to their surprise some wide dissimilarities among their children as well as some striking resemblances.

One sometimes hears the observation that a certain child inherited his father's or grandfather's ears or nose or eyes. Sometimes this is no more than fancy, but even if it is true, what it really means is that with a limited number of obvious physical traits there is a clear-cut dominance of one influence over another. Only one-quarter of the genes inherited by a child can come from any one grandparent, yet that fixed portion might contain a high percentage of dominant genes relating to prominent physical characteristics. This would account for any striking surface resemblance. It must be remembered that every individual contains thousands of other hereditary influences, many of which are subtler and far less prominent. We see only the dominating influences of an individual (his or her phenotype), but the complete genetic make-up (the genotype) is not always revealed. Disguised influences may appear in one's descendants in unforeseen ways.

There is still another mechanism that influences variations in related individuals. It is known as crossover. When the 23 chromosomes from the sperm and the 23 from the ovum pair, each member of a pair entwines itself lengthwise around its partner. This conjugation of homologous chromosomes from the two parents aligns their corresponding genes. Eventually the developing fetus will form its own germ cells, ultimately either sperm or ova. In the production of sperm or ova, the so-called diploid number of chromosomes (46) must be reduced to the haploid number (23) by a halving process known as meiosis. During meiosis, the two paired or intertwined chromosomes of a pair may break at corresponding positions. The separated portions may then reattach themselves to the conjugate member of the pair rather than to the chromosome they have broken away from. This crossing over or exchange of equivalent parts takes place only between paired chromosomes. It may result in the trading of anything from a few genes to almost an entire chromosome. While crossing over occurs only occasionally, it helps to ensure that characters from either parent are not inherited always in blocks.

Despite the possibility that all human beings must be related through common ancestry, not all of the genes now in circulation could have been present in the first few primordial ancestors of man. There has been evolution, and new inheritable characters have come into being through sudden changes known as mutations. Mutations can and do occur naturally in living organisms, but there is a greater likelihood of this occurring if the reproductive cells are subjected to ionizing radiation or to certain chemicals. Mutations are not purposeful and do not occur in response to some need of the species; they occur at random, and cannot be evaluated as "good" or "bad" on any moral or purposeful basis. Since it is presumed that the individual's genes have good survival value by virtue of their existence, deviations are harmful perhaps 99 per cent of the time. One hypothesis advanced for the disappearance of dinosaurs is that mutations resulted in a tendency to excessive size. The beasts became cumbersome and unwieldy, hence easy prey for smaller, more mobile animals. Perhaps more important, some of the outsized dinosaurs might have required so much food to satisfy their metabolic requirements that they gradually starved in the midst of plenty. We should not regard dinosaurs condescendingly—after all, they lasted almost 150 million years!

Many mutants drop by the wayside—the affected individuals may not live to reproductive age. Untold numbers of defective as well as desirable genes must have been purged in this manner. Of course, some genes do confer an advantage, and these tend to be perpetuated, since they increase the individual's chances for survival.

Through the years, scientists have painstakingly compiled a list of dominant and recessive characters in the human. These are tabulated in Appendix D. Although there are numerous exceptions, by and large desirable genes are dominant and undesirable ones recessive. This may be because natural selection has eliminated many undesirable traits. All of us are mixtures of dominant and recessive genes, so-called hybrids. If closely related persons marry, there is a greater than usual risk that two recessive (and usually undesirable) genes will coincide in the offspring, resulting in a higher incidence of congenital anomalies and early deaths. In certain states it is unlawful for relatives closer than first cousins to wed. Even this may provide only a dubious safety factor. In isolated parts of the country (and in Japan) marriage of close relatives (consanguinity) is still common, with the result that certain hereditary traits are prominent. Like the history of the royal dynasties of Europe, such pedigrees have provided valuable information about the mechanics of inheritance, but they affirm all the more the desirability of diverse heritages from the standpoint of survival. A deliberate mongrelization enables many undesirable or recessive traits to be obscured by the dominant member of each homologous pair of genes. Hybrids, which arise through the mixing of pure breeds, are almost invariably healthier, more fertile, and longer-lived than purebreds or thoroughbreds. All humans are hybrids to some degree. The likelihood of deleterious mutations that become homozygous (that is, inherited from both parents), and hence phenotypic (expressed in the child), is always greater in children of closely related people. Childhood abnormalities are more frequent, as is also sterility.

The degrees of shared heredity are summarized in the following table:

50 Per Cent	25 Per Cent	12.5 Per Cent	6.25 Per Cent
father	grandparent	great-grandparent	great-grandparent's parent
mother	grandchild	great-grandchild	great-grandchild's child
son	uncle	grand-uncle	grand-uncle's child
daughter	aunt	grand-aunt	grand-aunt's child
brother	nephew	grand-nephew	grand-nephew's child
sister	niece	grand-niece	grand-niece's child
		cousin	cousin's child (first cousin once removed)

Eye color in man   B = Brown—dominant, b = blue—recessive. Another actual pedigree of eye-color inheritance shows both parents to have brown eyes (solid black) but since they had blue-eyed children we know immediately that neither parent was pure (homozygous) for brown eyes but both carried the recessive gene known as blue (b) eye, or Bb heterozygous. But this apparent confusion is resolved for the parents but not for the brown-eyed brothers and sisters because they could be Bb or BB; in either case they would express the brown eyes but could be like their parents, heterozygous (Bb). The only way to tell would be to see how their own children of the next generation turned out.

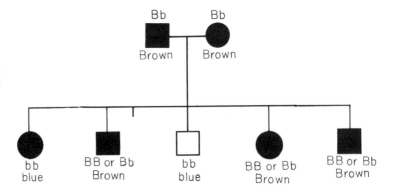

As things stand, nothing can be done to alter the genetic make-up of an unborn child. Its heredity was fixed at the moment that a particular sperm fertilized a particular ovum and every gene paired with its corresponding gene. There is a most fortunate aspect to this situation. It would be disastrous if the misbehavior, debauchery, ill temper, and maiming accidents of one generation could make their imprint on the next. Wars kill, but they can also leave many a man with no arms or legs, sight gone, hearing impaired, much of his internal organs removed. Yet none of this mutilation has any effect on a man's germ cells. If he is physically able to procreate, his sons and daughters will be born without these tragic souvenirs acquired during his lifetime.

Characters acquired during one's lifetime are never transmitted to one's offspring. The only voluntary influence a person can have on the heredity of his or her child lies in the selection of a spouse. This is seldom done scientifically, as in animal breeding, because the driving impetus is still primarily emotional rather than intellectual. Civilization has yet to evolve to the stage where individuals choose their mates at least in part on the basis of hereditary potential. No amount of education, financial support, or love can rectify the wrong combination of genes.

There is a simple scheme by which anyone can work out certain inheritance probabilities. Some physical characters, like those for ordering the basic structure of the heart, can't vary much without leading to abnormality, but most can have varied expressions. One obvious example is eye color, which is merely a range in the amount of pigmentation; darkness means a richness of pigment, blueness a lack. Since the tendency to develop dark-brown eyes always suppresses any simultaneous tendency to develop light-blue eyes when the two characters are present in the same individual, the former is clearly dominant, as is borne out by ample statistical evidence. We generally designate the dominant character of a pair by the capital letters of the name and the recessive by the lower-case letter. Thus in this case B would stand for brown, b for blue.

It stands to reason that a blue-eyed person has two genes for blue eyes (bb), since his (or her) eyes would be brown if a single B were present. Every brown-eyed person must have at least one gene for B, but he could be either BB or Bb. Knowing the color of his parents' and grandparents' eyes might resolve the ambiguity: if one parent has blue eyes, the brown-eyed child must be a Bb rather than a BB because that parent could contribute only a b gene. Of course, if both parents have brown eyes, there is no ready answer; he could be either Bb or BB. Thus one cannot always tell from a person's appearance (his phenotype) what his genetic make-up (his genotype) really is, since recessive genes are masked and emerge only when they are inherited from both parents. If a brown-eyed Bb man marries a brown-eyed Bb woman, their children's eyes may be either brown or blue. The probability is that out of four children, three will have brown eyes (one BB and two Bb) and one blue eyes (bb). However, such statistical probabilities apply only in families of large size. Further, the proud parents will not be able to tell immediately what this color will be, since it takes several weeks of exposure to light for the pigment to come out fully in the newborn infant.

What has just been illustrated is called the Second Mendelian Law of Inheritance (after Gregor Mendel, a nineteenth-century Austrian monk who observed inherited tendencies in flowers he was cultivating). This law emphasizes that there are at least two possible divergent influences for every hereditary character. The duality is a clear-cut one: a Bb child has eyes just as brown as if he were BB. The two genes do not merge, for when that child's germ cells mature he will be capable of passing either a B (brown) or a b (blue) tendency to his own offspring. Neither gene is altered by their sojourn together for one generation; there is no dilution or contamination of either tendency.

Most parents do not particularly care about the color of their children's eyes. But they are very much concerned about more vital characters. A number of these characters are presented in Appendix D, together with an indication of which alternative of each pair is dominant. By means of this table one can make some interesting predictions about the probability of

Inheritance of eye color in man B = Brown—dominant, b = blue—recessive. This actual pedigree of eye color inheritance shows that the father (square) has brown eyes (solid black) while the mother (circle) has blue eyes (clear). It is stated that brown (B) is dominant over blue (b). Note that this couple had two children, one with blue eyes (the boy) and one with brown eyes (the girl). The only way this could happen would be for the brown-eyed father to carry a recessive gene for eye color, namely the blue-eyed tendency. This proves that the father's genotype (Bb) is different from his phenotype (B) meaning that even though he is brown-eyed he covers up a hereditary tendency that he can give to his children, namely the (b) blue-eyed tendency. One could then say that the father was heterozygous for eye color (Bb) while the mother was homozygous (bb) meaning the pairs are identical. This also shows that eye color is inherited in the same manner by either son or daughter, hence is not sex-linked (i.e., associated with the sex or X chromosome).

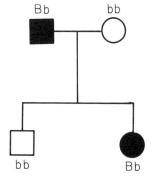

Bb bb

bb Bb

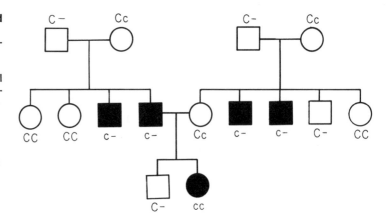

whether a child will be blue-eyed or brown-eyed, or whether it may exhibit other characters.

Recessive genes have been implicated in most (but by no means all) hereditary defects. It has been found that the *majority of inheritable abnormalities* are associated with nine particular chromosome pairs (numbers 4, 5, 13, 14, 15, 17, 18, 21, and 22). One such chromosomal abnormality is a condition known as trisomy—the presence of an extra chromosome related to one of the 23 pairs. About 8 per cent of all spontaneous abortions are caused by the contribution of an extra chromosome from the spermatozoon or the ovum. However, for some reason an individual can survive the period of gestation if his or her extra chromosome belongs specifically to pairs 13, 18, or 21. In other words, these trisomies are tolerable. It is estimated that 1 in every 200 persons is born with an extra chromosome.

In the original and by now classic studies of the fruit fly Drosophila (favored by geneticists because its life cycle is short and its chromosomes are few in number and relatively huge, hence more easily observable), an occasional fly was seen to have an extra y chromosome. Since this made it Xyy instead of Xy, it was called a "supermale." This trisomy of the sex chromosomes has recently been shown in humans to be prevalent among certain types of habitual criminals. The "supermale" human is more likely than most to be tall, not particularly bright, and tending toward antisocial behavior. One possible example is Richard Speck, who was convicted in Illinois for murdering eight nurses. Whether the presence of an extra y chromosome will ever be accepted by the legal profession as an automatic defense for psychopathic behavior, rather than merely as a sociobiological explanation, is purely conjectural at this time. In various courts around the world juries have thus far rejected such notions put forth by defense counsels. When there is an extra X, as in XXy, the result is called an "intersex," and physical males of this sort often exhibit cryptorchidism (testes retained in the body) and generally have low intelligence. It appears that the more the X chromosomes, the greater the possibility of retardation, and when there is at least one y chromosome, the possibility of bodily anomalies becomes greater with each additional X chromosome.

There are other possible intersex types—XXX and XO, among others. The XXX trisomy results in a "superfemale." Contrary to what one might expect, however, the superfemale is not an abundantly endowed woman (large breasts, rounded shape, long fertile period, and so forth). Instead, she tends to have underdeveloped breasts and small genitalia, and she either doesn't menstruate at all or else stops at an early age. In an XO female one sex chromosome is missing. This condition (Turner's syndrome) is generally accompanied by short sta re and subnormal development of the breasts and ovaries. It s ems as though the superfemale atrophies—"burns herself out '—and enters her menopause before or soon after she reaches puberty, whereas the XO female is hypotrophied—that is, she is incomplete because she never develops at all. With another X chromosome she would have become a normal female, but with a y chromosome added she would have become a normal male instead. There is no male or neuter counterpart to this—a yO or OO would abort in the embryonic stage.

The condition known as Mongolism has been associated

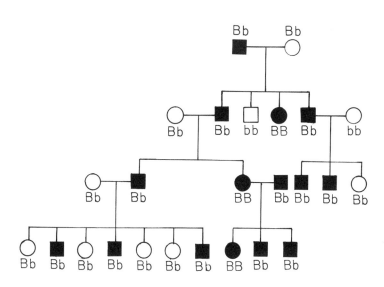

Inheritance of baldness (black), a sex-influenced character. Baldness (B) is dominant in men and recessive in women. In certain cases it may be due to a disease but the usual so-called "pattern baldness" seems to be due to inheritance. It is more common in men than in women; so that there must be some relation to sex. A bald man generally transmits baldness to half of his sons but very rarely to his daughters. If B represents a gene for Baldness, and b for nonbaldness, and B proves to be dominant in men but recessive in women, then the above pedigree chart can be fully explained. This is a case of what is called a sex-influenced character since the same genotype has a different expression in men and in women. Check the above chart and see how the genetic makeup of the original parents can be determined.

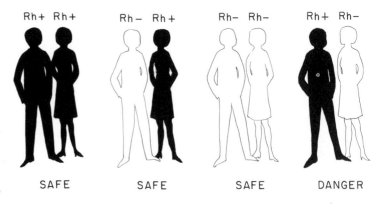

Rh+ Rh+   Rh− Rh+   Rh− Rh−   Rh+ Rh−

SAFE   SAFE   SAFE   DANGER

Rh factor problem   The agglutinating factor in human blood known as the Rh factor is generally identified by testing against an agglutinogen in monkey (Rhesus) blood. It can be positive (Rh+) as it is in 85% of Americans, or negative (Rh−) as it occurs in the other 15% (among Orientals the Rh− ratio is 5%). If Rh+ blood is transfused into an Rh− person, the recipient develops an immunizing effect against Rh+ blood so that further transfusion of the same type of blood may cause death.

But Rh factors can pass from an embryo through the placenta into the blood of the mother and if the embryo is Rh+ and the mother Rh−, the mother becomes immunized against further Rh+ invasion. If, for instance, an Rh+ man marries an Rh− woman, she will be immunized against Rh+ blood but will usually deliver her first child. However, she will retain her immunity against further children carrying the Rh+ from the same father, and this will cause agglutination and hemolysis of the fetal blood so that she may lose her second and succeeding children. The condition is known as erythroblastosis and is recognized, if the child is delivered, by anemia, jaundice, the accumulation of fluids in the tissues (edema); but often death of the fetus occurs some weeks before expected birth.

An average of 1 in 12 pregnancies is like that of the fourth couple in the diagram, hence carries the threat of erythroblastosis. Note that three of the possible Rh combinations do not carry any threat to the fetuses, or children born to these couples.

with the presence of an extra chromosome—number 21 in the numbering scheme used by geneticists. This is called Trisomic 21 of Mongolian idiots. Occasionally one of the parents will acquire a 24th chromosome in his or her sperm or ova. If this excess chromosome is number 21, then a Mongoloid child will result. Mongolism can be detected even before birth. It occurs much more often with mothers in their forties than with younger women. There is, however, a second mechanism by which Mongolism may come about, and this one is independent of age. For some reason one member of the 21st pair of chromosomes in a primitive germ cell of either parent may become linked with one chromosome of pair number 15. Although the amount of DNA is in no way altered, in effect there are only 45 chromosomes (one a number 15 chromosome that is attached to an unwanted passenger). Should this happen, that person could become a carrier for Mongolism when it is his or her turn to have children. When germ cells divide, 23 chromosomes normally go with each spermatozoon or ovum. But a carrier could pass either a single 21st chromosome (which would be normal) or a 21st chromosome plus a second 21st chromosome that was riding on the 15th. These two number 21 chromosomes, together with the number 21 chromosome from the other parent, would add up to three—the fateful trisomy that inevitably results in Mongolism.

There are other possible trisomies. An extra chromosome of the 13–15 series results in extra fingers, hemorrhages of small capillaries, cleft palate, and various eye defects. An extra chromosome of the 17–18 series results in a reduced jaw, malformed ears, spasticity, and various skeletal anomalies. Chromosomal aberrations lead to a quantitative imbalance of the individual's hereditary (genetic) potential, and this can be expressed in a variety of ways, including anomalies.

It is possible for two intellectually normal or even superior individuals to conceive a certain kind of feeble-minded child if they both carry the recessive gene for that abnormality. Only 25 per cent of the children of such parents would possibly be feeble-minded, and then only if they had many children. However, 50 per cent of their children, although coming from normal parents, would be carriers for the gene that produces feeble-mindedness. The remaining 25 per cent would not only be completely normal but would also be genetically untainted by the recessive tendency to this feeble-mindedness. Parents may wish to avoid the risk of Mongolism or feeble-mindedness in their children, and might avoid further pregnancy if the first child turns out abnormal, thus revealing the masked presence of undesirable genes. A more positive and intelligent decision would be to consult an obstetrician or genetic counselor (a new breed of medical specialist). Feeble-mindedness is sometimes congenital rather than hereditary in origin, or it might be due to a chemical deficiency. It should also be borne in mind that Mendelian probabilities are not ironclad, especially with a small sample. Statistics are always based on large numbers. Parents might start out with two or three feeble-minded children in a row, or they might have children who are all phenotypically normal. The trouble with raw statistics is that they may lead to irrational decisions—like the European woman who stopped having children after her third because she had heard that every fourth child born in the world was Chinese!

There is no way to test the mental acuity of a newborn child. The inheritance of a tendency to feeble-mindedness will be revealed gradually as the child fails to develop along with his contemporaries. He simply doesn't have the physical potential to develop his intellect in a normal manner, no matter what is done for him, although he can improve within the limits of his unfortunate condition.

The feeble-minded child might inherit structural deficiencies in his brain, and possibly in other related systems as well. He might display poor motor coordination because he isn't capable of exercising effective nervous control over his muscles. He might be insensitive to all sorts of stimuli. His circulation might be poor. These are all physical properties that develop to different levels of perfection in different individuals. His feeble-mindedness, then, could reflect a composite of inherited deficits. It might also be the result of a deficiency of some chemical needed by the nervous system. No doubt someday some of these conditions will be rectifiable. The point is that intelligence is not inherited per se, but is dependent upon a normal physical foundation.

Society would like to improve its bank of hereditary potential. This means not only culling undesirable traits but increasing the proportion of favorable ones. Why could we not have a great many more musicians, for example? Unfortunately, while musical potential is inherited, it is not inherited as a unit, and the components are all recessive. There seem to be separate genes influencing perfect pitch, tonal memory, rhythm, and sensitivity to harmony or discord. Unless all of them are inherited together and homozygously, the individual is unlikely to become an accomplished musician. This may explain why despite having 20 children (by two musical wives) Johann Sebastian Bach's genetic legacy seemed to be dissipated in one or two generations: several sons, but not grandsons, showed musical talent that approached his own. Right now the only thing we can do with a man (or woman) fortunate enough to possess all of these recessive genes concomitantly is to subsidize him financially so that he can develop his potential to the limit. Perhaps at some future date scientists will learn how to enable him to bequeath his genes unfailingly.

The prospects for dealing with hereditary disabilities are by no means hopeless. More than one disease passed through the parents' genes has proved amenable to therapy or even to prevention. A case in point is the inherited blood factor (named Rh factor after the rhesus monkey used in the experiments that led to the discovery). About 85 per cent of the general population carry this blood factor and therefore are called Rh-positive; the 15 per cent who do not have it are called Rh-negative. The Rh-positive character is the genetically dominant one.

If the mother is Rh-positive, there is nothing to worry about, regardless of the father's Rh factor. There is likewise no risk if both parents are Rh-negative. But each year there are more than 200,000 marriages between Rh-negative women and Rh-positive men in the United States. Until quite recently these couples were unknowingly courting trouble and even tragedy.

Nothing untoward is likely to happen to the first child of such a union. But during its fetal development this child produces Rh-positive blood because that is the dominant tendency. The presence of the Rh factor is something foreign to the mother's own blood, and this stimulates the mother's body to produce antibodies against the invading substance. The fetus will not be affected by these antibodies unless they get into its bloodstream in considerable quantity, and this seldom happens. The second fetus, however, is not so fortunate, for by this time the mother is already equipped with a considerable capacity to produce antibodies to Rh-positive blood. These antibodies pass through the placenta into the bloodstream of the next fetus. The build-up of a substance known as bilirubin will attack its blood, producing anemia, jaundice, brain damage, and even heart failure in many instances. About 10,000 babies die each year because of this blood incompatibility, known as erythroblastosis fetalis. But 15 to 20 per cent of intrauterine fetuses with erythroblastosis die between 20 and 36 weeks. This disease, which need not be fatal if treated in time, may affect 10 per cent or more of the second pregnancies of such marriages; subsequent children are in increasingly greater danger because the amount of bilirubin builds up.

The knowledgeable obstetrician is alert to complications of this sort and takes proper precautions to try to save the lives of these children. If a critical level of anti-Rh antibody in the mother's blood is reached, it calls for immediate treatment of the fetus. This involves massive blood transfusion (to counter the antibody which is destroying the Rh-positive blood in the fetus), and if the pregnancy is in the eighth or ninth month the obstetrician may deliberately induce premature delivery, followed by an exchange transfusion. Suspected women are generally screened beginning at 26 weeks and continuing to 40 weeks. Usually the infants (if they survive) are monitored closely for the first three or four weeks after delivery, and booster transfusions are given as necessary.

Until a few years ago the only way to save any of these babies was to replace virtually 100 per cent of the blood following birth. But this was often too late to prevent death or brain damage. Then Dr. A. William Liley of New Zealand discovered how to transfuse Rh-negative blood into the body cavity of the fetus (at or after 30 weeks) with a long hypodermic needle. A radiologist would stand by at the fluoroscope and guide the obstetrician so that he would avoid piercing heart, lungs, or liver with the hypodermic needle. The technique is credited with saving about 35 per cent of the babies[5] who were destined to die without it.

Why, we may ask, can't something be done to protect the

5. So treated at the Columbia Presbyterian Medical Center in New York City by Dr. Vincent Freda and Dr. John Gorman.

blood of the fetus against the blood-destroying agents which can develop in the mother's blood? After all, doesn't the problem seem to be bound up with the broader question of allergies, immune antibodies, and the rejection of foreign tissue? The antibodies produced by the Rh-negative mother against the Rh-positive fetus are protein substances in the blood which can destroy the Rh-positive but not the Rh-negative red blood cells. Recently, after five years of intensive research, Drs. John Gorman and Vincent Freda of the College of Physicians and Surgeons, Columbia University, and Dr. William Pollack of the Ortho Research Foundation succeeded in releasing a new blood extract or immunoglobin known as Rhogam. This substance can be injected into any Rh-negative mother who has already had an Rh-positive child and who expects to become pregnant again by the Rh-positive father. Rhogam is usually given 24 hours after such a woman has experienced either a normal delivery or a miscarriage of an Rh-positive fetus (her first offspring). Mothers who have already been sensitized by this prior pregnancy cannot themselves benefit from the vaccine, but their blood will be useful as donor blood to other mothers faced with the prospect of losing their children to erythroblastosis. A foreign patient had one normal child, but then lost the next eight children because of this affliction, and a Toronto woman had fourteen living children before losing her fifteenth in this way. The obstetrician cannot predict the liability for any unborn child after the first, but he can test the mother's blood to determine whether it possesses a critical level of the antibodies to the Rh factor, and he can make certain that Rhogam is furnished within 24 hours of each miscarriage or birth.

Chemically, Rhogam is a gamma-globulin fraction that is rich in Rh antibodies. These antibodies are identical to those developed by the Rh-negative mother whose first baby had an Rh-positive father. When Rhogam is administered, her body reacts entirely differently from the way in which it would respond to the Rh factor—her blood does not produce a considerable number of immune bodies, since the intrusion is by the antibodies in the Rhogam rather than by the chemical they are trying to suppress. In effect the body is tricked into reducing the level of antibodies. This reduces the danger to future Rh-positive fetuses (which she can always expect with an Rh-positive husband). The inoculation method is obviously more desirable —as well as more successful—than the ingenious but hazardous fetal transfusion procedure. When properly carried out, the administration of Rhogam should be 99 per cent effective in protecting the lives of babies who might otherwise develop erythroblastosis.

There are other blood incompatibilities that may jeopardize the health of a fetus. For example, if the mother's blood is of type O and that of her fetus is of type A, the latter may develop jaundice (a condition which is not always fatal). Human blood can be classified in more than 2,764,800 different ways, and its component inheritance follows the usual Mendelian pattern, remaining unchanged through the life of the individual. The simpler categories are O, A, B, AB, M, N, and P. Because of this diversity of blood type combinations a specific individual can be identified positively from a sample of his or her blood, just as with the more than 190 million different fingerprints filed with the FBI.[6] This adds still more weight to one of our major contentions, namely, that no two babies can be alike in physical detail (except identical twins, who have contributed much to our understanding of human heredity).

Finger, palm, and foot prints are never duplicated among individuals. The palm creases appear in the fetus by three months, and by four months the fine palm lines have formed so as to unmistakably and permanently identify it—even five months before birth. Closely related people tend to have similar but never identical fingerprints.

Already more than 100 human skeletal mutations and another 100 eye variations have been described, most of which are tolerable. In fact mutations have been described for more than 200 specific genes among the estimated 24,000 or more found in the human. It has recently been estimated that the number of phenotypically possible different human beings would exceed a number made up of 1 followed by at least 143 zeros—far in excess of all humankind that has ever existed.

It is obviously possible for Rh-negative women to avoid complications in their offspring by deliberately not having a child by an Rh-positive man, and similar thinking can be applied to avoid other problems introduced by heredity. However, in this age in which man has unlocked the energy of the atom and set foot on the moon, anything may be possible. It is natural to wonder whether man can also modify his genes to rid them of tendencies to diabetes, gout, epilepsy, chorea, and a host of other afflictions which are recessive and may be due to faulty metabolism only. It is estimated that 5 per cent of the population carry paired genes for diabetes, and 10 per cent of American Negro males have red cells that are susceptible to

6. Information in correspondence from J. Edgar Hoover.

hemolysis by certain drugs because of a genetically determined enzyme defect.

What, then, does the child inherit? He inherits a vast array of potentials from each parent, grandparent, great-grandparent, etc., most of which are never realized. He inherits the physical basis or equipment for various levels of possible achievement and excellence in a variety of directions. Along with his composite inheritance which, because he exists, has survival value, he most assuredly also inherits undesirable or handicapping potentials which he can tolerate. Civilization and education afford this child opportunities to develop his talents. If only he could make the most of those opportunities!

"Many and diverse are the modes of interaction between heredity and environmental influences. And many and diverse are the resulting measurable human traits. The manifold combinations of these traits result in the most infinite diversity of human individuality, a diversity we are just beginning to comprehend."[7]

7. L. H. Snyder, *Principles of Heredity* (1949).

APPENDIXES

APPENDIX A *human embryo and fetus*
relation of age to crown-rump length and weight[1]

POST CONCEPTION AGE	LENGTH inches	LENGTH millimeters	WEIGHT ounces	WEIGHT grams
19 days	$\frac{1}{50}$	0.7		
20 days	$\frac{1}{25}$	1.5		
21 days	$\frac{1}{16}$	2.0–2.3		
22 days	$\frac{1}{8}$	2.5–3.0		
3–4 weeks	$\frac{1}{8}+$	2.8–3.8		
4 weeks	$\frac{3}{16}$	4–5	0.0007	0.02
5 weeks	$\frac{5}{16}$	7–8		
6 weeks	$\frac{1}{2}$	12–13		
7 weeks	$1\frac{1}{16}$	16–20		
8 weeks	$1\frac{1}{8}$	22–30	0.035	1.0
9 weeks	$1\frac{1}{2}$	35–45		
10 weeks	$2\frac{1}{8}$	48–55		
11 weeks	$2\frac{1}{2}$	64–66		
12 weeks	3	75–80	0.5–0.70	14–20
13 weeks	$3\frac{5}{8}$	91–93		
14 weeks	$4\frac{3}{16}$	105–107		
15 weeks	$4\frac{3}{4}$	119–121		
16 weeks	$5\frac{1}{4}$	132–134		
17 weeks	$5\frac{3}{4}$	147±	3.7–4.2	
18 weeks	$6\frac{1}{4}$	160±		
19 weeks	$6\frac{3}{4}$	173±		
20 weeks	$7\frac{1}{4}$	185±		
21 weeks	$7\frac{3}{4}$	197±	7.0–10.9	200–310
22 weeks	$8\frac{3}{16}$	208±		
23 weeks	$8\frac{1}{4}$	219±		
24 weeks	$9\frac{1}{4}$	236±	1 lb. 6 oz.	635–650
28 weeks	$10\frac{5}{8}$	270±		
32 weeks	$11\frac{3}{4}$	310±	2 lbs. 10 oz.	1,080–1,225
36 weeks	$13\frac{5}{6}$	346±	3 lbs. 10 oz.–4 lbs.	1,670–1,700
38 weeks	$14\frac{1}{2}$	362±	4 lbs. 12 oz.–5 lbs.	2,240–2,400

1. These measurements are only averages and may not apply to any specific case, although they may be very close.

APPENDIX B *drugs and pregnancy*

Medication Taken by the Mother	Possible Effects on Fetus or Newborn
Adrenaline	Bradycardia
Amethopterin	Anomalies, abortions
Ammonium chloride	Acidosis
Amyl nitrite	Increased fetal heart rate
Androgens (male hormones)	Masculinization of fetus
Anesthetics	Depression of fetus, asphyxia
Antiemetics, antidepressants, tranquilizers, sedatives	Effects similar to those of Thalidomide are possible
Antimetabolites	Hydrocephaly, cleft palate, infertility of the newborn
Antihistamines	Abortion or malformations
Aspirin	Persistent truncus arteriosus, abnormal heart
Barbiturates	Depressed breathing, drowsy fetus affected to 6 days
Bishydroxycoumarin (Dicoumarol)	Hemorrhage, fetal death
Blood pressure depressants	Respiratory problems, death
Chlorambucil (Leukeran)	Eye defects, abortions, absence of kidneys or ureters
Chloramphenicol, an antibiotic (Chloromycetin)	"Gray" syndrome, death, leukemia, damage to chromosomes
Chloroquine phosphate	Retinal and auditory damage, thrombocytopenia (?), death*
Cortison acetate	Anomalies, cleft palate (?), withdrawal syndrome
Cyclophosphamide	Anomalies
Demerol	Brain damage (?)
Dicoumeral	Hemorrhage, fetal death
Diuretics and potassium-depleting agents	Polycystic kidney disease
Erythromycin	Liver damage (?)
Estrogens (female hormones)	Malformations, hyperactivity of fetal adrenals
Ethyl bicoumacetate	Hemorrhage and fetal death

* Where the (?) is used it denotes that the evidence is taken from experimental animals rather than from human beings. It is obvious that some of the following will have to be modified or amended as further evidence comes in. It is probably correct to assume that all drugs are toxic in certain doses, and that they can, in most cases, reach the fetus by way of the mother and do damage to this relatively sensitive organism.

Medication Taken by the Mother	Possible Effects on Fetus or Newborn
Gantrisin	Hyperbilirubinemia (a blood disorder)
Heroin and morphine	Convulsions, tremor, neonatal death
Hexamethomium bromide	Neonatal ileus
Insulin shock	Fetal loss
Intravenous fluids in excess	Electrolyte imbalance, abnormalities
Isophenoxic acid	Elevation of serum protein-bound iodine
Lead	Anemia, hemorrhage, abortion, lead line in teeth
LSD (d-lysergic acid diethylamide)	Chromosomal anomalies, deformed babies
Methimazaole	Goiter and mental retardation
Methotrexate (Amethopterin)	Anomalies, abortion
Morphine	Addiction, respiratory depression, withdrawal symptoms
Nitrofurantoin	Hemolysis, dissolution of blood, hyperbilirubinemia
Norethisterone or Enovid	Androgenesis, masculinization
Novobiocin	Jaundice
Oral progestogens Androgens Estrogens	Secondary sex anomalies (?) Masculinization Feminization
Phenacetin	Anemia, death
Phenformin hydrochloride (DBI)	Lactic acidosis (?)
Phenobarbital in excess	Asphyxiation, brain damage (?), neonatal bleeding, death
Phenothiazines	Hyperbilirubinemia (?)
Potassium iodine	Goiter and mental retardation
Progestins	Masculinization of females
Propylthiouracil	Goiter and mental retardation
Protoveratrine	Fetal bradycardia
Quinine	Thrombocytopenia, congenital deafness, abnormal 8th nerve
Reserpine	Stuffy nose, drowsiness, hypothermia, respiratory problems, death
Salicylates, in excess (aspirin)	Neonatal bleeding, cardiovascular abnormalities possible, heart transposition (?)

Medication Taken by the Mother	Possible Effects on Fetus or Newborn
Smoking (nicotine)	Stunting, accelerated heartbeat, premature birth, organ congestion, fits and convulsions
Sodium salicylate (aspirin)	Abnormalities, particularly of the heart (?)
Sodium seconal	Electrical depression of brain waves
Stilbesterol	Virilization of females
Streptomycin	Damage to auditory nerve
Sulphameoxypytifozine	Brain damage possible
Sulfonamides	Jaundice, kernicterus
Sulfonylurea derivatives	Anomalies (?)
Thalidomide	Hearing loss, abnormal appendages, death
Tranquilizers	Retarded development (?)
Thiazine (diuretics)	Thrombocytopenia, polycystic kidney disease
Thiouracil	Affects fetal thyroid
Vaccination, influenza	Increases anti-A and -B titers in mother's blood
Vaccination, smallpox	Fetal vaccinia
Vitamin K analogues, in excess	Hyperbilirubinemia, jaundice in prematures

APPENDIX C *maternal diseases and the fetus*

Maternal Infection	Possible Effects on Fetus or Newborn
Chicken pox or shingles	Chicken pox or shingles, increases abortions and stillbirths
Congenital syphilis (Treponema palladium)	Miscarriage
Coxsackie B virus	Inflammation of heart muscles
Cytomegalovirus (salivary gland virus)	Small head, inflammation and hardening of brain and retina, deafness, mental retardation, enlargement of spleen and liver, anemia, giant cells in urine from kidneys
Hepatitis	Hepatitis
Herpes simplex	Generalized herpes, inflammation of brain, cyanosis, jaundice, fever, respiratory and circulatory collapse, death
Influenza A	Malformations
Mumps	Fetal death, endocardial fibroelastosis, anomalies
Pneumonia	Abortion in early pregnancy
Polio	Spinal or bulbar polio, acute poliomyelitis of the newborn
Rubella (German measles)	Anomalies, hemorrhage, enlargement of spleen and liver, inflammation of brain, liver, and lungs; cataract, small brain, deafness, various mental defects, death
Rubeola	Increased stillbirths and abortions
Scarlet fever (streptococcus)	Abortion in early pregnancy due to high maternal temperature
Smallpox	Smallpox, increased abortions and stillbirths
Specific nonviral infections; several viral infections	Prematurity
Syphilis	Premature, stillborn, or congenitally syphilitic baby

Maternal Infection	Possible Effects on Fetus or Newborn
Toxoplasmosis (protozoan parasite)	Small eyes and head, mental retardation, water on the brain (encephalitis), heart damage, fetal death
Tuberculosis bacillus	Fetal death, lowered resistance to tuberculosis
Typhoid fever	Abortion in early pregnancy
Vaccination	Vaccinia, increased abortions
Western equine encephalitis	Encephalitis, idiocy

APPENDIX D *characters in man with evidence of heritability*

Dominant Characters	Recessive Characters
Skin and Hair	
Dark-brown hair	Light-brown and red hair
Black hair	All other colors
Curly hair	Straight hair
Skin spotted with white	Uniformly colored
Ichthyosis (scaly skin)	Normal
Epidermolysis (blistered skin)	Normal
Keratosis (cornified areas of feet and hands)	Normal
Monolithrix (beaded and fragile hair)	Normal
Hypotrichosis (absence of hair on body)	Normal
Hypertrichosis (lanugo 4–10 inches persists)	Normal
Normal	Ichthyosis fetalis (skin thick, split, fissured)
Normal	Anhidrotic ectodermal dysplasia (absence of sweat glands, sex-linked)
Pattern baldness (dominant in males)	Baldness (recessive in females)
Normal skin pigmentation	Albinism
Eyes and Ears	
Brown eyes	Blue eyes
Normal	Pigment degeneration, iris
Hereditary cataract	Normal
Normal	Night blindness (sex-linked)
Normal	Red-green color-blind (sex-linked)
Astigmatism	Normal vision
Hyperopia (far-sightedness)	Normal
Aniridia (absence of iris)	Normal
Nystagmus (rolling eyeball)	Normal
Glaucoma (increased intraocular tension)	Normal
Blue sclerotic (thin sclera, fragile bones)	Normal
Otosclerosis (spongy bone in ear capsule)	Normal

Dominant Characters	Recessive Characters
Eyes and Ears *(cont'd)*	
Labyrinthine deafness	Normal
Normal color	Albinism
Normal	Optic atrophy (Leber's disease)
Normal	Deaf-mutism
Normal	Day blindness (sex-linked)
Retinoblastonia	Normal
Normal	Microphthalmas (small eyes)
Skeleton	
Round head	Long head
Brachydactlyly (shortened fingers)	Normal
Polydactyly (extra fingers)	Normal
Syndactyl (fusion of fingers webbed)	Normal
Symphalangy (extensive fusion of fingers)	Normal
Fragility (tendency of bones to break)	Normal
Absence of collarbone	Presence
Protruding jaw	Normal
Cleft palate	Normal
Normal stature	Dwarfism
Normal	Spina bifida (split tail)
Lobster claw	Normal
Absence of kneecap	Presence
Double-jointedness	Normal
Congenital dislocation of hip	Normal
Achondroplasia (short arms and legs, big head)	Normal
Normal	Clubfoot
Kidneys	
Diabetes insipidus (malfunction of the pancreas)	Normal
Normal	Alkaptonuria (black urine)
Phenylketonuria	Normal
Nervous	
Huntington's chorea	Normal
Normal	Feeble-mindedness

Dominant Characters	Recessive Characters
Nervous *(cont'd)*	
Lack of musical ability	Musical ability
Normal	Cerebral sclerosis
Epilepsy	Normal
Migraine	Normal
Normal	Friedreich's ataxia
Cerebellar ataxia (hereditary)	Normal
Primary degeneration of cerebellum	Normal
Wilson's disease (cirrhosis of the liver)	Normal
Paralysis agitans (Parkinson's disease)	Normal
Essential tremor, hereditary	Normal
Manic-depressive (psychosis)	Normal
Dementia praecox (old age presenility)	Normal
Mongolism	Normal
Normal	Microcephaly (small head and brain)
Normal	Amaurotic idiocy (paralysis and loss of vision, death by 2 years of age usual)
Muscular	
Family periodic paralysis	Normal
Myotonia congenita	Normal
Dystrophia myotonia	Normal
Normal	Progressive muscular dystrophy
Normal	Hypertrophic neuritis
Normal	Infantile muscular atrophy
Normal	Hereditary spastic
Normal	Spinal paralysis
Normal	Gowers' muscular atrophy
Diseases and Susceptibilities	
Diabetes insipidus	Normal
Renal glycosuria	Normal
Endemic goiter	Normal
Hypertension	Normal

Dominant Characters	Recessive Characters
Diseases and Susceptibilities	
Migraine	Normal
Normal	Diabetes mellitus
Normal	Exophthalmic goiter
Normal	Susceptibility to scarlet fever
Immunity to poison ivy	Susceptibility to poison ivy
Diseases of Blood and Storage	
Multiple telangiectasia (capillary dilation)	Normal
Eosinophilia (increase in blood eosinophils)	Normal
Hemolytic ecterus (jaundice and dissolution of red cells)	Normal
Pernicious anemia (reduction in red cells of the blood)	Normal
Sickle cell anemia	Normal
Gout	Normal
Normal	Hemophilia (sex-linked)
Normal	Erythroblastic anemia
Normal	Erythroblastosis
Normal	Gaucher's disease (anemia, hemorrhage, enlarged spleen)
Normal	Christian's disease
Normal	Tay-Sach's disease (amaurotic family idiocy)

APPENDIX E   *inheritance of cancer susceptibility*

1. Identical twins tend to have cancer at the same stage of development, of the same type, and in the same organs. This suggests hereditary factors.

2. Cancer apparently due to trauma in one member of identical twins generally appears later in the other twin and in the same region.

3. Tumors appearing in various members of the same family tend to appear at the same age.

4. Tumors tend to affect the same organ or organs in the various members of the same family.

5. The same type of tumor tends to affect various members of the same family.

6. Animal experimentation substantiates the familial tendency to tumor development.

glossary

The following terms are likely to be included in any discussion concerned with pregnancy. The definitions are brief but are designed to give the most pertinent information available.

ABORTION   The premature (spontaneous or induced) expulsion of the fetus from the uterus before the time when the baby can live by itself.

ABORTUS   Products of an abortion, whether alive or otherwise.

ABSTINENCE, SEXUAL   Complete avoidance of all sexual activity.

ACTIVATION   Process of initiating development of an ovum, normally achieved by a spermatozoon of the same species but also accomplished artificially (parthenogenesis); stimulation of a spermatozoon to accelerated activity by chemical means.

ADRENAL GLANDS   Two endocrine (ductless) glands, located one above each kidney; produce hormones which affect body functions; one hormone called androgen influences development of secondary sex characteristics and sex drive and is produced in both sexes.

AFTERBIRTH   Placenta and membranes extruded from the uterus after the birth of a baby, and composed mainly of the placenta, amniotic sac, and umbilical cord.

AFTER-PAINS   Cramplike pains which result from contractile efforts of the uterus to return to its proper condition after expulsion of the afterbirth; may last several days.

ALBUMIN   Protein found in nearly every animal and characterized by being soluble in water and coagulable by heat; abnormally found in urine during pregnancy.

ALLANTOIS   Saclike organ of respiration and excretion in embryos and fetuses which develops from its hindgut and contributes to the formation of the umbilical cord and placenta.

AMNIOCENTESIS   Tapping of the amnion for fluid sample to determine sex, chance of erythroblastosis, or presence of polyhydramnios.

AMNION   Transparent, thin, but tough membrane comprising the sac or "bag or waters," which produces the amniotic fluid in which the fetus grows and can move. It acts as a shock absorber protecting the fetus within the uterus, and its spontaneous rupture is usually an indication that labor will soon follow.

ANDROGEN   Masculinizing hormone produced by the testis in the male and adrenal glands of both sexes. Ovarian secretion estrogen is the androgen counterpart in the female. Normal sex development, sex drive, bone growth, and other secondary sex characters are believed to be dependent upon proper balance of these two hormones.

ANTENATAL   Occurring or forming before birth; prior to birth.

ANTEPARTUM   Prenatal in the sense that it occurs before delivery of the child.

APGAR SCORE   On a scale of 1 to 10, a means of evaluating within 60 seconds the survival probability of a newborn child. With 5 categories, each having value of 0, 1, or 2, a judgment can be made as to how the baby can be expected to function. It assesses the heart rate, respiratory effort, muscle tone, reflex irritability, and color, giving critical evaluation almost immediately. A score of 10 is perfect; 7 is quite normal; but 3 or less calls for emergency measures.

ARCHES, BRANCHIAL   Bars of dense tissue seen in the 5-week-old human embryo located on the sides of the face and neck between the so-called temporary gill slits; become parts of jaws, ears, and throat.

ASCHEIM-ZONDEK TEST Test for pregnancy in which a small amount of urine from a woman in her first weeks of pregnancy (or suspected) is injected for each of 2 days into infantile female mice, causing follicular ovarian hemorrhages which can be taken as indicative of pregnancy; examination made in 4 days; presence of corpora lutea is 97 per cent accurate diagnosis of pregnancy.

ASPERMIA Total absence of sperm; male sterility of one type.

AUTOSOME Any ordinary paired chromosome as distinguished from a sex (X or y) chromosome.

AZOOSPERMIA Total absence of sperm in the semen, form of sterility.

BABY RASH Temporary red spots on the skin of the newborn.

BAG OF WATERS Term formerly used to refer to the fetal amniotic membrane which encloses the fluids in which the fetus develops, and which ruptures early in labor.

BIRTH Process in which the baby is expelled from the mother's uterus and begins its independent life. In humans it usually occurs about 9 months, 266 days after conception or 280 days after the first day of the last menstrual period.

BIRTH CONTROL Deliberate limitation of the number of children conceived, by way of a variety of means.

BIRTH RATE Number of births per 1,000 population.

BISEXUAL Having gonads of both sexes (hermaphrodite) or having both male and female interests or characteristics.

BLASTOCYST The developing ovum during the second week after fertilization in the human, when it is a small hollow ball of cells.

BLASTODERM Stage in the development of the early embryo in which it is a disc of cells from which the primary germ layers are derived.

BLASTULA State in development of the early embryo which is a hollow single-layered sphere of cells immediately following the morula stage.

BLOOD ISLANDS Small areas of tissue within the yolk sac membrane of the early embryo in which the blood vessels and blood cells first appear.

BRANCHIAL ARCHES Remnants of ancestral gills which are seen temporarily in the neck region of the human embryo and which later contribute to the jaw apparatus.

BREASTS Paired mammary (milk) glands between the third and seventh ribs of the female which produce milk for the newborn child. Breast development is one of the early signs of sexual maturity in girls, but even the rudimentary breasts of the newborn male child may secrete a bit of milklike substance in response to the female hormone derived from the mother.

BREECH   The buttocks or nates; a breech delivery is one in which the buttocks appear first instead of the head.

CAESAREAN SECTION   Delivery of the baby through the abdomen by means of a surgical incision through the abdominal and uterine walls. Indicated in certain cases of toxemia or pregnancy, prior Caesarean sections which may have weakened the uterine muscles, an inadequate pelvic basin for normal delivery of child of excess size, or for other extenuating circumstances.

CAP, CRADLE   Thin, waxy, light-brown crusty patch (or patches) on the baby's scalp 2 to 3 days after birth, due to hyperactivity of the sebaceous or oil glands.

CAPACITATION   Sum of anatomic and physiologic changes which take place in the epididymal sperm before they become capable of fertilizing an ovum.

CASTRATION   Complete surgical or infectional removal of the sex glands (spaying) of either sex.

CAUL   Part of the amnion which may cover the baby's face at birth.

CELL   Basic unit of protoplasm, therefore of all life and reproduction. Each cell consists of a central nucleus containing the hereditary elements called chromosomes, cytoplasm surrounding this nucleus, and a cell membrane. In general there are two kinds of cells which make up the body: reproductive or sex cells which can unite to form another organism and somatic cells which are all the other vast variety of body cells.

CERVIX UTERI   The lower portion of the uterus which extends into the vaginal cavity and possesses a small canal which connects the uterus with the vagina; also called "neck of the womb."

CHANGE OF LIFE   *See* Climacteric.

CHORION   Outermost of the fetal membranes. Externally it develops finger-like villi which become embedded in the uterus and acquire blood vessels which carry on metabolic interchanges between the fetus and the mother, such as nourishment and waste discharges. It is a part of the placenta.

CHROMOSOMES   Small, stainable, rodlike bodies found in the nuclei of all cells during their process of division. They carry the genes. The numbers differ with the different animal species but are always in pairs except in the mature germ cells. Man possesses 46, in 23 pairs, one of each coming from each parent at the moment of fertilization.

CILIA Minute vibratile hairlike processes attached to the free surface of a cell; sometimes create a directional current, as in the Fallopian tube (oviduct).

CIRCUMCISION Surgical removal of the foreskin or prepuce of the penis; generally done before the child leaves the hospital. Usually performed for hygienic reasons, although it is a rite among the Jews and a traditional practice among the Moslems and some primitive tribes. Thought to reduce the possibility of cervical cancer in the marriage mate, as well as penile cancers.

CLEAVAGE The mitotic division of the fertilized ovum or zygote, resulting in blastomeres; segmentation or cell division.

CLEFTS, BRANCHIAL "Gill clefts," grooves or clefts on the side of the neck in 5-week embryo, comparable in form and position to the gill slits in other animals.

CLIMACTERIC "Change of life," a combination of somatic, endocrine, and psychic changes occurring at the end of the reproductive period of the female (menopause) or accompanying the normal reduction of sexual activity of the male.

CLITORIS Small, elongated erectile body situated anterior to the vulva in the female; a center of sexual sensation. It is homologous (similar in origin) to the penis of the male.

COFFEE-COLORED MARKS Abnormal pigmentation spots on the skin of the newborn child.

COITUS Copulation or sexual union (intercourse) between individuals of the opposite sex; the sexual act of insertion of the penis of the male into the vagina of the female and the ejaculation of semen from the penis.

COLOSTRUM Thin, slightly greenish-colored, milky fluid secreted by the mammary glands a few days before or after delivery; drop for drop it is almost as nutritious as breast milk, but its maximum rate of production is about one per cent of the normal output of milk in the lactating mother.

CONCEPTION Fertilization of the ovum by a spermatozoon, thus initiating the development of an embryo and starting pregnancy.

CONCEPTUS Products of conception, the fetus and placenta.

CONFINEMENT Labor; childbirth; the lying-in period.

CONGENITAL Existing at, and usually before, birth; a deviation from the normal in fetal development which is not hereditary.

CONTRACEPTION   Prevention of conception by any means, chemical or mechanical.

CORONAL   Relating to the crown of the head.

CORPUS LUTEUM   Secretory structure which forms in the Graafian follicle of the ovary after the ovum has been extruded; deteriorates if the egg is not fertilized, matures and grows if it is. Its function is to produce the pregnancy hormone progesterone, which causes the thickening of the uterine lining in preparation for the embryo.

CROWNING   The moment during the second phase of labor when the baby's head stretches the vulva to its maximum and the baby's crown becomes visible; at this moment the obstetrician can often bring the birth to completion by a little manual aid.

CRYPTORCHIDISM   Developmental defect in which the testes remain within the pelvis instead of descending into the scrotal sac. In man this could cause sterility because of the heat of the body.

CYTOPLASM   Protoplasm of the cell other than that of the nucleus.

DECIDUA   Uterine mucosa (lining) of pregnancy, thrown off after birth.

DEFECT, BIRTH   Any abnormality present at birth that will deprive the child of physical and/or mental health.

DELIVERY   Expulsion of the child by the mother from her uterus, or the extraction by the obstetrician. Can refer to delivery of the placenta also, after birth.

DELIVERY, ABDOMINAL   Delivery of a baby by abdominal surgery (Caesarean section) when the pelvis is too narrow or for other reasons when the normal birth would endanger the life of either the mother or the baby.

DELIVERY, BREECH   Fetus is presented buttocks first during labor and in delivery.

DELIVERY, FORCEPS   The extraction of the fetus from the maternal passages by the application of forceps to the child's head.

DELIVERY, PREMATURE   The delivery of a premature infant weighing less than 5½ pounds.

DEOXYRIBONUCLEIC ACID   DNA: nucleic acid present in the nucleus and active in chromosome duplication.

DIAPHRAGM   Transverse muscular and membranous partition which separates the chest cavity from the abdominal cavity and plays an important role in breathing; also a contraceptive device.

DILATATION   Stretching. Dilatation of the cervix is done by curettage; dilatation of the cervix is a measure of the progress of labor.

DIPLOID   Having two sets of homologous chromosomes, pairs, normally found in the body, or somatic, cells of all higher animals.

DIURETIC   Drug which increases the production of urine and thereby decreases the volume of body water, reducing tissue edema.

DOMINANT   In genetics, refers to a gene which is capable of expression when carried by only one of a pair of homologous chromosomes; it is "dominant" in expression over the other paired chromosome.

DOUCHE   Stream of water, gas, or vapor directed into a cavity or against a part; often referred to in relation to its use in cleansing the vagina, for contraception or to combat infection.

ECTODERM   The outermost of the three primary cell layers in the early embryo; gives rise to the skin, nervous system, and sense organs.

EDEMA   Presence of abnormally large amounts of fluid in the intercellular tissue spaces of the body; may accompany toxemia of pregnancy.

EFFACEMENT   Shortening of the cervical canal, originally 1 to 2 centimeters in length, to complete absence of a canal, leaving only a circular orifice. Occurs during the first stage of labor and is also called "obliteration" or "taking up" of the cervix.

EJACULATION   Generally refers to the forcible and sudden expulsion of semen from the male genital tract at the climax of the sexual act.

EMBRYO   Early stage of development of an organism. In humans it is regarded as development from the 3rd to the 5th week of gestation, after which it is called a fetus. It is the period of organ differentiation.

EMBRYONIC DISC   A flat, disc-shaped plate of cells which represents the future body of the embryo during the second week of development.

EMBRYONIC MEMBRANES   Those enclosing membranes such as the amnion and chorion which develop between the embryo and the mother.

ENDOCRINE GLANDS   Special type of glands without ducts which secrete potent chemicals into the bloodstream and which control the activity of organs or tissues in another part of the body, such as the adrenals and pituitary or thyroid glands.

ENDODERM   Innermost of the two or three layers of the very early embryo; the layer from which are derived the lining of the digestive tract and all of its adjuncts.

ENDOMETRIUM   Mucous membrane lining the uterus which is shed during menstruation. During pregnancy it forms a bed for the embryo and later becomes incorporated into the placenta.

ENGAGEMENT   In obstetrics, the entrance of the fetal head or presenting part into the superior pelvic strait and beginning of the descent through the pelvic canal. In the firstborn this occurs early in labor; in subsequent pregnancies it occurs later.

EPISIOTOMY   In obstetrics, a surgical incision of the vulvar orifice prior to delivery in order to control tearing; applied in about 75 per cent of hospital deliveries. Generally sutured immediately after delivery.

EPITHELIUM   Covering of internal and external surfaces of the body, including the lining of vessels and small cavities.

ERYTHROBLASTOSIS   Disease which may affect infants born to Rh-negative mothers and Rh-positive fathers and characterized by destruction of the red blood cells and compensatory excessive development of hematopoietic tissue, often fatal unless proper blood is transfused.

ESTROGEN   Hormone secreted by the ovary and placenta throughout the menstrual cycle and pregnancy; essential for the feminization of the body; regulated by the master pituitary gland.

EXTRAEMBRYONIC   All structures related to but not within or incorporated within the embryo; refers principally to the membranes and the placenta.

FEEDING, ARTIFICIAL   Feeding of a baby with food other than mother's milk.

FEMALE SEX ORGANS   External organs, or vulva, include the inner and outer lips (labia), clitoris, and opening of vagina. Internal organs include vaginal canal, cervix, neck and body (or fundus) of the uterus, Fallopian tubes (oviducts), and ovaries.

FERTILITY   Ability to produce offspring; power of reproduction.

FERTILIZATION   Fusion of sperm with ovum, the beginning of pregnancy. Entrance of an active sperm into a mature ovum and their fusion to form a zygote which has the potentiality of developing into an organism such as a human being; conception or impregnation.

FETUS Human development from 5th week to birth; sometimes after the 3rd month regarded as an unborn child only because most of the major organs have been formed, but it cannot survive outside of the uterus at this time.

FONTANELLE Quadrangular space between the frontal and two parietal bones in the upper part of the skull of very young infants, known as the "soft spot," just above the baby's forehead. There is another between the occipital and parietal bones (posterior). The anterior soft spot may remain for 18 months, but the posterior closes by 2 months.

FSH Abbreviation for "follicle-stimulating hormone" which is derived from the pituitary gland and which stimulates the growth and maturation of Graafian follicles in the ovary or the seminiferous tubules in the testis.

GAMETE Either of the two mature germ cells (ovum or sperm) which, when they unite, forms a zygote which develops into a new individual. Germ cell.

GASTRULA Embryonic stage following the blastula. It is formed by the invagination of the blastula and consists of two cell layers, the outer ectoderm and inner endoderm, with a central cavity, the primitive gut.

GENE Hereditary unit on a chromosome which determines some physical characteristics.

GENETIC Inherited. Used in describing certain physical conditions which are believed to be carried in the genes of the parent as potentialities, such as hair and eye color or some types of epilepsy.

GENITALIA Reproductive or sexual glands or organs, both external and internal.

GENOTYPE Fundamental hereditary constitution (assortment of genes) of an individual rather than merely his appearance (phenotype).

GERM CELL Gamete. The reproductive cell which combines with that of the opposite sex to form a new life. Sperm or ovum.

GESTATION Pregnancy; gravidity. The period from fertilization to birth.

GONAD Ovary or testis; germ-cell-producing organ.

GRAAFIAN FOLLICLE Vesicle, small, usually spherical and growing in the ovary, containing a maturing ovum (egg).

GYNECOLOGY Medical specialty dealing with the problems of the female sexual and reproductive organs.

HAPLOID   Having a single set of chromosomes, as normally found in a gamete, or having one complete set of non-homologous chromosomes.

HEAT SPOTS   Sebaceous glands of the baby's skin may appear as raised red spots called "heat spots" where the outflow of sebum may be hampered; may cause boils, pustules, furuncles, impetigo, acne, etc.

HEMORRHAGE   Excessive bleeding which, at birth, causes 19.9 per cent of maternal deaths.

HEREDITARY   Transmission of traits and characteristics from parents to offspring. accomplished by the combining of genes from the respective parents at the moment of fertilization.

HERMAPHRODITISM   Bisexual condition in which the gonads or other sexual organs of both sexes are present in one individual; ability to produce both sperm and ova.

HETEROSEXUAL   Pertaining to the two sexes, or attraction for the opposite sex. Opposed to homosexual.

HETEROZYGOTE   An individual possessing different genes in regard to a given character, such as for brown and blue eyes.

HOMOZYGOTE   Individual possessing an identical pair of genes with respect to a particular character (two blue-eyed genes).

HORMONE   Chemical substance produced by a ductless gland in one part of the body, carried by the bloodstream to affect an organ in another part of the body. Produced by endocrine glands.

HYDRAMNIOS   Excess amniotic fluid which, if not drained off, will often cause the congenital anomaly known as anencephaly (without a head).

HYMEN   Membranous fold which partially or wholly covers the external opening of the vagina; typically found in a virgin.

HYPERTENSION   High blood pressure. In pregnancy the blood pressure higher than 140/90.

HYSTERECTOMY   Surgical removal of the uterus.

HYSTEROTOMY   Incision of the uterus, as in the performance of a late therapeutic abortion by Caesarean section.

IMPLANTATION   Invasion of the lining of the uterus by the developing embryo 6 or 7 days after fertilization of the ovum.

IMPOTENCE   Inability on the part of the male to perform sexual intercourse owing to inability to achieve and maintain an erection. Orgasm is rarely attained without erection, though possible.

IMPREGNATE To fertilize or to make pregnant.

INBREEDING Breeding for generations by continual mating of those who are closely related, such as brother and sister matings.

INFANCY Period from birth to the end of the second year of life.

INFANT A baby; child under two years of age.

INFERTILITY Sterility; condition of being unable to produce offspring.

INSEMINATION, ARTIFICIAL Placing of male sperm into the vagina and the cervix of a woman by the use of a syringe.

INTRAUTERINE Within the uterus.

IN UTERO Inside the uterus.

INVOLUTION Return of the uterus to its normal size and condition after the birth of a child or after an abortion.

LABIA Plural of *labium,* meaning lips or liplike epithelial folds lateral to the vaginal opening, homologous to male scrotum.

LABOR Parturition; the process of childbirth; the series of processes by which the products of conception are expelled from the mother's body, usually in 3 stages: (1) ends with complete dilatation of the cervix (8–16 hours); (2) ends when the baby has moved through the vagina and out into the air (1–2 hours); (3) ends with the complete expulsion of the placenta and membranes (afterbirth).

LACTATION Act or period of giving milk; the secretion of milk; the time or period of secreting milk. Usually begins 3 days after birth.

LANUGO The fine downy hair found on nearly all parts of the body of the fetus except the palms of the hands and soles of the feet; seen first at 5 months and persisting to 9 months, disappearing usually before birth.

LH Abbreviation for "luteinizing hormone" produced by the pituitary gland; stimulates the corpora lutea in the ovary to secrete estrogen and progesterone.

LIGHTENING Sensation of decreased abdominal distention produced by the descent of the fetal head into the pelvic cavity, occurring 2 or 3 weeks before the onset of labor.

LIMB BUDS Moundlike swellings occurring in pairs on the sides of the body in the one-month-old human embryo; later develop into arms or legs.

MALE SEX ORGANS External organs include the penis and the scrotum, which contains the paired testes; internal organs are the prostate gland, sperm ducts, seminal vesicles, Cowper's glands, and urethra.

MASTITIS   Inflammation of the breast; may occur shortly after the beginning of breast-feeding.

MATURATION   Process of cell division and metamorphosis of reproductive cells which results in a fully fertilizable sperm or ovum, and during which the (diploid) number of chromosomes is reduced to half (haploid) so that when fertilization occurs the normal number of chromosomes is restored. Each species has a characteristic number.

MECONIUM   Dark-green mucus and dead cells found in the intestine of the full-term fetus or newborn infant; mixture of cells and secretions of the intestinal glands and mucus and some amniotic fluid.

MEIOSIS   Special type of cell division occurring only in the germ cells (sex cells) as they mature, during which the diploid set of chromosomes is reduced to half (haploid) by the separation of member pairs. In *mitosis* there is no such reduction, each daughter cell being identical with that of the parent cell.

MEMBRANE   Thin, usually tough layer of tissue which covers a surface or divides a space or organ, such as the amnion or chorion.

MEMBRANES, FETAL   Membranous structures that serve to protect the embryo and provide for its nutrition, respiration, and excretion; they include the yolk sac, allantois, amnion, chorion, decidua, and placenta.

MENOPAUSE   Period when menstruation ceases from natural causes, the female "change of life" or "climacteric"; usually occurring between the ages of forty-five and fifty; marks the end of the reproductive period but not the end of sexual desire or activity.

MENORRHAGIA   Abnormally profuse menstrual flow.

MENSES   Periodic monthly discharge of blood from the uterus.

MENSTRUATION   Monthly discharge of endometrium and blood from the uterus because no fertilized ovum is present to engage this uterine lining, when it reverts to the normal state; takes place from puberty to menopause usually at regular (lunar) intervals of 28 days but with variations. The onset occurs on the average of 13.2 years.

MESODERM   Middle or intermediate layer of the three primary germ layers of the early embryo, lying between the outer ectoderm and the inner endoderm layers. From it are derived muscles, bones, skeleton, excretory system, and many glands.

MESONEPHROS Second of three succcessive stages in the fetal development of the kidney; present at 2 months in the human, but degenerates as the third and final kidney (metanephros) develops. Certain parts of this temporary and fetal kidney remain as parts of the adult reproductive system.

METANEPHROS The "third kidney" or final kidney which remains to function as the kidney of the postnatal individual.

MIDWIFE A woman who assists at childbirth; practice of midwifery.

MIGRATION The normal passage of an ovum from the ovary to the uterus through the oviduct; also, the passage of primitive germ cells from the yolk sac to the final abode, within the reproductive organs, ovary or testis.

MISCARRIAGE Spontaneous abortion; premature expulsion, accidental ending of a pregnancy before a living child can be delivered. About 20 per cent of all pregnancies end in miscarriage during first three months, and one-fifth of these will miscarry again (4.4 per cent of all pregnancies). About 1 per cent miscarry three times in succession.

MITOSIS Indirect cell division; typical mode of division of somatic (body) cells, and germ cells not in meiosis. The four phases or steps are prophase, metaphase, anaphase, and telophase.

MOLDING Shaping of the baby's head so as to adjust itself to the size and shape of the birth canal; mild and temporary overlapping of the cranial (head) bones may occur.

MONGOLISM Form of congenital physical and mental abnormality caused by a genetic defect involving an extra chromosome (number 21), making it triploid instead of diploid. Sometimes called "fetalism" because of facial resemblance to a fetus. Mongoloid children are usually lively and imitative but do not develop intelligence much beyond childhood, and have a short span of life. This condition can be determined at birth by the microscopic examination of the chromosomes in blood cells.

MORO REFLEX An embracing or startling reflex of the baby caused by any sudden change in body position or by sound waves. *See also* reflex.

MORTALITY, PERINATAL Stillbirths; combined infant mortality during pregnancy, labor, and newborn to 20 weeks or older.

MORTALITY RATE, MATERNAL Number of maternal deaths per 1,000 births. Average 4.1 per 10,000 live births; 2.8 for white and 11.8 for nonwhites. Major reasons are hemorrhage, puerperal infection, and toxemia of pregnancy.

MULTIPARA   Woman who has borne several or many children.

NATAL   Pertaining to birth.

NAVEL   Umbilicus, or shriveled remnant of umbilical connection.

NEONATAL   Newborn; pertaining to the newborn, usually first 4 weeks.

NEURAL PLATE   Flat plate of thickened ectoderm cells found in the 3-week human embryo; gives rise to the central nervous system and to parts of the eyes.

NIPPLE   Projecting tip of the breast which contains the outlets of the milk ducts and through which the infant receives the mother's milk by sucking.

NULLIPARA   Woman who has not yet borne any children.

OBSTETRICIAN   Medical doctor who specializes in the management of pregnancy, labor, delivery, and puerperium.

OÖGONIUM   Primordial cell from which the ovarian egg arises, before it becomes a primary oöcyte.

OSSIFICATION   Process of conversion of fibrous or cartilaginous tissue into bone, beginning at about 2 months of age in the human fetus.

OVA   Plural for ovum, or egg.

OVARY   Sexual gland or organ of the female in which ova are produced; two in each normal female, one on each side of pelvis near kidneys. Produces estrogen, which governs the female sex characteristics.

OVULATION   Growth and expulsion or discharge of the ovum from the ovary prior to its fertilization by a spermatozoon. Occurs between 10 and 16 days after onset of a normal menstrual cycle of 28 days; controlled by a complicated glandular interrelationship of the master pituitary and the thyroid and other glands.

OVUM   Female reproductive cell, the egg, produced only in the ovary and usually once every 28 days, measuring about 1/175 inch in diameter. After fertilization called a zygote or early embryo.

OXYTOCIN   Hormone secreted by the posterior lobe of the pituitary gland which stimulates the uterine musculature to contraction and is used to induce active labor or to cause contraction of the uterus after delivery of the placenta.

PARTHENOGENESIS   Unisexual reproduction or reproduction by the development of an ovum without its being fertilized by a spermatozoon.

PARTURITION   Act or process of giving birth to a child.

PATERNITY   Being a father; relation of father to child.

PEDIATRICIAN   Doctor who specializes in the care of children.

PELVIMETRY   Measurement of the dimensions of the pelvis, as well as its capacity; achieved by pelvic examination, X-ray radiography, or fluoroscopy.

PELVIS   Bony girdle that encloses the lower part of the abdomen; hipbones, sacrum (behind), and pubic bone (in front). A bony ring interposed between the trunk and the thighs; also refers to cavity which contains the generative organs, particularly uterus and vagina of the female.

PENIS   Phallus; male external sexual organ for copulation; organ for intromission of the vagina during coitus.

PERINEUM   Area between the vagina and rectum in women, between the anus and scrotum in men.

PITUITARY   Hypophysis of the embryo; endocrine or ductless gland at the base of the brain, its secretions affecting growth, sexual development and function. Known as the master gland because it is responsible for the proper functioning of other glands.

PLACENTA   Flat, circular, vascular structure in the pregnant uterus which constitutes the place of exchange of respiratory, nutritive, and excretory products between the mother and the fetus through the umbilical cord; the afterbirth.

POSITION   In obstetrics, position of the fetus within the pelvis usually designated with respect to the right or left side of the mother.

POSTNATAL   Occurring after birth.

POSTPARTUM   Following childbirth.

POSTTERM   Infants born after 41st gestation week.

PREFORMATION   Theory of early physiologists that the fully formed animal exists in minute form in the germ cell; opposed to epigenesis.

PREGNANCY   From Latin meaning "previous to bringing forth"; period between conception and birth when the embryo and then the fetus develop within the uterus of the mother; approximately 266 days, 10 lunar or 9 calendar months.

PREGNANCY, ECTOPIC   When fetus develops abnormally outside of the uterus in the interstitial portion of the Fallopian tube, in rudimentary horn of the uterus, in cervical region, abdomen, or even in the ovary. Cause of about 7 per cent of maternal deaths; must be surgically interrupted.

PREGNANCY TEST   Test based upon the response of the ovary of the tested animal (mouse, rat, rabbit, or toad) to the injection of the urine of suspected patient; generally takes 6 to 48 hours and is reliable only in the hands of experts (*see* Ascheim-Zondek Test). Two-hour urine or blood tests are now available.

PREMATURE INFANT   One which at delivery weighs less than 5½ pounds and arrives before calculated time of delivery.

PRENATAL   Term used to distinguish life before birth from life after birth (postnatal).

PRESENTATION   Term referring to that part of the fetus nearest the os cervix or felt by the obstetrician when examining internally and presented first at birth.

PRESENTATION, BREECH   When a baby is presented buttocks first.

PRESENTATION, CEPHALIC   When a baby is presented head first; may be any part of the head, such as face, brow, or top (occiput)—the most frequent situation.

PRETERM   Infants born before 38th week is completed.

PRIMIGRAVIDA   Woman who is pregnant for the first time.

PRIMIPARA   Woman who has given birth to her first child.

PRIMORDIAL   Primitive or original, simplest or undeveloped.

PROGESTERONE   Hormone produced by the corpora lutea of the ovary whose function is to prepare the lining of the uterus for the reception and development of the fertilized ovum; prevents further ovulation and menstruation during pregnancy and is often regarded as the "pregnancy hormone."

PRONEPHROS   The "first" kidneys of three pairs which develop successively in the embryo, and fetus, no part of which remains as kidney but a tubular portion of which may remain as the oviducts of the female; originally known as the Müllerian ducts; become the Fallopian tubes.

PROTOPLASM   Original primordial living substance, capable of breathing, reproducing, and reacting to stimuli as well as growing. The major constituent of all cells (cytoplasm and nucleoplasm).

PUBERTY   Age at which the reproductive organs become functionally active. In boys from thirteen to sixteen years, girls from twelve to fourteen years. It is started by an unexplained action of the pituitary gland which sets off the sex glands (ovaries or testes) and the sex hormones start the rapid physical growth at this period, as well as emotional vagaries.

QUICKENING   Mother's first perception of any movement on the part of the fetus, usually in the fourth to sixth month of pregnancy.

RABBIT TEST Test for pregnancy, using the rabbit. See Ascheim-Zondek Test.

RECAPITULATION Theory that during the development of man (or any animal) there is evidence of his (phylogenetic) ancestry in some of the temporary structures that appear, such as gill slits, tail bud, etc.

RECESSIVE In genetics, refers to genes which are incapable of expression unless they occur in the absence of their counterpart; blue-eyed genes are recessive to brown-eyed genes, being expressed only when pure and exclusively blue-eyed genes are present.

REFLEX Automatic, uncontrolled neuromuscular response to external stimulation. Present in fetus.

REPRODUCTION Process of producing offspring in basic likeness to itself.

Rh FACTOR Abbreviation for *rh*esus monkey; an inherited antigen or antibody in human blood of about 85 per cent of the white population in the U.S. Those possessing it are said to be Rh-positive, and those lacking it are Rh-negative (15 per cent). (See Chapter 13.)

RhoGAM Commercial name for a specific gamma globulin containing an anti-Rh antibody used to protect the fetus against fatal erythroblastosis fetalis often found in children after the first when an Rh-negative woman marries an Rh-positive man. Rhogam obviates the necessity of blood transfusions to save the lives of blood-conflict babies.

SECONDARY SEXUAL CHARACTERISTICS Physical traits apart from the primary sex organs (ovary or testis) which distinguish male from female, such as distribution and growth of pubic and facial hair, level of voice, muscular development, breasts, etc. These differences make their appearance at puberty under the influence of pituitary and sex hormones.

SEGMENTATION Process by which a fertilized ovum divides, thereby forming increasing numbers of cells, before they are arranged in layers.

SEMEN Fluid containing sperm secreted by the male reproductive organs and ejaculated from the penis during orgasm; believed to consist of fluids from the testes, prostate, seminal vesicles, Cowper's glands, and small glands in the urethra.

SEX Difference between those individuals which produce ova and those which produce sperm, including primary and secondary characters.

SEX DETERMINATION   Mechanism by which the sex of the child is predetermined before it develops in the fetus; sperm are of two types, one male-producing and the other female-producing. If a y-carrying sperm fertilizes any ovum a boy will result; if an X-carrying sperm fertilizes any ovum a girl will result.

SEX-LINKED   Character transmitted by genes carried on the sex-determining chromosomes.

SEX RATIO   Rate of male to female production in a statistically adequate population; average human ratio is about 106 to 100.

SHOW   Blood-tinged mucous discharge from the vagina before or during labor.

SKELETON   Basically the bony foundation upon which all of the soft tissues are built, and to which they adhere; that part of the body which gives it rigidity; may be cartilage, bone, or both.

SOMITES   Blocks of mesoderm, the intermediate layer of embryonic cells, found paired along the back as early as 3 weeks; give rise to the skeleton and the major muscles of the body.

SPERMATOZOON   Mature male germ cell, specific output of the testes. It is microscopic, motile, the only cell which can stimulate and fertilize the mature ovum; has head, middle piece, and tail; takes about 2 weeks to travel from testis through the sperm duct to point of ejaculation during coitus; each ejaculation may contain from 2 to 10 cubic centimeters of semen and roughly half a billion spermatozoa.

STILLBORN   Born without life; born dead. *See also* Mortality, Perinatal.

SYNGAMY   Sexual union of germ cells in fertilization; actual merging of their respective nuclei and contents.

TERM   Pregnancy is "at term" between the 38th and 42nd weeks, from 2 weeks before to 2 weeks after the due date; preterm delivery occurs before the 38th week.

TESTES   Paired reproductive or sex glands of the male which produce both germ cells (spermatozoa) and a hormone (testosterone) which stimulates in the male the development of his secondary sexual characters.

TESTICLE   One of the paired sex glands of the male usually located in the scrotum.

TISSUES   Groups of similar cells, generally with a common function such as muscle tissue, nerve tissue, etc.

TRIMESTER Period of three months, one of three phases of nine months' pregnancy.

TROPHECTODERM Outer layer of cells of early embryonic blastodermic vesicle.

TROPHOBLAST Special layer of outer cells of the embryo at one month; aids the embryo in invading the mucous lining of the uterus (womb) and then aids in the formation of the placenta. "Feeding layer."

TWINS, DIZYGOTIC Fraternal twins, derived from two separate ova simultaneously fertilized by different sperm; never identical.

TWINS, MONOZYGOTIC Twins derived from one fertilized ovum which, for hereditary or other reasons, separated at the two-cell stage into two identical cells, each giving rise to a separate individual, complete and whole in every respect. Each is an image of the other since they arose from the same fertilized ovum.

UMBILICAL CORD Cord connecting placenta with the fetus; contains two arteries and a large vein encased in Wharton's jelly; may be about ½ inch in diameter or more, and as much as 20 inches in length.

UTERUS Thick-walled muscular organ of the female reproductive system (womb) which serves as the abode and place of nourishment and growth of the embryo and fetus during its development; about the size of the woman's closed fist prior to her first pregnancy.

VAGINA Canal in the female from the vulva to the cervix, through which the child passes during delivery; birth canal; canal into which the penis is inserted during coitus.

VASECTOMY Surgical procedure for sterilizing the male whereby the sperm duct is cut and tied; short and simple minor operation which has no effect on sexual activity but makes insemination impossible.

VERTEBRAE The 33 small bones which comprise the backbone.

VIABLE Able or likely to live; applied to the condition of the child at birth.

VULVA External genitals of the female.

WHARTON'S JELLY Soft jelly-like mucous material which fills the bulk of the umbilical cord, supporting the blood vessels.

WOMB Common name for uterus.

X-CHROMOSOME The sex-determining chromosome carried by half of the sperm and by all of the mature ova produced in humans. Its presence in double form determines that the child will be a female.

Y-CHROMOSOME   The sex-determining chromosome carried by half of the sperm and never by the ovum, whose presence (along with the other sex or X chromosome) predetermines that the child will be a male.

YOLK SAC   Small and yolkless in the human attached to the abdomen of the embryo at one month; remnant of an ancestral structure from which all germ cells of the fetus arise before one month of development.

ZONA PELLUCIDA   Transparent nonliving membrane which surrounds the early fertilized ovum.

ZYGOTE   Single cell resulting from combination of mature ovum and mature sperm at fertilization; fusion of pronuclei.

bibliography

Apgar, Virginia. "Drugs in Pregnancy," *Journal of the American Medical Association,* 190 (1963), 840–884.

Auerbach, A. B., and Arnstein, B. S. *Pregnancy and You.* Child Study Ass'n. of America, 1962.

Bing, Elizabeth. *Six Practical Lessons for an Easier Childbirth.* New York: Grosset & Dunlap, 1967.

Blue Cross Association. *The Modern Baby.* Chicago, 1965.

Buxton, C. Lee. *A Study of Psychophysical Methods for Relief of Childbirth Pains.* Baltimore: Williams & Wilkins, 1962.

Calderone, M. S. *Manual of Contraceptive Practice.* Baltimore: Williams and Wilkins, 1966.

Cavanaugh, John R. *Fundamental Marriage Counselling.* Milwaukee: Bruce, 1963.

Chertok, L. *Psychosomatic Methods for Painless Childbirth.* New York: Pergamon, 1959.

Consumer Union of the United States. *The Consumer Union Report on Family Planning.* Mt. Vernon, N.Y., 1962.

Corner, G. W. *Ourselves Unborn: An Embryologist's Essay on Man.* New Haven, Conn.: Yale University, 1944.

Countryman, B. A. *Breast Feeding.* New York: Bobbs-Merrill, 1960.

Davis, M. E., and Maisel, F. *Have Your Baby, Keep Your Figure.* New York: Stein & Day, 1963.

Day, B., and Liley, H. M. I. *Modern Motherhood: Pregnancy, Childbirth, and the Newborn Baby*. New York: Random House, 1967.

Day, R. L. *Fertility Control: A Social Need, a Medical Responsibility*. New York: Planned Parenthood Association, 1966.

Demarest, R., and Sciarra, J. *Conception, Birth, Contraception*. New York: McGraw-Hill, 1969.

Dickinson, R. L., and Belskie, A. *Birth Atlas*. New York: Maternity Center Association, 1943.

Douglas, R. G. *A Baby Is Born*. New York: Maternity Center Association, 1957.

Eastman, N. J. *Expectant Motherhood*. Boston: Little, Brown, & Co., 1940.

Finch, B. F., and Green, H. *Contraception Through the Ages*. London: Peter Owen, 1963.

Fishbein, M. *Birth Defects*. Philadelphia: J. B. Lippincott, 1963.

Fitzpatrick, E., and Eastman, N. J. *Obstetrics for Nurses*. Philadelphia: J. B. Lippincott, 1960.

Flanagan, G. L. *The First Nine Months of Life*. New York: Simon and Schuster, 1962.

Fraiberg, S. *The Magic Years*. Rev. ed. New York: Scribner's, 1965.

Gelb, Barbara. *The ABC of Natural Childbirth: A Manual for Expectant Parents*. Englewood Cliffs, N.J.: Prentice-Hall, 1954.

Genne, W. H. *Husbands and Pregnancy*. New York: Association, 1956.

Gilbert, M. S. *Biography of the Unborn*. Rev. ed. New York: Hafner, 1963.

Gilbreth, Lillian M., Thomas, R. M., and Clymer, F. *Management in the Home*. New York: Dodd, Mead & Co., 1966.

Goodrich, F. W. *Maternity*. Englewood Cliffs, N.J.: Prentice-Hall, 1959.

———. *Natural Childbirth*. Englewood Cliffs, N.J.: Prentice-Hall, 1950.

———. *Preparing for Childbirth: A Manual for Expectant Parents*. Englewood Cliffs, N.J.: Prentice-Hall, 1966.

Gruenberg, Sidonie. *The Wonderful Story of How You Were Born*. New York: Doubleday, 1952.

Guttmacher, A. F. *Babies by Choice or by Chance*. New York: Doubleday, 1959.

———. *Planning Your Family*. New York: Macmillan, 1963.

———. *Pregnancy and Birth: A Book for Expectant Parents*. New York: Viking, 1957.

Hall, Robert F. *Nine Months of Reading: A Medical Guide for Pregnant Women*. New York: Doubleday, 1960.

Havemann, E. *Birth Control*. New York: Time, Inc., 1967.

Heardman, Helen. *Relaxation and Exercise for Natural Childbirth*. Edinburgh: Livingston, 1959.

Himes, N. E. *Medical History of Contraception*. New York: Gamut Press, 1963.

Hooker, D. *The Prenatal Origin of Behaviour*. Lawrence: University of Kansas, 1952.

Hutchins, C. M. *Life's Key—DNA*. New York: Coward-McCann, 1961.

Jacobson, F. *How to Relax and Have Your Baby*. McGraw-Hill, 1959.

Jenkins, G. *These Are Your Children: How They Develop and How to Guide Them*. Chicago: Scott, Foresman, 1953.

Karmel, M. *Thank You, Dr. Lamaze: A Mother's Experience in Painless Childbirth*. Philadelphia: J. B. Lippincott, 1959.

Kennon, J. *Educational Proceedings of the International Symposium on Rhythm*. Washington, D.C.: Family Life Burnam Act, 1965.

Kleinman, R. L. *Medical Handbook: Contraception*. London, International Planned Parenthood Federation, 1965.

Lader, L. *Abortion*. New York: Bobbs-Merrill, 1966.

Levine, M. I., and Seligmann, J. H. *A Baby Is Born*. Wayne, N.J.: Golden Press, 1966.

Levy, J., and Monroe, R. *The Happy Family*. New York: Knopf, 1938.

Liley, H. M. I. *Modern Motherhood*. New York: Random House, 1967.

Little, W. A. "Drugs in Pregnancy," *American Journal of Nursing*, 61 (1966), 1303.

Masters, W., and Johnson, V. *Human Sexual Response*. Boston: Little, Brown & Co., 1966.

Maternity Center Association. *Preparation for Childbearing*. New York, 1969.

Muller, H. J., Little, C. C., and Snyder, L. H. *Genetics, Medicine, and Man*. Ithaca, N.Y.: Cornell University, 1947.

Nilsson, A. L. *A Child Is Born*. New York: Delacorte, 1967.

Offen, J. A. *Adventures in Motherhood*. New York: Simon & Schuster, 1964.

Ogg, Elizabeth. *A New Chapter in Family Planning*. New York: Public Affairs Pamphlets, 1964.

Ortho Pharmaceutical Corporation. *Understanding Conception and Contraception*. Raritan, N.J., 1967.

Prenatal Care. Washington, D.C.: U.S. Government Printing Office, 1949.

Rainwater, Lee. *And the Poor Get Children*. Chicago, Quadrangle Books, 1960.

Read, G. D. *Childbirth Without Fear: The Principles and Practice of Natural Childbirth*. New York: Harper & Row, 1959.

———. *Introduction to Motherhood*. New York: Harper Bros., 1950.

Richardson, F. H. *The Nursing Mother*. New York: McKay, 1953.

Rugh, R. *Vertebrate Embryology: The Dynamics of Development*. New York: Harcourt, Brace & World, 1964.

Sanger, Margaret. *Woman and the New Race*. New York: Blue Ribbon Books, 1920.

Shettles, L. B. *Ovum Humanum*. New York: Hafner, 1964.

Spock, B. *Baby and Child Care*. New York: Pocket Books, 1969.

Stern, C. B. *Principles of Human Genetics*. San Francisco: W. H. Freeman, 1960.

Stone, H. M., and Stone, A. *A Marriage Manual*. New York: Simon & Schuster, 1952.

Suitters, B. *The History of Contraception*. Chile: IPPF, 1967.

Swartzm, D. P., and Vande Wiele, R. L. *Methods of Conception Control: A Programmed Instruction Course*. Raritan, N.J.: Ortho Pharmaceutical Co., 1965.

Thomas, H., and Lawrence, R. *Understanding Natural Childbirth*. New York: McGraw-Hill, 1950.

Thoms, H. *Childbirth with Understanding*. Springfield, Ill.: C. C. Thomas, 1962.

————. *Training for Childbirth*. New York: McGraw-Hill, 1950.

Tietze, C. "The History of Contraceptive Methods," *Journal of Sex Research*, 1 (1965), 69.

————. "Induced Abortion and Sterilization as Methods of Fertility Control," *Journal of Chronic Diseases*, 18 (1965).

U.S. Government Children's Bureau. *When Your Baby Is on the Way*. Washington, D.C.: Government Printing Office, 1961.

Velardo, J. T. *Essentials of Human Reproduction*. New York: Oxford, 1958.

Villay, P. *Childbirth Without Pain*. New York: E. P. Dutton, 1960.

Weidenbach, E. *Family Centered Maternity Nursing*. New York: G. P. Putnam, 1967.

Wolf, K. M., and Auerbach, A. B. *As Your Child Grows: The First Eighteen Months*. Child Study Ass'n. of America, 1955.

Woollam, D. H. M. "The Effect of Environmental Factors on the Foetus," *Journal of the College of General Practitioners*, Suppl. 2, 8 (1964), 46.

World Health Organization. *Basic and Clinical Aspects of the Intra-Uterine Devices*. (Tech. Rep. Ser. 332.) Geneva, 1966.

————. *Clinical Aspects of Oral Estrogens*. (Tech. Rep. Ser. 326.) Geneva, 1966.

Wright, E. *The New Childbirth*. New York: Hart, 1961.

index

ILLUSTRATION CREDITS

Color photographs: Plate 1, opposite page 54, from L. B. Shettles, *Ovum Humanum,* Hafner Publishing Company, N.Y., 1960. All others by Roberts Rugh
Title page: Courtesy Bristol Laboratories
page 5. L. B. Shettles, *Ovulation: Normal and Abnormal,* International Academy of Pathology, Williams and Wilkins, Baltimore, 1962
6. R. Rugh
7. L. B. Shettles, *Ovum Humanum*
8, 9. L. B. Shettles, *Fertility & Sterility,* 12:20, 1961
10. L. B. Shettles, *Ovum Humanum*
11. Modified and redrawn from Patten's *Human Embryology*
18. L. B. Shettles, *Ovum Humanum*
19. R. Rugh, *Vertebrate Embryology,* Harcourt, Brace & World, N.Y., 1964
20. L. B. Shettles, *Ovum Humanum*
21. Courtesy Carnegie Institution, Washington
22. (Human embryo) L. B. Shettles, *Ovum Humanum*
25. Courtesy Carnegie Institution, Washington
27. Carnegie Institution Publication #525, Embryology Series #184, 1941
30. Courtesy Dr. E. W. Page
34. (Top and bottom) courtesy Dr. Hideo Nishimura
36. (Human embryo) courtesy Carnegie Institution, Washington. Modified and redrawn from Patten's *Foundations of Embryology*
37. Redrawn and modified from Jordan & Kindred, *Textbook of Embryology,* Appleton-Century Co., N.Y.

41. Courtesy Dr. E. Ludwig, Basel
42. Courtesy Dr. Hideo Nishimura
43. Courtesy Dr. E. Ludwig, Basel
44. (Top and bottom) courtesy Carnegie Institution, Washington
45. (Human embryo at 5 weeks) courtesy Carnegie Institution, Washington
46, 47. R. Rugh
48, 49. Modified and redrawn from Patten's *Human Embryology*
50. Courtesy Dr. Hideo Nishimura
51. Courtesy Carnegie Institution, Washington
52, 64. R. Rugh
86. Redrawn from Louise Zabriskie, *Obstetrics for Nurses,* Lippincott, Montreal, 1960
89. Radiograph by Dr. W. W. Parke, courtesy of William and Wilkins Co.
96. R. Rugh
98. Courtesy of Dr. T. R. Harlan
99, 100, 101. R. Rugh
102. Elizabeth Wilcox
103, 106, 107. R. Rugh
116. (Top) courtesy of J. Schneider, New York
122-127; 171-179. Redrawn, courtesy Maternity Center Association
191. Redrawn, courtesy Ortho Pharmaceutical Corp.
192. R. Rugh
203. Courtesy O. J. Miller and W. R. Berg